MW00606248

THE HUMBLING OF JOB

Meditations on Finding Comfort Through Affliction

Craig K. Svensson

Unless otherwise noted, Scripture quotations are from the ESV® Bible (The Holy Bible, English Standard Version®), copyright © 2001 by Crossway, a publishing ministry of Good News Publishers. Used by permission. All rights reserved. The ESV text may not be quoted in any publication made available to the public by a Creative Commons license. The ESV may not be translated in whole or in part into any other language.

Scriptures references marked KJV are taken from the King James Version (KJV): King James Version, public domain.

The Humbling of Job: Meditations on Finding Comfort Through Affliction

Copyright © 2023 Craig K. Svensson

All rights reserved. No part of this publication may be reproduced, stored in a retrieval system, or transmitted in any form by any means electronic, mechanical, photocopy, recording, or otherwise except as brief quotations embodied in critical articles and reviews.

Cover design: Cathi Stevenson, Book Cover Express

Paperback ISBN: 978-1-7327069-3-4
e-book ISBN: 978-1-7327069-4-1

Library of Congress Control Number: 2023935311

Consilium Publishing
West Lafayette, IN

To my beloved Sue, who has brought comfort to me by being faithful to her wedding vows to me in sickness and ...in sickness.

Contents

INTRODUCTION

Where do you turn when the pain won't stop? Is there a healing balm for the ache of soul that comes from the loss of a child? Where can one find solace from haunting memories of a traumatic experience? What is the source of light when darkness has engulfed your mind? In other words, is there help for those who live with a world of hurt? Thankfully, there is. In fact—lots of it.

From Genesis to Revelation, the Bible repeatedly addresses the troubling problem of human suffering. The betrayal of Joseph by his brothers, the burden of Israel as slaves in Egypt, the agony of the widow Naomi, the unjust treatment of David by Saul, the despair of Elijah, the lamentations of Jeremiah, the captivity of Daniel, the sufferings of the Messiah, the persecutions of Paul, and the tribulations of the church at Smyrna all have much to teach us about human suffering in its various forms. But it is in the book of Job that we face the perplexity of the problem of persistent suffering. More than any other, Job wrestles with the tough questions and the anguish of soul that comes when the pain won't stop. In remembering "the steadfastness of Job" (James 5:11), we can find help and hope in our times of suffering.

Reading Job is tough sledding. The dialogue is dense and difficult. While we may recognize the patience of Job, it also takes patient endurance to read this ancient treatise with care. But forbearance in mining its prose and poetry will bear treasure worthy of the effort. You cannot take a minimalist approach when grappling with the hard realities of human suffering. A brief memo from on high will not suffice. We must wrestle with the hard facts and heart-wrenching feelings surfaced by suffering. Job will help us do this. The truths are deep and their implications profound. These are truths that will lead us from turmoil to trust, from perplexity to peace.

The renowned reformer John Calvin preached 159 sermons on the book of Job. While brevity is not a characteristic any knowing person would attach to Calvin, his volume of pastoral material reveals something of the depth of truth to be found through a study of Job. Calvin was not a man to fill the air with empty words. His extensive treatment of Job speaks of the bountiful fruit that can be harvested from a thoughtful consideration of this ancient book.

Some might argue the extreme experience of Job is so unusual that it is hard to connect his story with our experiences. Surely, losing all your possessions and children in the blink of an eye is unusual—though far from unique. Somali Christians living in refugee camps in northeast Kenya lost all in relatively short order. The congested and unsanitary conditions in which they now live leaves them plagued with a host of physical ailments. The recent experience of Christians in parts of Iraq and Syria parallels the depth and severity of Job—as Islamic radicals plundered and punished those who refused to bow the knee to the terrorists' master. Like Job, the physical and emotional suffering of these brethren is deep and abiding. But more importantly, it is illogical to create a mental scale by which to compare the intensity of suffering between people. Like surgery, suffering is only minor when it occurs to someone else.

Job is the story of just one man and his suffering. Nonetheless, the discourse it contains probes the anguish and confusion wrought by suffering like no other book of the Bible. Many scholars argue it is unparalleled in ancient or modern literature. Of greater significance is that the God who was sovereign in Job's suffering is sovereign in ours. And through Job's story we can learn important truths about this God and the tangled web of thoughts that arise in our hearts in response to suffering.

Yet, the last verse of Job is not God's final word on the subject of suffering. We who live this side of the cross of Calvary must not view suffering solely through the lens of Job. The One who bore our griefs and sorrows had much to say to those who suffer—as did his Apostles. We must, therefore, see Job through the victory gained and proclaimed by the empty tomb. For we have help and hope that Job did not know.

I am neither a Hebraist nor a theologian. So, I leave to others better equipped than I the task of explicating the text line upon line and revealing nuances borne from studying this book in its original language. I am but a fellow pilgrim, with some experiential knowledge of suffering, who has found much help and hope in the story of Job. As I have described elsewhere, my journey through adulthood has included collecting a series of incurable ailments—producing pain and other discomforting sensations that serve as my companions 24/7/365.[1] I also live with the agony of soul from the death of a son—whose demise was the tragic end of a tortuous fifteen-year journey watching him descend into the depths of drug abuse and the unimaginable consequences that come with it.[2] My reading of Job is through the lens of a sufferer—physically, emotionally, and spiritually. Admittedly, I have little interest in debates about the timing of its writing, the process by which this book found its way into the canon, or intricate dissections of the literary genre included in its forty-two chapters. There is a time and a place

---

1   See CK Svensson, *When There Is No Cure: How to Thrive While Living with the Pain and Suffering of Chronic Illness.* Consilium Publishing, 2019.

2   This journey is described, in part, in my book, *The Painful Path of a Prodigal: Biblical Help and Hope for Those Who Love the Wayward and Rebellious.* Shepherd Press, 2019.

for debate about such topics. But the sufferer who comes to Job needs its timeless truths to temper their troubled soul.

This collection of meditations on Job is offered in the hope that it will help those who are in the midst of suffering, as well as those who minister to them. As an author, I have taken as my charge the call to "comfort those who are in any affliction, with the comfort with which we ourselves are comforted by God" (2 Corinthians 1:4). I have experienced that comfort through tears brought on by the never-ending siren of physical pain screeching its presence in my body for over two decades. I have known it while pounding the door of heaven with petitions that seem ill-equipped to move the hand of God. And I have sensed that comfort in the midst of the anguish of soul when faced with the death of my beloved but prodigal son—not to speak of the years of comfort through the agony of enduring his painful journey.

In the turmoil of suffering, comfort is our immediate need. Rescue would be nice, but not necessary. If relief does not come, knowing the "God of all comfort, who comforts us in all our affliction" (2 Corinthians 1:3) will suffice. Indeed, it is more than adequate. There is a sense in which experiencing God's comfort through the crucible of affliction makes him more precious to us than the blessing of prosperity could ever accomplish. This, in part, is the message of Job.

But what is this comfort we seek and are promised in times of trouble? Our English word *comfort* derives from the Latin *confortis*, which means "strong with" or "brave together." Comfort comes from another who helps you bear a burden. They bring strength and bravery you do not possess by yourself. If God is the One providing the comfort, it means he is the One who comes alongside us. Indeed, this is why the translators of the King James Version of the Bible used the term *Comforter* to refer to the Holy Spirit (John 14:26; 15:26).

Another way to understand what is meant biblically by comfort is by hearing how Paul describes the comfort he experienced in trials:

> *If we are afflicted, it is for your comfort and salvation; and if we are comforted, it is for your comfort, which you experience when you patiently endure the same sufferings that we suffer. Our hope for you is unshaken, for we know that as you share in our sufferings, you will also share in our comfort.*
>
> *2 Corinthians 1:6-7*

Do you see how Paul speaks of comfort in these verses? Comfort is not escape *from* affliction. Comfort is experienced *through* affliction. Specifically, when we patiently endure suffering. Comfort is that consolation that comes to us in the heat of the battle—that allows us to rise above the pain, the sorrow, and the suffering. It is serenity in the midst of apparent turmoil. It is the gift given to Job at the end of his lengthy ordeal of suffering (see Job 42:11). Walking with Job through his journey will enable us to see what this comfort really means.

Here's a promise: careful reflection on Job will change you. It will deepen your understanding of suffering. Job will enlighten you about extreme responses we can fall into while on a journey through affliction. This ancient book will also help you be a better comforter to those who suffer. Most of all, meditating on Job will expand your vision of the sovereign God who is behind all suffering. But to gain these benefits, you must truly enter the drama that is the story of Job.

The opening verses of Job reveal to us a man who lived east of the Promised Land. But he was not just any man. His life seemed to display the calculus by which you and I would design life on this earth. After revealing that he was "blameless and upright," the author recounts his wealth— wealth that accorded him the highest status of all the men of the east. That, we often think, is how it should be. The godly should prosper. Living life in the fear of God and shunning evil should be rewarded with blessing from God. Naturally, that blessing will show itself materially, we reason.

Such was the life of Job. Prosperous by all measures, life was good. So was life for his children. Having a wealthy dad left them to enjoy the fruit of his blessings—including celebrating together on a regular basis. But verse 5 of the first chapter reveals that Job knew there was a danger lurking in the shadows. Prosperity brought its own risks. He feared this hidden enemy would grab his children in the secret chambers of their hearts. The irony is that what he feared for his children was the very thing that his wife and Satan tempted him to do—to curse God. This was also what he ultimately was accused of doing by his three friends. And it is his fear of this danger that opens a window into the soul of Job and his agony of suffering.

1

THE PERIL OF PROSPERITY

Read Job 1:1-5

The "American dream" is a lie that sometimes turns into a nightmare. Prosperity and worldly success is not the end-all. It does not ensure living happily ever after. And we are foolish if we buy into the lie that it does. Not just foolish, but blind. Endless are the examples of the rich and famous who implode in public. Their self-destruction should serve as a clarion call to reject the folly of thinking wealth and health leads to bliss. Many have sacrificed family, friendships, personal integrity, and health in the elusive pursuit of success.

But such errant notions are not just an American phenomenon. Seeing prosperity as the ultimate measure of life runs far and wide. Nor is this perspective limited to the irreligious. Equating prosperity with blessing from on high has deep roots. It is at the core of the dialogue between Job and his friends in the chapters to follow. In their minds, those who prospered showed they were right with God. The destitute were seen as devoid of a right standing before God—their physical want reflecting his retribution for their evil. Hence, the conundrum of an apparently righteous man reduced to shambles in both his possessions and his person.

The portrait of Job's life in these opening verses sets the stage for *everything* that follows. The incongruity of suffering in a prosperous man, who by all appearances lives a godly life, is at the heart of the story. It is what creates the tension. And every good story has tension. But if we look closely, we realize there was anxiety in Job long before Satan began his assaults. Job's actions described in verse 5 reveal that he knew all may not be well in the land of Uz.

We are told that Job was concerned his children may have "cursed God in their hearts." Clearly, their sibling celebrations were devoid of drunkenness and debauchery—otherwise he would have made sacrifice for their outward sins. While all appeared well on the surface, he knew that what transpired in their hearts was what mattered most. Though living in outward prosperity, he was concerned that their souls prosper. This was not a mild concern. After each of their feasts, Job collected his children and consecrated them.

He would rise early in the morning and offer burnt
sacrifices according to the number of them all.

Can you picture this scene? Son number one steps forward. Job, as the family priest, places the offering on the altar and sets it ablaze.[3] Smoke tears their eyes and the aroma of burning fat tingles their nostrils. Standing in the heat of the flames, they all watch as the sacrifice is roasted in the inferno. And then it is gone. Now son number two steps forward. Another offering is placed on the altar, the fire lit, and the scorching blaze holds their gaze as the sacrifice is wholly consumed. And so, the ritual is repeated ten times, one for each son and daughter. "Thus Job did continually."

After each of their festal gatherings, Job called them together and led them in this same ceremony. Tying the timing of the sacrifices to their sibling celebrations does not mean he feared they did something requiring sacrifice in the context of their party. It may simply have been the means to create the cycle of regularity for the offerings, taking advantage of the times when they could all be gathered together. But this regular cycle of sacrifice demonstrates his understanding of the peril of living in prosperity. All may appear well on the outside—while corruption can flourish

---

3   That Job ministered these burnt offerings suggests he was either ignorant of the Mosaic Law
     or lived before it was given. Hence, like the patriarchs, he offered sacrifices on behalf of his
     household.

below the surface. The Lord's assessment of Job shows that one can be godly and wealthy. But Job's concern for his children shows that material prosperity did not provide Job comfort about his children's spiritual prosperity.

We who suffer physically, emotionally, and spiritually may see restoration to our unafflicted state to be what is best. If I have lost my health, restoration to a state of wellness is what I need. If I am plagued with traumatic thoughts, a mind clear of such torturers will surely be the deliverance God would want for me. If I struggle with the silence of heaven despite my earnest pleas in prayer, the arrival of answers—in the manner I think best— will rid my life of the turmoil I feel. If fire, war, or pandemic has left me destitute, restoring my possessions will enable me to thrive again. If I long for my lonely journey through the land of singleness to end, fulfilling my desire for a spouse will make all well in the world, most especially in my soul.

But not so fast. Good health, a stable mind, quick answers to prayers, an abundance of things, and a life partner are not the keys to eternal bliss. Indeed, they may put our eternal bliss at risk. For they tempt us to be satisfied with lesser things than God himself. Job understood this. And we should as well.

Jesus shocked his disciples when he declared,

> it is easier for a camel to go through the eye of a needle
> than for a rich person to enter the kingdom of God.
> *Matthew 19:24*

This truth upset their equation for life that linked prosperity with blessing from God—indeed as a key outward sign that all is well with one's soul. But this is not the only time he shattered their sense of the implications of social hierarchy. Recall the account of the rich man and Lazarus. When the rich man cried out to Father Abraham in the torment of his state after death, he is told,

> Child, remember that you in your lifetime received
> your good things, and Lazarus in like manner

received bad things; but now he is comforted here,
and you are in anguish.

Luke 16:25

With whom would you trade places? Sometimes the comforts of this world keep us from the comfort of God.

Prosperity is, in fact, a danger. We should not wish it upon anyone, especially ourselves. If a man with the wisdom of Solomon could not handle material blessings without in turn abandoning God (cf. I Kings 11:4, 6), what chance do you and I stand? Well did Agur, the son of Jakeh, declare,

> *give me neither poverty nor riches;*
> *feed me with the food that is needful for me,*
> *lest I be full and deny you and say, "Who is the Lord?"*
> *or lest I be poor and steal and profane the name of*
> *my God.*

Proverbs 30:8-9

Stripped of lesser things, we grab hold of what alone is able to see us through to eternity. And that *what* is actually a *who*. As the Apostle Paul put it,

> *I count everything as loss because of the surpassing*
> *worth of knowing Christ Jesus my Lord.*

Philippians 3:8

So, my friend, can you see the loss that has brought suffering into your life as a blessing in disguise? Can it be the instrument by which our Lord refines you into the image of his Son? May your loss of health or wealth be what is best for this season—that the next may be richer than ever imagined?

> *Whether it be loss of what I once had or hoped to be,*
> *it may be that loss is better for me.*
> *Yes, loss is often better than prosperity.*

2

BEHIND THE CURTAIN

Read Job 1:6-12

People are enamored with transparency. Citizens want it in their government. Unions want it from employers. Students and faculty want it from the leaders of their schools. Shareholders want it from the company CEO. We all want to know everything we want to know. We feel it to be our right. But we will not receive it from God, much as we may desire otherwise. There are things he does not tell us and will not show us. We do well to remember this while living life on this speck of dust we call home.

The book of Job reminds us that there is an unseen world of happenings that, apart from an occasional glimpse, remain hidden behind a curtain. A thick, dark, impenetrable curtain— at least impenetrable for those who live on the terrestrial side. Things go on within that other side that are, so to speak, hidden from his children. Apparently, it is best that it be that way. At least for now, for most of us, and for most of the time.

The author of Job, enabled by the One who rules on both sides of the curtain, was given a glimpse of goings-on beyond Job's sight. And this peek reveals that sometimes what goes on over the other side does not stay there. It passes over and into our side of the curtain. When it does, things can get messy. Quite messy, in fact.

With frustrating brevity, the author of Job tells us of a specific gathering of the Divine Council—a collection of spiritual beings hinted at throughout Scripture.[4] The ancients

---

4   For a brief introduction to the Divine Council, a helpful summary is provided by Bible Project at: https://youtu.be/e1rai6WoOJU.

among the people of God acknowledged the existence of a company of spiritual beings dwelling in the heavenly realm. Unseen by us earthlings, they populate the heavenly kingdom and were created before the physical universe. Moses alludes to their presence at the creation of man when he tells us, "Then God said, 'Let us make man in our image, after our likeness'" (Genesis 1:26). Though sometimes seen by modern commentators as inter-Trinitarian discourse, the plurality spoken of here would have been seen differently by those to whom Moses wrote and for many generations afterward. The plural nature of the statement (us ...our) is better understood as the Lord declaring to his Divine Council his intent to form the crown of his creation—man.

Further pronouncements by God to this council are made as the story of man's rebellion unfolds. After the Fall, we are told, "Then the Lord God said, 'Behold, the man has become like one of us in knowing good and evil'" (Genesis 3:22). In declaring judgment due to the efforts of men at the Tower of Babel, the Lord said, "Come, let us go down and there confuse their language, so that they may not understand one another's speech" (Genesis 11:7). Knowledge of this spiritual realm with whom and through whom God speaks and acts was not limited to Moses. The Psalmist tells us,

> God has taken his place in the divine council;
> in the midst of the gods he holds judgment
>
> *Psalm 82:1*

Elsewhere, the Psalmist asks who is like him,

> a God greatly to be feared in the council of the holy ones,
> and awesome above all who are around him?
>
> *Psalm 89:7*

These and other whispers throughout Scripture remind us there is a complex spiritual world about which we know very little. In ways mysterious, the Father periodically invites them to join him in making and carrying out decisions. He seeks their input. He sends them on errands. Job and his friends were not ignorant of the existence of these celestial gatherings. In his second refutation of Job's lament, Eliphaz asks, "Have you listened in the council of God?" (15:8). (Note it is *council*, not *counsel*.) In subsequent verses Eliphaz makes the point that since Job has not been privileged into this heavenly council, he does not possess wisdom beyond that of his three friends. Eliphaz knew that Job's presence in this council, were it to happen, would have given him wisdom that evades others. Later, in his own answer to Job, the Lord asks,

> *Where were you when I laid the foundation of the earth?...*
> *when the morning stars sang together*
> *and all the sons of God shouted for joy?*
>
> *Job 38:4, 7*

Job was not present when God created the earth, but others were—the "morning stars," the "sons of God." Job, like other Old Testament members of the family of God, knew this unseen realm existed and played a role in God's kingdom. But their role in his experience of suffering was unknown to him.

With all going well for Job, an event takes place behind the curtain that will bring unbearable affliction into his prosperous life. A gathering of these spiritual beings occurs that seems akin to subservient workers coming to report to the master of the realm. Some may be serving with gladness, while others do so as recalcitrant wanderers. They report and are asked questions. That is when things take a troubling turn—at least for Job. To say he was blindsided by the outcome from this heavenly huddle would be an understatement. It is plain that Job was oblivious to what transpired. As an audience, we are granted a front-row seat—though the curtain is only slightly parted and the glimpse of what we see leaves much untold. But as the adversary is dismissed to do his damage, we find ourselves wanting to rise from our seats and yell, "Look out, Job!" But it will do no good, it will prevent no harm. Poor Job will not know what hit him nor why. He never knew about the cosmic conflict that caused his calamity.

The point is this: there is much that transpires that we do not understand. There is a realm of happenings beyond our gaze. Herein lies the reason we often do not know the why behind our sufferings. It is not simply that we *do not* understand why, but that we *cannot* understand why. Our knowledge is far too limited to grasp the heights and depths of all that the Father is doing. And this is where trust arrives. Job understood this, at least at moments in his terrible trial. That is why he declared, "And after my skin has been destroyed, yet in my flesh I shall see God" (19:26).

The why behind our suffering tends to unsettle us. In the tumult of our soul, we seek a tangible source for our trouble. Was it because I did this? Is this because I failed to do that? Is this the fruit of lessons I have failed to learn? Is that why the suffering does not stop? Often, no such answer can be found. Rather than searching every crevice of our soul for a hidden reason—which our mind is far too likely to conjure up—better that we learn to live with the tension of mystery. I do not suggest we ignore obvious instances of reaping what we have sown. Repentance is the right response for such moments. More often than not, though, no link between our suffering and our sin is obvious. In such times we do well to remember that we know little of what goes on behind the curtain, and its reaching through to our side. And that's okay. Because our Father rules on both sides, I can live with the reality that much remains hidden from me. My Father knows. I trust him completely. So, I can leave it with him.

But it is not him alone with whom I leave it. We who live this side of the cross have a comfort unknown to Job. The writer of Hebrews reminds us that we have a source of refuge, a wellspring of strong encouragement, of which Job knew not:

We have this as a sure and steadfast anchor of the soul, a hope that enters into the inner place behind the curtain, where Jesus has gone as a forerunner on our behalf, having become a high priest forever after the order of Melchizedek.

Hebrews 6:19-20

Today, at this very moment, there is one on the other side of the curtain who is our intercessor. He knows what life is like on our side. He is able "to sympathize with our weaknesses" (Hebrews 4:15). So, do not let the unknown unsettle you. Jesus is for you. He is with you. He will never leave you nor forsake you ...no matter how dark things may get.

3

OUR GREAT ADVERSARY

Read Job 1:6-12

Everyone is not your friend. Some are enemies. In the beauty of the innocence of childhood, this hard reality is unknown. One of the painful experiences of parenthood is watching your child awaken to this troubling truth. Because this knowledge changes so much, most especially our interactions with others. Sadly, we sometimes misclassify friends for foes—and vice versa. Getting this wrong leads to all sorts of problems.

President Franklin Roosevelt and Commander of the Allied Forces Dwight Eisenhower both miscalculated in their plans for the final stages of World War II—because they did not measure Stalin for the enemy that was later unmasked. The city of Troy was blissfully ignorant that the gift of a wooden horse was a ruse that led to their ruin. Western literature would never have known the phrase *Et tu, Brute?* had Julius Caesar recognized Marcus Brutus as a foe rather than friend.

Yet more troubling is that so many are blind to the reality of an adversary among adversaries—a great enemy of us all whose schemes and power far surpass any earthly enemy. His swath of destruction began in the Garden of Eden and will continue its ruinous conquests until the King of kings returns to bind him forever. The Satan.

We know little of those who make up the unseen realm who usually inhabit the other side of the curtain. A few who have had a special role as messengers of God to men and women are named—Gabriel and Michael. But we also know that among the "sons of God" are those who did the unthinkable. They became turncoats. Rebellious they are, and ruinous are their schemes. They prey upon those who dwell on this earth. Indeed, it seems they have especially devoted themselves to deceiving men onto the path of destruction.

The ringleader of this rebellious horde of heavenly hosts jumped into action shortly after the creation of Adam and Eve. Embodying a beast who instilled no alarm in Eve, "that ancient serpent, who is called the devil and Satan, the deceiver of the whole world" (Revelation 12:9) took the first step in his long war with God over the souls of men. His bent is toward bondage—enslaving men to himself as the prince of this world. Isaiah tells us he does "not let his prisoners go home" (Isaiah 14:17). And poor Job was to experience the weight of this adversary.[5]

As members of the Divine Council report before the Lord, he probes the Satan with a question:

Have you considered my servant Job, that there is none like him on the earth, a blameless and upright man, who fears God and turns away from evil?

Satan's response reveals the reason for his title—which in Hebrew is "the Adversary."[6] True to form, he neither commends nor acknowledges the godliness of this servant of servants in the terrestrial realm. Instead, he questions Job's integrity. "Does Job fear God for no reason?" His insolence implies his injurious intent. Job, he argues, is godly for the goods he gets. "Take that stuff away," the Adversary asserts, "and he will curse you to your face." Satan's approach toward the children of God is simple, he "accuses them day and night

---

5   Some Bible scholars do not believe *the satan* of Job is Satan, or the devil, spoken of in the New Testament—but rather one of many adversaries populating the heavenly realm. In other words, the torturer of Job is *an* adversary but not *the* Adversary. Regardless of one's view on this matter, the implications of the text for believers today seem not to differ significantly.

6   While the Hebrew text includes the article "the," indicating a title, not a proper name, I will follow the convention of modern translations—omitting the article and referring to this adversary simply as Satan.

before our God" (Revelation 12:10). Why does God tolerate the presence of this accuser? That is part of the mystery of goings-on within the other side of the curtain. What is of no mystery is that his schemes are designed to bring ruin in the realm of men.

All is not well on this terrestrial ball. Roaming to and fro across the globe is a great adversary, along with his minions. He wreaks havoc among the sons of men. He is the source of much suffering. Job experienced this firsthand. It is clear that Job's experience in suffering finds its causation in the great adversary of our souls. Yes, our souls—not just Job's.

The Bible makes plain that all human suffering arises as the fruit of the initial deception Satan used to ensnare Eve. The catastrophic consequences of that singular event are incalculable. Like the ripples on a pond after its surface is violated by a stone, the ripple effects of the Fall continue into our day. Yet it is also true that specific suffering sometimes finds its source in the ongoing schemes of this destroyer. Of that fact the New Testament, especially the Gospels, is as clear as crystal.

Numerous are the accounts in which people experienced physical affliction from demonic activity. Demons made men mute (Matthew 9:32), blind and mute (Matthew 12:22), epileptic (Matthew 17:15), and chronically contorted in their physical appearance (Luke 13:11-16). Others were severely mentally disordered (Mark 5:1-15) or simply described as "severely oppressed" (Matthew 15:22). Physical and mental affliction were a common manifestation of demonic activity in the New Testament era. Whether Paul's thorn in the flesh was physical or something different, it is evident this was "a messenger of Satan" (2 Corinthians 12:7).

In the same way that Satan sought to sift Job—and in so doing make his allegiance to God falter—the Adversary also sought to sift the Apostles of Jesus (Luke 22:31).[7] But his efforts did not

---

7   The "you" in "sift you like wheat" is plural, indicating his intent to sift all the Apostles, not just Peter.

end with them. Paul speaks of not being "outwitted by Satan; for we are not ignorant of his designs" (2 Corinthians 2:11). He also warns the saints at Ephesus to "Put on the whole armor of God, that you may be able to stand against the schemes of the devil" (Ephesians 6:11). Peter warns us that he "prowls around like a roaring lion, seeking someone to devour" (I Peter 5:8). And John's Revelation reveals the aggressive pursuit of the saints perpetuated by Satan.

You and I live in a battle zone. There is an ongoing war for the souls of men. The weapons used in this war are diverse and powerful. Like all wars, there will be casualties. Sometimes we are direct targets, other times collateral damage.

Am I suggesting your affliction is rooted in this rebel from heaven? Indirectly it certainly is. For all affliction on this earth is linked by a thread weaved through all of human history from the initial deception in the Garden. Whether your current affliction is due to the immediate action of Satan and his devilish host we cannot know. It may be, but perhaps not. Whether his hand has directly caused it or not, you may be sure he wants to use it to sift you. He will whisper in your ear, "This God of yours does not care. Who treats children they love like this?"

Do not fall for words from the father of lies. For there is another who has passed through the curtain to our side. This one:

> did not count equality with God a thing to be grasped, but emptied himself, by taking the form of a servant, being born in the likeness of men. And being found in human form, he humbled himself by becoming obedient to the point of death, even death on a cross.
>
> Philippians 2:6-8

In his incarnation, death, and resurrection, Jesus has conquered the evil forces that have entered the realm of men.

He will build his church and the gates of hell will not prevail against it. Therefore, we do not fear what goes on within the other side of the curtain ...nor those who traverse to our side. Some skirmishes we may lose, but ultimately victory is assured. In the words of great reformer Martin Luther:

> And though this world with devils filled
> should threaten to undo us,
> We will not fear, for God hath willed
> His truth to triumph through us[8]

---

8   Lyrics from *A Mighty Fortress Is Our God* by Martin Luther.

4

THE PROTECTIVE HEDGE

Read Job 1:10

Being inconspicuous has its advantages. In trench warfare, keeping your head down can be lifesaving. Doing the same in the business or academic world can keep you out of the ugly fray of office politics. In other cases, being inconspicuous makes it unlikely you will be selected for distasteful duties. In contrast, rising above the crowd often puts a target on your back. Standing out can make you the object of disdain, activating opponents who long for your downfall. Sadly, this was Job's experience.

Job was the opposite of inconspicuous. He stood out from among the men of the east. In fact, "this man was the greatest of all the people of the east" (v. 3). As a blameless man, his reputation was beyond reproach. The accounting of his possessions makes it clear that he had an abundance of wealth. His character and possessions put him head and shoulders above everyone else. And that made him a special target of Satan.

Job was targeted particularly because he was godly. Not just in the eyes of his fellow citizens, but in the eyes of God as well. The Lord said, "[T]here is none like him on the earth, a blameless and upright man, who fears God and turns away from evil" (v. 8). He lived with the same temptations as we do, perhaps even more because he was so wealthy. But his life was lived in constant defiance of the destructive deception Satan began in the Garden. The Lord, in a sense, threw this fact in Satan's face: "Have you considered my servant Job?"

This is unlikely the kind of attention Job desired. Riled by the question, Satan unleashes his accusation.

Yet Job faced a frustrated foe. From his reply, it is evident that this adversary had not only noticed Job, he had scouted out this servant of God—looking for a beachhead from which to launch an assault. But none was to be found. For the Lord had "put a hedge around him and his house and all that he has, on every side." Satan may have been free to roam the earth, but there was territory he was unable to penetrate. God established and sustained a protective ring around Job, his family, and his possessions. Satan, wily he may be, could not go where God forbid.

The message here is indisputable—the Adversary could not touch Job apart from God removing his hand of protection. Satan did not possess the power or insight to penetrate the hedge the Lord established around Job. His only hope to do so was to gain God's permission. And that he did acquire.

Was Job unique in having a ring of safety around him? Did his extraordinary godliness earn him special care from God, or can we who follow Jesus expect similar protection? Does the great adversary need God's approval to touch us? Scripture gives us confidence that the reach of Satan only extends where God permits. This is the only credible conclusion when considering the entire testimony of Scripture.

First, the most pervasive truth of the Bible—from Genesis to Revelation—is that the Lord God of heaven rules over all. Nothing happens outside his authoritative rule. Nothing. His divine permission is needed for the actions of the highest ruler to the lowliest of servants. This is *the* fundamental truth of the Bible. It is the foundation for *everything*.

Second, we who have been redeemed by the blood of the Lamb reside in the Father's hand. All who belong to Jesus dwell in his protective care, and "no one is able to snatch them out of the Father's hand." (John 10:29). No one. Not even Satan. Satan cannot conduct a stealth assault outside the gaze of our Father. He will not catch our Shepherd in a time of slumber. We are in the Father's hand—and there is no safer place to be.

Third, all things work together for our good (Romans 8:28). Satan seeks to ruin us, while the Father seeks to refine us. Left to his own devices, any assault of the devil would leave us as damaged goods. Only if controlled and constrained by the hand of God could Lucifer's assaults produce good in us. A scalpel in the hand of a murderer brings harm, but the same scalpel in the hand of a surgeon brings healing. If Satan does touch us, it is for the Father's purposes.

The Lord's shield protects all his children. That is the comfort pronounced many times in the book of Psalms. The Psalmist declared,

> But let all who take refuge in you rejoice;
>   let them ever sing for joy,
> and spread your protection over them,
>   that those who love your name may exult in you.
> For you bless the righteous, O Lord;
>   you cover him with favor as with a shield.
>   Psalm 5:11-12

Repeatedly, the Psalmist refers to God as our fortress. Twenty times he speaks of the Lord as our shield. Whether the enemy be earthbound or one who passes from the other side of the curtain, God is our shield against them all. He is our protector.

And yet, there is also an explicit promise that touches directly on this subject:

> We know that everyone who has been born of God does not keep on sinning, but he who was born of God protects him, and the evil one does not touch

him. We know that we are from God, and the whole
world lies in the power of the evil one.

1 John 5:18-19

When John says "he who was born of God protects him," he is referring to Jesus. He is our protector and defender—most especially against the evil one. Our Advocate guards us from assault by the adversary. Don't miss this assertion. Of those who belong to Jesus, John says, "the evil one does not touch him."

What profound implications arise from this truth. When I reside in my good Father's hand, how can I fear loss? For if loss does come, it has first been sifted through his hand and serves a greater purpose. The Enemy of enemies will never bypass my Father's control. He will not climb over or through the hedge unawares. Though this is certainly not an encouragement to carelessness, I need not fret over my well-being or that of my family or treasure. There is no cause to worry about the future, not that such worry would accomplish anything anyway. And I certainly should not spend time wondering what might be happening on the other side of the curtain, what plans are being hatched that have been hidden from me.

This does not mean we should ignore the devices of this deceptive tyrant who assaulted Job so long ago. We do not just sit passive in the face of this adversary. No, there are far too many warning passages in the New Testament for us to in turn give way to a slothful state when it comes to this great seducer of souls. We must be like good soldiers and "put on the whole armor of God" (Ephesians 6:11). We must not do things that make us susceptible to his temptations (see 1 Corinthians 7:5). We must resist him (James 4:7). Confidence in our Father's care does not translate into ignorance of the designs of the deceiver (2 Corinthians 2:11). Yet it does mean his power over us is restrained. His attacks never catch our Father unawares.

Like Job, we face a formidable foe. But he is a defeated demon. The work on the cross has been completed and the tomb is empty. We know the Victor. He is ours and we are his. He keeps us in his ever-present protective care. In that, there is much comfort.

5

BAD THINGS HAPPEN TO GODLY PEOPLE

Read Job 1:8

The suffering of apparently innocent people has long troubled the human psyche. Decades ago, Rabbi Harold Kushner wrote a book entitled *When Bad Things Happen to Good People*. It sold over four million copies—showing that many are troubled by the hard reality of human suffering and the why behind it all. Borne out of his own experience of tragedy, his theological conclusions are dismissive of the central claims of the message of the book of Job. Sadly, he sees God as either uncaring about or unable to stop suffering. Some Christians have deconstructed the very premise of Kushner's argument by asserting that there are no good people. For "all we like sheep have gone astray" (Isaiah 53:6). Hence, any pain we experience is less than we deserve if the Righteous Judge were to distribute justice based on our personal merit. But the story of Job will not let us off so easily.

It is interesting that, when he desired to point Satan to something noteworthy, God did not point to the beauty or power in the creation that this interloper had surely seen through his travels across the earth. Like a grandfather admiring his grandchild, the Lord asks Satan, "Have you considered my servant Job?" There is something most precious in the Lord calling Job *my* servant. He does not hesitate to call this man one of his own. The Lord is pleased with Job.

Our Lord himself characterized Job by saying, "[T]here is none like him on the earth, a blameless and upright man."

Furthermore, God defends the integrity of Job when the latter is falsely accused by Satan. Job's integrity was not just commendatory, it was exemplary. This man was one of a kind, for his day at least. I have read and heard many who try to soften the power of the Lord's statement about Job—seeking to nuance the words to limit their plain meaning. But such gamesmanship with the text violates sound biblical interpretation. It also robs the story of its force, since the core of the conflict is that of a godly man experiencing profound suffering. Francis Andersen, author of one of the most respected commentaries on Job, summed it up well when he said, "The book of Job loses its point if the righteousness of Job is not taken as genuine."[9]

Before his three protagonists enter the scene with their ill-founded reasoning, we are provided the setting for the story: a godly man who does not merit punishment. He is one in whom the Lord finds no fault. That is the plain meaning of the way he is described by God himself. His suffering does not arise from personal shortcomings. And therein lies an incredibly important message often missed through the ages.

We live in a world largely governed by cause and effect—as designed by our gracious creator. The book of Proverbs is filled with sayings rooted in this foundation; "If you do this, this is what will happen." For example, "Whoever works his land will have plenty of bread" (Prov 12:11). Elsewhere the Bible speaks about the principle of sowing and reaping. Actions bring consequences. Because some causes produce a specific effect, we are inclined to err by tracing things backwards. We look at the effect and seek to discern the cause—thus repeating the error of Job's three friends.

The Bible is clear that sometimes physical suffering is punishment for personal sin. Miriam's leprosy was punishment for her ethnic prejudice (Numbers 12). Is everyone suffering from leprosy similarly guilty of ethnic

9   Andersen, Francis I. *Job*. Tyndale Old Testament Commentaries, Donald J. Wiseman (ed), IVP Academic, 1976, p. 69.

prejudice? That would be an unjustified application of the principle of cause and effect. Members among the congregation in Corinth had defiled the Lord's Table. As a result, some were sick while others had died (1 Corinthians 11). Does that mean all people in the church in Corinth who were ill or had died had participated in this defilement? Obviously not. It is wrongheaded to look at physical suffering and conclude the person is being punished for some specific sin. The Lord made this clear when his disciples asked whether it was the blind man or his parents who had sinned—resulting in his blindness from birth. Jesus replied, "It was not that this man sinned, or his parents, but that the works of God might be displayed in him" (John 9:3).

The words of Jesus should forever end the errant notion that those who suffer are simply receiving their just desserts. Yet this mindset is hard to put to death. It is sometimes expressed indirectly. While not seeking to pin suffering on a particular sin, some will argue, "Yes, what you are experiencing is bad, but it is less than you deserve—which is the fire of hell itself. So, you can be grateful it is not worse." I've never been sure how this was supposed to help the sufferer bear the load. Nonetheless, this is errant theology for those who know Christ. The price was paid on Calvary. There is no further punishment to be paid. The debt I owed has already been cancelled out (Colossians 2:14)—paid in full by the Savior. I owe no penance for wrongdoings for which Jesus died. God does not exact retribution from men for sins covered by the blood of his Son. He does not.

Oh my Christian friend, discard any notion that your suffering is retribution from God. There is no further payment for sin. As the author of a famous hymn wrote:

Jesus paid it all, all to him I owe
Sin had left a crimson stain
He washed it white as snow[10]

---

10   Words from *Jesus Paid It All* by Elvina Hall, 1865.

Child of God, the price has been paid. His Son bore *all* the wrath merited by our sin. He will not exact payment from you that has already been paid by his Son. For there is no more debt. The ledger was wiped clean by Jesus' blood. In fact, it is an insult to God to see a Christian's suffering as retribution for sin. For in so doing, we deny the efficacy of what Jesus accomplished on the cross.

Does that mean there is never any relation between sin and suffering in the life of a Christian? No, it does not. The law of cause and effect still rules in God's creation. For example, if a Christian commits sexual immorality and thereby contracts a sexually transmitted disease, they will reap what they have sown. It is a biological consequence of sinful behavior. I met a Christian woman in Kenya who contracted AIDS through her husband's infidelity. Her ailment was the fruit of her husband's sinful activity. Sinful behavior brings consequences because it violates the divine order of things. Sometimes we bear that consequence personally, sometimes it is borne by others.

There are also times when a Christian may suffer as chastening from God to halt their sinful behavior that may bring harm to themselves or others. It may look like punishment, retribution for sin, but it is not. When an owner swats their dog for relieving itself inside the house, it is intended to train, not to exact vengeance for its misdeed. Likewise, whom the Lord loves, he chastens (Hebrews 12:6)—that he might rid us of the dross that pollutes our lives. In such moments we are undergoing refinement, not retribution. We are being purified, not punished. Other times suffering comes to keep us from sin. Paul's thorn in the flesh was not punitive, it was preventive. The intent of his persistent affliction was to protect him from arrogance. There are times when suffering is like a vaccine—it is meant to keep us well.

The point is this: the godly do suffer, including those made godly through faith in Jesus. But they do not suffer as an act of retribution from God—for that was all laid on his Son on Calvary. When we suffer as Christians, we must dispel the notion that it is retribution from God for our sin, for no retribution is required.

Job's experience warns us to reject the reward-retribution paradigm; that prosperity reveals goodness and suffering reveals sinfulness. The reasons for suffering are far too complex to be deduced from such a simple formula.

6

THE MULTIFARIOUS CAUSES OF SUFFERING

Read Job 1:9-22

I wrote these words while isolated at home under orders from the governor of Indiana, orders designed to keep us safe from a global pandemic caused by a little microbe named SARS-CoV-2. There are heated debates over whether such protective measures make a difference. You see, the trouble with microbes is they go where they want to go and grow where they want to grow. Despite our predictive models and protective measures, viruses tend to do their own thing without asking our permission. But is all the suffering across the globe from this pandemic the result of the unprogrammed wandering of some virus? Unless you were isolated without internet, television, or radio signal during this time, you know that many have asked or attempted to answer the question of whether God brought this pandemic. Job helps us answer this question by the clarity with which he sees the cause of his own suffering.

But to understand this element of Job's story, we are best served by three words: *proximate, penultimate,* and *ultimate.* These are not part of most people's daily vocabulary. Nonetheless, they are words we must grasp if we are to understand the causes of human suffering. The last of the three is where comfort is found. So, allow me to expand your lexicon—with apologies to my English teachers who bore with my inattentiveness during my school days. It turns out some lessons did penetrate that stubborn head of mine.

Proximate means close in relationship. In our context, it refers to the immediate cause of events. Penultimate means almost last, or next to last. It is the cause closest to the true origin of what provoked the chain of events resulting in the calamity we observe. Ultimate speaks of the final or decisive cause behind all events. It turns out that all calamities that befall us are multifarious—meaning many parts play a role before they appear in our lives. This is clear from Job's experience, as is readily seen from how the story unfolds.

Job's first loss was from a marauding band of Sabeans who "struck down the servants with the edge of the sword" and made off with his livestock. His second loss came from fire that "burned up the sheep and the servants and consumed them." Then came the Chaldeans, who "formed three groups and made a raid on the camels and took them and struck down the servants with the edge of the sword." The final blow struck when "a great wind came across the wilderness and struck the four corners of the house, and it fell upon the young people"—who all died. The Sabeans, the fire, the Chaldeans, and the wind were the proximate causes of Job's loss. Natural disaster and wicked men were the forces that robbed him of his possessions and posterity.

Yet we know an evil force was behind the scenes pulling the lever for all these events. Unbeknownst to Job, Satan was using these to provoke him to curse God. Satan was the penultimate force bringing the loss of Job's livestock, servants, and children. There were evil doings behind these events. This reality was hidden from Job. But God has revealed it to us.

Most important though, we find that Job was not only unknowing of the penultimate cause, he was unconcerned about the proximate cause. He heard the report. He knew the tribes of enemies who pillaged his possessions. He heard the reports of the devastating fire and wind. But he attributes the cause elsewhere: "The Lord gave, and the Lord has taken away."

God, Job knew, was the ultimate cause of all these things.

The resounding message of the book of Job—from the first chapter to the last—is that God is the ultimate cause of everything. For thousands of years, theologians have debated whether words like *desire* and *decree* should be attached to this causal role on the part of God. But the simple faith of Job is clear. He knew that God was the ultimate cause of his trouble. That was also the undisputed assessment of his friends, which was later confirmed by God himself.

When trouble strikes, we can often see the proximate cause. A meandering microbe. A drunken driver. A slip on the stairs. An evil enemy. The tremor of tectonic plates. And it is true—they play a very real role in our loss. Moreover, when the proximate cause is an evil act by a person, justice demands consequences for their deeds. Whether we will see it on this earth is uncertain. But the God of heaven will hold them accountable in his timing, even though the causes are deeper than them alone.

Whether the evil one or his minions play a role behind the scenes of our suffering is usually indiscernible to us. That the Lord God of heaven is ultimately the cause is undebatable. This is the core truth of the Bible. The Creator of all things is in control of all things. He even determines whether calamity occurs.

> *I form light and create darkness;*
> *I make well-being and create calamity;*
> *I am the Lord, who does all these things.*
>
> *Isaiah 45:7*

He not only controls the events of the world in which we live; he determines our physical afflictions:

> *Then the Lord said to him, "Who has made man's mouth?*
> *Who makes him mute, or deaf, or seeing, or blind?*
> *Is it not I, the Lord?*
>
> *Exodus 4:11*

41

Even those things wherein the proximate cause is with evil intent, the Lord is in control. He is the ultimate cause. Recall Joseph's response when confronting his brothers—the ones who sold him into slavery: "As for you, you meant evil against me, but God meant it for good" (Genesis 50:20). Therein lies the secret of Joseph's contentment through the many trials whose proximate cause was the deed of his jealous siblings. He knew God's hand was behind it all. He knew it served a greater purpose. And he trusted the One who was in control.

Job understood this as well. This is why he responded to his wife's pleadings to give up with the retort: "You speak as one of the foolish women would speak. Shall we receive good from God, and shall we not receive evil?" (Job 2:10). Though not understanding the why behind his suffering, he knew the Who behind it all. And ultimately, that is all that should matter for us.

It is okay to struggle with the tension created by a good God who brings suffering into our lives. We'll spend much time on the mat wrestling with this issue in the pages ahead. But Job begins where we must end—acknowledging that God is the ultimate cause of all that enters our lives. Not just acknowledging it, but embracing it. Job's testing did not turn into temptation, causing him to sin because he stood on this bedrock truth. God's will is decisive in all things.

Like Job, it is most likely you will never know the why behind the affliction that besets you—at least not as long as you dwell on this side of the curtain. Few ever do. But you must not allow the proximate causes of your suffering to distract you from the ultimate causer. It is so easy to spend our time cursing the disease, bemoaning the disaster, or damning the devils whose hands have robbed us of health or wealth. Yet for Job, these don't really matter. Not in the long run nor the short term. For these are foes without freedom. What matters is that all is from God. It is all from his hand. My Shepherd has brought this rod upon my back. And with him I will fear no evil. He will walk with me through the dark valley. And in him I can find my comfort. Or, to express it poetically:

I may not know the reason why,
   Nor whether through it I live or die.
But through his hand calamity is here,
   So, I accept without discontent or fear.

7

TRUE TREASURE

Read Job 1:11-22

The book of Job would be a treasure even if it closed with chapter 1. One reason for this is the perspective it gives about possessions. The message is simple: it is dangerous to treasure our treasure. It can all disappear in a flash. Whether that treasure is material or persons, we can hold it too tightly and love it too dearly. If we do, disaster may bring destruction to our soul. So, don't cling to it.

Satan accused Job of seeing God as a celestial Santa Claus. It was the stuff Job loved, not God. The Adversary asserts that Job's piety is produced by his prosperity—his allegiance to God is rooted in his material gain. Quite sure of himself, Satan declares, "[S]tretch out your hand and touch all that he has, and he will curse you to your face." So, the Lord gave him leave to grab Job's goods. Some have referred to this as God's Wager, or a cosmic bet—as though Satan coaxed the Lord into betting on his favorite horse. Such a view is not just a crass characterization; it expresses an unsound exegesis. The outcome was not in question. Nor was this a game of one-upmanship. It was a test of truth, a proof of Job's piety. The Lord was not rolling dice. "You are wrong, I am Job's treasure, not his stuff," declared the Lord. And with this correction, Satan is granted permission to make Job's possessions vanish.

The swiftness with which Job lost his children and wealth is staggering. The rapid-fire reporting of the calamitous events shows Satan wasted no time unleashing his assault.

He pounced the moment he gained permission. In staccato fashion, Job receives the reports of the damage. Though the attacks wrecked his world, that was not where Job's treasure was found. When all was lost, we are told:

Then Job arose and tore his robe and shaved his head and fell on the ground and worshiped. And he said, "Naked I came from my mother's womb, and naked shall I return. The Lord gave, and the Lord has taken away; blessed be the name of the Lord."

Which takes our breath away—his loss or his worship? Worshiping in response to loss? Honoring God in response to his humbling? Blessing God on the heels of losing all his children? Who does that?

Job mourned his loss—after all, it was the Lord who had given him his possessions and children. It was not ill-gotten gain. The Lord had "blessed the work of his hands." But he knew his ownership was temporary. He knew he would take none of it with him when he exited this life. And the Lord who gave it all could take it away at any moment. So, he blessed the Lord in the face of his loss. When tested, he proved his piety. His treasure lay with the ruler in heaven, not with the fleeting pleasures of this earth. The assault of the Adversary failed. God was proven right.

How would we fare in the face of a similar assault? How would we respond to the loss of everything—even our children? Would we still bless the Lord when humbled before the world? Would we quickly worship or find ourselves unable to utter praise in the face of poverty? We miss an important message from Job if we do not ponder this potential.

The Bible contains many warnings about the polluting power of possessions. Being rich in the things of the world can be dangerous for our eternal well-being. It can actually be a barrier that keeps us out of heaven. Nowhere is this more explicitly stated than in Jesus' encounter with a rich young ruler.

And behold, a man came up to him, saying, "Teacher, what good deed must I do to have eternal life?" And he said to him, "Why do you ask me about what is good? There is only one who is good. If you would enter life, keep the commandments." He said to him, "Which ones?" And Jesus said, "You shall not murder, You shall not commit adultery, You shall not steal, You shall not bear false witness, Honor your father and mother, and, You shall love your neighbor as yourself." The young man said to him, "All these I have kept. What do I still lack?" Jesus said to him, "If you would be perfect, go, sell what you possess and give to the poor, and you will have treasure in heaven; and come, follow me." When the young man heard this he went away sorrowful, for he had great possessions. And Jesus said to his disciples, "Truly, I say to you, only with difficulty will a rich person enter the kingdom of heaven."

Matthew 19:16-23

Worldly riches will not grease the gates of heaven. They have no purchasing power when it comes to eternal things. Worse than that, they misalign our affections. Jesus said, "For where your treasure is, there will your heart be also" (Matthew 6:21). Or, even more pointedly, "You cannot serve God and money" (Matthew 6:24). We must choose. There is no room for divided allegiances. God or money? It is either-or, never both.

We who live in the affluent West must in particular battle the inclination toward the love of money. We have treasure by the ton. The distinction between want and necessity has become blurred. Much of our lives are consumed by acquiring things and taking care of them. The allure of earthly treasure invades our lives incessantly. It is sometimes hard to tell whether we own stuff or the stuff owns us. Constant vigilance is needed to prevent our hearts from treasuring all these goods. If Jesus' warnings on the matter of money don't trouble us, there is a deep problem within us.

What does all this have to do with suffering? Affliction always brings loss. Always. Loss of health or wealth, loss of dreams or schemes, loss of things we hold dear. Whether the affliction is physical, relational, emotional, or spiritual, it is always associated with the loss of something we value. And that value may be honorable. It was good and right that Job cared deeply about his children. After all, "children are a heritage from the Lord, the fruit of the womb a reward" (Psalms 127:3). Something would have been amiss in Job had he not grieved their loss. But in grieving the loss, "Job did not sin or charge God with wrong."

How we deal with loss is determined by what we treasure. If we treasure what is lost, nothing short of its return will satisfy. That means misery will be our companion. We will begrudge the loss and give way to bitterness. What we once had will hold us, even when it is gone. But if we treasure the Lord above all else, his presence will comfort in the face of loss. Restoration of what we had will not be foremost in our minds. It is okay to regret loss—Job did. But pining for the past is a problem.

If we are in the midst of affliction and thereby suffered loss, what has it revealed about what we treasure? What has it exposed about our heart? What has our testing uncovered? Are we even asking ourselves these questions?

The loss and pain of Job were real. But they did not rob him of his greatest treasure—his God. This is why his loss of family and possessions did not lead to a loss of faith. And, at the end of his trial, it was in the Lord that Job found his consolation.

Others have also gone through tremendous trials that tested their source of treasure. Perhaps none more than the Apostle Paul. Yet he would confess, "I am content with weaknesses, insults, hardships, persecutions, and calamities" (2 Corinthians 12:10). What enabled him to see things this way? Simple—he treasured Christ above all else:

> *Indeed, I count everything as loss because of the surpassing worth of knowing Christ Jesus my Lord. For his sake I have suffered the loss of all things and count them as rubbish.*
>
> *Philippians 3:8*

All things rubbish in comparison to Christ. What a way to put it. What a way to live. What can I do to be like that?

The tie to treasure can tether us to what is transient. Job shows us a better path—a perspective that comforts in the face of loss. All that we have is from God, and our true treasure is found in him. This is a perspective that will preserve our souls.

8

GRIEVING LOSS WITHOUT SINNING

Read Job 1:20-22

The Stoics were wrong—at least the distorted perception of their virtues in the modern era. Showing emotion is neither wrong nor weak. There is no inherent goodness to avoiding verbal or other expressions of pain and grief. I write this aware that those who know me best would tell you that I most often lean in with the Stoics. It is hard for me not to shrink from others' strong expressions of sorrow.

Job was a virtuous man who gained the respect of his society. His life was admirable in word and deed. In fact, the Lord characterized his life as "blameless." This is not a reputation gained by a person known for emotional swings. He was not a man driven by his feelings. Yet when loss quickly piled upon loss, he displayed his distress for all to see: "Then Job arose and tore his robe and shaved his head and fell on the ground and worshiped."

The act of tearing one's clothes as an expression of grief sounds quite odd to our ears. But it was a common response in the Near East. A semblance of this is retained among Jewish communities today who practice the *Kriah*—the Hebrew term for "tearing" or "rending."[11] When Jacob learned of the feigned demise of his son Joseph, "Jacob tore his garments" (Genesis 37:34). In response to those who sought to dethrone Moses and find a leader to take them back to Egypt, Joshua and Caleb "tore their clothes" (Numbers 14:6). Upon hearing

---

11   *Kriah*, or Keriah, is a mourning practice of wearing torn clothing or a cut black ribbon for seven days. When the one lost is immediate family, it is worn on the left side to signify a heart deeply torn by the loss.

of the death of King Saul, "David took hold of his clothes and tore them" (2 Samuel 1:11). This pattern of expressing public grief, and even shock, carried into the New Testament era. When Paul and Barnabas learned those at Lystra were preparing to make sacrifices, as though they were gods, "they tore their garments" (Acts 14:14). There is a deep tradition for such a response.

Job not only tore his robe, he also shaved his head and prostrated himself on the ground. The text implies his ritual response was as rapid as his reported losses. First, he was struck by disaster. Then he was struck by grief. "In all this, Job did not sin." There is no fault in his public display of deep sorrow.

Public expressions of grief vary among cultures and time. For some, wearing black shows sorrow. Others place a black drape over the doorway to their home. Job, as was the custom of his day, displayed his grief by rending his robe and shaving his skull. But he did not do what scholars tell us was common in Near Eastern culture—he did not perform any act of self-harm, such as cutting.

But there is something else Job did not do. He did not curse God—the very thing Satan was certain he would do. In fact, Satan's assault was designed to provoke a profane response. Do not forget this. Satan schemed to get Job to curse God. Nonetheless, it did not work. Job expressed dismay but did not deny his God. Quite the opposite—he blessed the Lord. He blessed him, knowing full well that God was the ultimate causer of his loss.

When disaster strikes, when loss looms heavy, most will give outward expression to their grief. This is fine and good. What we must not do is what the devil wants us to do in a time of testing—curse God. Seething with anger and expressing our rage at him is sin. Doing so dishonors him before devils and mocks him before men.

Sadly, I have seen those who turn on and from God when calamity comes into their lives. Bitterness takes root as they mourn their loss by targeting their blame at the Almighty. This is a dark descent from which some do not return. It is a ruinous route. But those who start down this road can reverse course. I have watched some recover their steps.

If fist-shaking at God has gripped you, you need to gain hold of your heart. You must repent of your rage and renew your resolve to rejoice in all things. To stop drinking the waters of bitterness, you need to quench your soul through the biblical pattern of lament.[12] The Psalms are filled with the voice of lament. They all follow two simple stages. First, talk to God about your feelings. Second, talk to your feelings about God. Time and again, the psalmists voice their pain with penetrating honesty. Consider the opening of Psalm 13:

> *How long, O Lord? Will you forget me forever?*
> *How long will you hide your face from me?*
> *How long must I take counsel in my soul*
> *and have sorrow in my heart all the day?*
> *How long shall my enemy be exalted over me?*
> *Consider and answer me, O Lord my God;*
> *light up my eyes, lest I sleep the sleep of death,*
> *lest my enemy say, "I have prevailed over him,"*
> *lest my foes rejoice because I am shaken.*
>
> *Psalm 13:1-4*

Can you feel David's anguish in these verses? Does his appeal to God draw you into his despair? Yet David does not stay there. He turns and steadies his soul with truth about the God he knows and serves. His renewed resolve is inspiring:

> *But I have trusted in your steadfast love; my heart*
> *shall rejoice in your salvation.*
> *I will sing to the Lord, because he has dealt bountifully*
> *with me.*
>
> *Psalm 13:5-6*

12　For those unfamiliar with the biblical practice of lament, Mark Vroegop's book *Dark Clouds, Deep Mercy: Discovering the Grace of Lament* (Crossway, 2019) is a helpful guide that will nourish your soul.

David moves from pain to praise, from travail to trust. He speaks to God about his pain and confusion, then to his soul about truth. This pattern, with varying complexities, is repeated again and again throughout the psalms of lament. It is a pattern we do well to memorize and mimic—so that we can give proper voice to our pain.

Suffering is inevitable. The sorrow of loss will one day come upon us all. And past sorrow is no shield from subsequent suffering—as Job soon discovered. So, it is best we prepare for this eventual experience. From time to time, dark clouds descend upon us all. We need to know the path to light when they do.

But the scaffold of lament can only work when it is erected on a strong foundation. Absent that, we will have no truths to preach to our soul when sorrow strikes. We must make sure the foundation of our faith is strong enough to withstand storms that are certain to come. This was the core message of one of the most important sayings our Savior pronounced:

> Everyone then who hears these words of mine and does them will be like a wise man who built his house on the rock. And the rain fell, and the floods came, and the winds blew and beat on that house, but it did not fall, because it had been founded on the rock. And everyone who hears these words of mine and does not do them will be like a foolish man who built his house on the sand. And the rain fell, and the floods came, and the winds blew and beat against that house, and it fell, and great was the fall of it.
>
> Matthew 7:24-27

If our lives are not built upon the foundation of gospel truth, they will not withstand the battering brought by the storms of life. We will find no anchor for our soul in the tempest of our trials. So, we must get ready. We must saturate ourselves with gospel truths at all times—for it will provide a reservoir we can draw from in our time of need.

In this sense, we have every reason to be better equipped than Job. The fact that neither he nor his friends quoted from the law suggests they did not possess this treasure. But we have the record of the doings of our God through the ages, along with his precious promises. The declarations and demonstrations of his sovereignty within the record of Scripture are too numerous to count. They should create within us an unmovable confidence of his control and goodness.

Job's faith did not falter when he was faced with his foe's assaults. Why? Because he lived with the unshakable confidence that God controls all things at all times. As a consequence, his time of testing proved his faith in God. That faith did not fold in the face of deep grief. Will ours?

9

OUR SUFFERING AND GOD'S HONOR

Read Job 2:1-3

No one likes to fail tests. We can all remember the tension tests created during our school days. We feared failure. The higher the stakes, the higher the stress. Truth be told, however, the stakes were not as high as we thought. It turns out spelling tests don't determine anyone's destiny.

Having left our school years behind, we can mistakenly believe we're done with tests. Nothing could be further from the truth. In some ways, life is one big test. Or maybe better seen as a continuous series of tests. Sadly, in the school of life, failure is common—even though the stakes *are* very high. The legacy of loss in a time of testing is lengthy, and colossal failures have had calamitous fallout.

When Adam and Eve were tested by the tempter, they failed and ruined it for us all. The entry to Eden was closed and death descended. Cain caved at the sin crouching at his door—culminating in committing a capital crime. Abraham and Sarah lost their patience, leading to a plot to gain an heir through Hagar. Their impatience produced perpetual conflict that continues into this century. When tested in the wilderness, Israel wilted and became wanderers for forty years. As Saul's patience was tried while he was waiting for Samuel, he took matters into his own hands—thereby losing his grip on the throne. And on we could go. The list of defeats is depressingly long.

How we respond to testing can be momentous—even when we don't realize it is a test. Job did not. He had no knowledge about Satan's plot underlying the disaster his life became. He did not realize his allegiance to God was questioned. Though unannounced, it was a test of his integrity. A test of the highest order. At stake was the honor of God.

Honor is both a noun and a verb. It is something inherent in God's person *and* something others give to him. He holds a place of honor by virtue of his being God. That place of honor is held whether recognized by others or not. In addition, his creatures give him honor—while at other times withholding it. Though he is not diminished by honor withheld, we are deluded if we think he doesn't care whether we give it or not.

The Bible is filled with calls to give honor (or glory) to God, as well as examples of those who do. The living creatures around the throne "give glory and honor and thanks to him who is seated on the throne" (Revelation 4:9). They further declare that he is "worthy" to *receive* honor (4:11). It is not simply something intrinsic to his being; it is also something ascribed to him by those who worship. Paul's wonderful doxology in his first letter to Timothy declares, "To the King of the ages, immortal, invisible, the only God, be honor and glory forever and ever. Amen" (1 Timothy 1:17).

One of the most important ways we honor God is by affirming the truth of what he has said. Of Jesus, he said, "This is my beloved Son, with whom I am well pleased" (Matthew 3:17). You cannot honor God apart from agreeing with this declaration, which is why Jesus said:

> For the Father judges no one, but has given all judgment to the Son, that all may honor the Son, just as they honor the Father. Whoever does not honor the Son does not honor the Father who sent him.
>
> John 5:22-23

Honoring the Father today is only possible through honoring Jesus. Honoring Jesus in suffering is determined by how we respond to suffering.

God is not pleased with platitudes. He does not want empty words that do not arise from the depth of our souls. There must be integrity to our words. They must be tethered to our hearts. The truth behind what we say is most surely shown in times of testing. This is at the root of Peter's encouragement to Christians facing the disdain of the world:

> *In this you rejoice, though now for a little while, if necessary, you have been grieved by various trials, so that the tested genuineness of your faith—more precious than gold that perishes though it is tested by fire—may be found to result in praise and glory and honor at the revelation of Jesus Christ.*
>
> *1 Peter 1:6-7*

There it is, plain as the nose on your face. As the genuineness of our faith is proven through testing, it redounds to the honor of God in Jesus Christ. When our faith is tested through affliction, we are presented with the marvelous opportunity to bring honor to God by how we respond. When God brings suffering, he is not doing something to us. He is doing something through us. He is bringing honor to his own name. Unless, of course, we don't pass the test.

Here is something that Job did not see,
   which explains his painful perplexity.
It was not a sin-wrought calamity,
   but a challenge for heavenly victory!
The honor of God was now at stake—
   would Job his integrity forsake?
False claims Satan rudely did make,
   Job's stuff he cruelly did take.
Stripped of possessions, his heart was laid bare,
   for earth's fleeting treasures, Job did not care.
The test of affliction, he humbly would bear,
   for he knew that his God, the Almighty, was there.

Job honored God by maintaining his integrity in the face of loss. Satan accused him of possessing a selfish motive for honoring God with his life. But when the test came, Job held fast. Satan refused to honor God. He would not admit the Omniscient One was right when he asserted the true nature of Job's heart. The stubborn slanderer refused to honor God in the face of evidence.

But we must not miss the other witnesses to this unfolding scene—another gathering "when the sons of God came to present themselves before the Lord." Much to his consternation, there was a cloud of witnesses to Satan's false claims. Others knew God had been vindicated by the integrity of Job in the face of assault. Surely, God was honored in their eyes—as he is in the eyes of the millions of believers who have read this account throughout history. Job's integrity mattered more than he ever knew.

I do not suggest our time of testing is as momentous as Job's—though one can never tell. But that does not mean the outcome is insignificant. It is easy to overlook the fact that there are witnesses to our suffering. There are always witnesses. Family, friends, coworkers, neighbors, and those with whom our encounters may be brief. How they see us handling a time of testing matters. When we hold fast to the faith in the face of trouble, we give cause for them to honor the God of all comfort—even if they refuse to do it until the glorious day of Jesus' return.

Do we see our suffering in this light? Do we see it as a testing of our faith, not our stamina? It is easy to lose focus in times of affliction. When the loss is great and the pain is deep, we get distracted from the main thing. We look for relief, when what we need is endurance. We pray for respite, when we what we need is strength to be steadfast. We ask to be freed from the affliction, but what we need is to be faithful for its duration. Instructing those experiencing afflictions, the writer of Hebrews declares, "For you have need of endurance, so that when you have done the will of God you may receive what is promised" (Hebrews 10:36).

Endurance, perseverance, and faithfulness are encouraged, are commended, and promise blessing throughout the New Testament. Hebrews 11 recounts those who have gone before and remained steadfast in a time of testing. Their choices in those times mattered. They matter to us—who are encouraged by their example—and they matter to God. James tells us that the steadfastness of Job showed "the purpose of the Lord, how the Lord is compassionate and merciful" (James 5:11). Thus, we should ask: What does our response to our suffering show the world about our Lord?

Every affliction is an opportunity to affirm our allegiance to Jesus. Let's not miss the opportunity affliction affords.

10

A PERSISTENT FOE

Read Job 2:1-5

Satan is a demon not easily dissuaded. He is persistent in his pursuits. Job experienced this the hard way. Having proved his adversary's accusations wrong, you'd think he might have received respite from further testing. But the worst was yet to come.

Another meeting of the Divine Council set the stage for Act 2 of the drama that unfolded in Job's life. It is plain that pride pervades the insolent fallen angel who accused Job of defective allegiance. He will not acknowledge defeat, he will not admit the Lord was right. No, in his corrupt mind, the problem was the severity of the test. The protective hedge is still there. This, he presumes, is why Job has not caved in and cursed God. So, Satan pleads for another go at him. For he is confident he has identified the weak spot.

This points to an important lesson for we who live for Jesus. The time of testing endures for as long as we live on this earth. We must, in a sense, prove our mettle every day. And this is why patient endurance is one of the most important characteristics in the Christian life, and why it is a critical lesson to take from the story of Job. When it comes to adversity, we are in it for the long haul. Thus, we must learn to endure.

No one is promised a trouble-free life. In his response to Job's lament, Eliphaz declared, "[B]ut man is born to trouble as the sparks fly upward" (Job 5:7). It's the sure path. The Lord Jesus said, "In the world you will have tribulation"

(John 16:33). The false prophets of the prosperity gospel are selling slander. Walking with Jesus does not ensure wealth or health. Like death and taxes, trouble is sure to come. And it comes in a variety of flavors.

Most germane to our present passage, sometimes trouble is an assault from the prince of this world. We may experience that directly or indirectly. But we must not be naïve about his strategies. He is in a battle for the souls of the image-bearers God has placed on this earth. If he cannot capture them for his fallen kingdom, he wants to render them ineffective for the kingdom Jesus is building. The war will not be won until our Redeemer returns in all his glory. Until then, the war goes on. And like all wars, that means battle after battle after battle. From time to time, there may be a lull in the action, but the enemy will not desist until fully defeated.

Job did not realize Satan was the penultimate cause of his calamity. But the enemy was there, pulling the levers of disaster. Scripture indicates he is often manipulating the events of our trials as well. The Apostles' flight upon Jesus' arrest and Peter's denial before the damsel may look like simple fear of men, but—as Jesus made clear—it was Satan's sifting (Luke 22:31). It is not surprising that Peter subsequently warned believers facing persecution: "Be sober-minded; be watchful. Your adversary the devil prowls around like a roaring lion, seeking someone to devour" (1 Peter 5:8). His warning was explicitly directed to Christians. He knew of what he spoke. Suffering for the faith always originates from the prince of this world—for he is the father of all who oppose King Jesus. But Job's story shows us that he is also the designer behind disaster, even those that seem "natural."

Sophisticated men sneer at simpletons who speak of Satan. Demons were the default explanation for scary happenings the ancients did not understand—or so we are told. But the deniers are the deluded ones. This formidable foe is real. No one spoke about this adversary more than Jesus. No one faced his onslaught more incessantly than the incarnate Son. Satan tempted him with his need for physical provision. He urged him to test the trustworthiness of his Father's promises. And he offered him authority over the world this fallen prince controlled. But Jesus would have none of it. Jesus' resistance caused a retreat—but the devil wasn't done: "And when the devil had ended every temptation, he departed from him until an opportune time" (Luke 4:13). He would be back.

Our Lord cast demons out of many—demonstrating his authority over them. Time and again he encountered people afflicted by demons. The afflictions they brought were physical, mental, and spiritual. And he warned that in the closing days of the drama on this earth, the onslaught of activity by these opponents would heighten. You cannot embrace the message of the Messiah and deny the devil's existence.

It is plain that the devious work of the devil did not end when the crucified one rose from the tomb in which his body rested for three days. Satan filled the hearts of Ananias and Sapphira to lie to the Holy Spirit (Acts 5:3). He continued to afflict people with unclean spirits (Acts 5:16; 19:11-17). And he opposed the proclamation of the gospel (Acts 13:8-12). He even hindered the Apostle Paul's travel plans (1 Thessalonians 2:18). So, we are repeatedly warned not to be unaware of his devices, to be wary of this wicked warrior who opposes the kingdom of God.

Men more learned may disagree, but I don't think Satan has accepted Jesus' victory. He does not accept the end as a foregone conclusion. He did not for Job, and he did not for Jesus. He actually tried to persuade the Son of God to switch allegiances. Was he delusional? Deluded he may be, but no dunce is he. For thousands of years he has observed the weaknesses of those who dwell in the realm of men. He knows their soft spots. He also knows repeated battering can accomplish what a single blow cannot.

Like it or not, we abide in enemy territory. We all were once his captives. But when we professed allegiance to King Jesus, we became traitors to the prince of this world. He does not take betrayals lightly. He will not ignore the threat of those who carry the message of the gospel in their hearts and on their lips. He wants to prevent further defections. This is best done by disabling us or distracting us. He doesn't need to get us to deny the faith, as long as he can divert our attention. That's why he trades in trials and temptations. He can, thereby, render us ineffective. And he relentlessly deploys this strategy.[13] If he fails in one approach, he will be back. Indeed, doesn't resistance make future assaults inevitable? He is, after all, persistent in his pursuits. For this reason, we must be careful not to proclaim victory prematurely.

Do you remember the boastful claim of Peter and the other Apostles when Jesus told of their coming betrayal?

> Then Jesus said to them, "You will all fall away because of me this night. For it is written, 'I will strike the shepherd, and the sheep of the flock will be scattered.' But after I am raised up, I will go before you to Galilee." Peter answered him, "Though they all fall away because of you, I will never fall away." Jesus said to him, "Truly, I tell you, this very night, before the rooster crows, you will deny me three times." Peter said to him, "Even if I must die with you, I will not deny you!" And all the disciples said the same.
>
> *Matthew 26:31-35*

Of course, we know what happened. They all fled and Peter made his shameful denials. Their overconfidence in their courage to stand the test proved hallow. In contrast, Jude reminds us that the archangel Michael is far from flippant in his words to our great adversary (Jude 9).

---

13   For a creative and challenging reflection on the strategies of Satan against men, see *The Screwtape Letters* by C. S. Lewis.

I am always troubled when I hear testimonies of victory over besetting sin. I understand the desire to praise God for work he has done. I get the joy of winning a battle. I appreciate the intent of providing hope to encourage others. But too often, I've watched the one who claimed victory wander into the same sin down the road. Healed wounds often remain weak—susceptible to future injury. They require special protection.

I am not sure we should be celebrating fighting well as opposed to finishing well. Celebrating victory should be reserved for heaven. Until then, the battle rages. Keep your guard up. The enemy won't lie low for long. Don't celebrate prematurely. The devil's not done.

11

SATAN'S DEVICES

Read Job 2:4-8

Satan is not used to losing. His early string of victories is undeniable. First, there was the deception in Eden that led to death for all. Then he grabbed hold of Cain's heart, leading to the first murder. Since those early days, he has tallied more victories than men can count. Again and again he has directed men onto the broad road to destruction. But there was this nagging problem of Job.

The reality of a blameless man in the land of Uz must have been burr in the slanderer's saddle as he surveyed the earth. The Master was pleased with this one. How to bring him down? The Adversary found no foothold to creep in with his corrupting designs. When the fence around the man contracted, he took what he could grab. "That should do it," he thought. But it didn't. Trust was strong in this one. The man was steadfast where others succumbed. There must be another way.

There are two strategies for defeating a resistant foe: either apply more force or identify a weak spot. Unless you can recruit help, the latter is the wisest path to victory. And it is precisely this path that Satan chose in his efforts to make Job curse God.

Physical pain presses a person like nothing else. When an enemy wishes to extract information from a captive, he begins with an assault on the mind. He coaxes, confuses, and coerces. When this fails, he turns to physical torture—inducing pain through barbaric techniques. He knows that pain screams for relief, and men will do what is otherwise forbidden to find it. The enemy of our soul also knows this. He knows the power of physical pain. Indeed, he declared, "Skin for skin! All that a man has he will give for his life. But stretch out your hand and touch his bone and his flesh, and he will curse you to your face."

Don't overlook who does the ultimate touching here. Troubling as its sounds, Satan knows the power to trouble frail flesh resides with God alone. It is from his hand that disease descends. If you live with persistent physical affliction, God has ordained it. It is, in some way, part of his plan for you and for his greater kingdom.

Yes, this truth raises many questions. No, there are no comfortable answers. But the text is plain. Equally plain is the choice of whether we are going to believe what it and other passages plainly say. There is no getting around it—though I have read many attempts to do so. The place this brings us to is simple: Are we going to believe God's word or not? And not just the comfortable parts, but all of it. We all must face this question.

But back to the story, the point is clear. Satan does not simply traffic in lies; he pounds the flesh. He knows physical disease will often accomplish spiritual destruction. We must recognize this tool of his trade. When plundering Job's possessions did not provoke Job to curse God, the Adversary battered his body. His persistent pain caused Job to falter, but he did not fall—he did not forsake God. As James reminds us, Job was steadfast.

I believe there is important truth in the stages of Satan's strategy, as well as the Lord's shielding. The tenderest spot was protected to the last—Job's body. For therein lay the ultimate test. The slanderer salivated when the shield was dropped and he could access Job's flesh. He struck Job with "loathsome sores." That even sounds gruesome. It surely felt worse.

Job was covered with these sores "from the sole of his

foot to the crown of his head." In other words, they were everywhere. His entire body was covered with painful, oozing sores. Job's act of scraping himself with broken pottery likely reflects incessant itching from the sores. Some have suggested sitting "in the ashes" means he removed himself from society and sat in the rubbish heap outside of town. Perhaps. But I'd suggest that sitting covered in ashes may have been to bring some measure of comfort by drying the oozing sores—much like calamine lotion is used today for people with poison ivy. Regardless, it is clear he was reduced to immeasurable misery.

If battering Job's body was the ultimate weapon of the Adversary, does this not tell us something important about the power of physical suffering to wreak spiritual havoc? Job's faith was sorely tested when his body was teeming with sores. Yes, he did not curse God as Satan intended. But—as we will see in the chapters ahead—as the misery persisted, he surely wobbled. It sent him into a dark pit of despair. He lost his joy in the Lord. He staggered, though he did not stumble. He did not sin, but he struggled.

Persistent pain pierces the soul like nothing else.[14] Losing your children and possessions is excruciating. Yet things distract you from your loss and you do not dwell on it constantly—though reminders may be frequent. But there is no place to hide from the piercing siren sound of physical pain. I have spent many years listening to patients with intractable pain. I have lived with pain every day for over two decades. Absent the experience, it is hard to understand just how pressing unrelieved pain becomes when it is your experience week by week, day by day, hour by hour, minute by minute, and second by second. Like a massive slow-moving grinding stone, pain can pulverize a person.

---

14 My use of the word *pain* should be taken in its broadest sense—to include burning, tingling, and itching; internal and external.

Those who live with persistent physical suffering, and those who minister to them, must recognize the threat to their spiritual well-being that physical ailments bring. What begins as a physical problem can quickly turn into a problem of the soul. Chronic conditions contort your view of things. They mess with your mind. That is just what Satan seeks.

Understandably, when pain becomes chronic, it can also become all-consuming. The world becomes very small. All that matters resides within the confines of your own skin. The picture painted of Job in the chapters to follow is of one who was abandoned by others and isolated. Understandably, his focus becomes his misery. As a consequence, he sits, sulks, and suffers.

Solitude can be dangerous for a troubled soul. For in that place you can talk yourself into all kinds of nonsense. And our adversary is great at offering lies. His lies are best battled with truth. That is why in times of testing, including physical testing, we need the fellowship of God's people and the public proclamation of his word more than ever. This is why the writer of Hebrews warns us to:

> consider how to stir up one another to love and good works, not neglecting to meet together, as is the habit of some, but encouraging one another, and all the more as you see the Day drawing near.
>
> *Hebrews 10:24-25*

The "Day" he refers to is the time of great testing, which will come when dusk descends and the depths of man's depravity is its darkest—just before the sky is set ablaze with the glory of the coming of Jesus. As that darkness descends, we will need one another and the encouragement from his word more than ever. And we also need it when the darkness descends on our individual lives in a time of personal testing.

It is, I suppose, natural to seek solitude when wounded. Trials tempt us to retreat—especially trials that are physical. We must be wary of giving into this inclination to isolation.

God has designed us to thrive in community. That sense and need for community has been elevated with the creation of the Body of Christ—the called-out ones who are part of his forever family. No part of your physical body will survive if cut off from the rest. Nor will we thrive if we are cut off from our spiritual body of fellow believers. I do not deny the special grace God has given believers like John Bunyan in their isolation in prison, but self-imposed isolation because of our pain is something different. We should not expect God's blessing there.

Satan would love to see pain push us into solitude. He knows we are most vulnerable when alone. And aloneness may come through being self-absorbed—even while surrounded by others. Take heed; don't fall into this folly. Get beyond your own skin, even when it screams with pain.

12

COLLATERAL DAMAGE

Read Job 2:9

Augustine assailed Job's wife as "the devil's assistant," while Calvin called her "Satan's tool." Preachers often dismiss her as a poisonous partner. Commentators cringe at her call for cursing. Often maligned—surely misunderstood—she merits a more measured judgment. Her experience and exasperation reveal an essential reality: the inevitability of collateral damage. Even when Satan hits his target, the blast injures bystanders.

We know little of this woman whose matrimony brought much wealth and prestige. Being married to the most noted man in the east had its perks. What woman wouldn't want the bliss of a blameless beau? Such was her joy in life. But then disaster struck. In the blink of an eye, all the children she bore perished. I know the pain of losing one child—but ten all in the same moment? Unthinkable. Unbearable. What greater disaster could befall? She carried each in her womb. She nursed them at her breasts. She bathed them, swaddled them, and comforted their cries. She saw their first steps and heard their first words. Year by year she guided and watched them grow into maturity. At the height of her joy, she was robbed of her delights. Oh, and add the violent destruction of her possessions to that painful loss. To top it off, her husband was reduced to a pitiful personage. How deep would be the despair into which we would descend if left destitute of children, spouse, and possessions?

Mrs. Job was not the target of the testing. But when Satan launched his sequence of salvos at Job, she was struck by the shrapnel. She was not just a witness to the terrible trial. Satan's assault assailed her life also. For what was Job's was hers and hers was his. As a consequence, they went down together.

But she was not alone in bearing the load that was launched at Job. Their sons and daughters left the land of the living—as did most of his servants. How many families were bereaved by the deaths in this disaster? Job's time of testing brought casualties beyond his own home.

Those who suffer affliction, whatever the nature or source, must realize that those we love suffer with us. Sometimes directly, sometimes indirectly. Our time of testing spills over into their lives. The physical pain we bear brings the pain of watching our suffering onto those who know us best. Our limitations change their lives immeasurably. Our loss is their loss. We must not overlook this. Indeed, studies have shown that spouses who have become caregivers often suffer from more depression and anxiety than their chronically ill partners.

Herein lies one reason we must fight for joy every day. There is more at stake than our well-being. It is easy for us to drag others down. If we live with a downcast soul, we will dispirit theirs. If we retreat from the world to wallow in our pain, we pull them into our mire. If our anger catches them in our anguish, we wound those we love most. Far too many force others to share their pain through harsh words and impatient retorts. But there is no room for self-pity. Affliction does not annul the admonition to love others and do good to them, most especially those in our own household.

It is easy to become self-absorbed and only see *our* suffering. I know, I've done it myself. Yet we must not ignore the collateral damage engulfing our entire family. They deserve our compassionate understanding and what comfort we can bring. Our familial roles and responsibilities are not removed when trials bring turmoil. We must show the patience with loved ones we would seek for ourselves. I believe Job displayed this in response to his dear wife.

The unraveling of her life with lightning speed must have left her in a daze. Watching his pain, hearing his moans, she let loose on Job: "Do you still hold fast to your integrity? Curse God and die." Interesting choice of words. Did she see deeper into the nature of his testing than his three friends to follow? Unlike them, she did not ask what hidden sin brought this calamity into their enviable life. She saw him as holding fast despite the torrential testing. Did she realize her pain was just a spillover from his testing, that he was the true target? Regardless, she just wanted all the pain to end. Can you blame her? Isn't that what Job subsequently asks for? But his response to her is measured: "You speak as one of the foolish women would speak."

The words of Mrs. Job were apparently out of character. He did not call her a foolish woman. Rather, she was speaking as they speak. This was not her speaking—as in not how she usually spoke. Then he reminded her, "Shall we receive good from God, and shall we not receive evil?" His tone of voice would have made a world of difference in how his wife received these words.

How we respond in our time of testing matters not only to God but also those we love. They need our help just as we need theirs. We need to realize we are in this tempest together— and the way to get through it is together. There will be days and moments where one of us has a tighter grip on truth than the other. The one stronger in the moment can prevent the other from falling overboard. Nowhere is this truer than in marriage. We must recognize this and face it head-on.

The tensile strength of a marriage is revealed through trials. Sadly, many marriages snap when stretched. The frequency of divorce is high when bankruptcy, chronic illness, a disabled child, or other trials strike the life of a couple. I've seen husbands and wives retreat into their own separate worlds when trials invade their lives. Instead of lashing themselves to one another to withstand the blast together, they lash out at one another—blindly striking blows at the one who should be dearest. But it doesn't have to be that way. Truth be told, it is easier to bear the load when another helps you:

> *Two are better than one, because they have a good reward for their toil. For if they fall, one will lift up his fellow. But woe to him who is alone when he falls and has not another to lift him up!*
>
> *Ecclesiastes 4:9-10*

A trial, whatever the source, must be seen as a threat to our marriage. Many marriages crumble in a time of testing. So, protect it. Call out reinforcements if necessary. If we wanted to add another story to our house, a builder would want to reinforce beams so they could bear the added weight. We need to reinforce our marital bonds if they are to bear the added load of trials.

This is true for other relationships as well. Children are often collateral damage. As they are trying to figure their place and way in a world that often confuses them, things are further confounded by trouble that befalls their family. It's hard to have a mom whose sickness places limitations on her mothering abilities. It's painful to watch a dad in despair over professional failures—and seeing his darkness envelop the whole family. It's embarrassing to have a sibling who has surrendered to a life of recklessness. Many are the ways children are afflicted when trouble comes. They need our help when they are forced to share our hurt.

It is also not easy to watch your children on the path of testing. You know they will grow through testing—you've experienced it in your own life—but you are no less anguished by their affliction. Even our parents bear a burden in our trials. Ignoring them in our pain only spreads the pain.

Our Lord Jesus is a marvelous example of avoiding self-absorption in our time of testing—recognizing that our testing impacts others. As the days and hours of the terrible affliction on Calvary drew near, he spoke gracious words to prepare the disciples for the travail ahead. He knew Satan would seek to sift them in his time of torment, so he prayed for them. When confronted by soldiers in the darkness of Gethsemane, he ensured their freedom by forcing the soldiers to acknowledge it was only him they had authority to arrest. Though his body was battered and bleeding, on his journey to Golgotha he warned of their coming pain to those who compassionately lamented his. At the height of his agony, with hands and feet pierced on a wooden cross, he paused to ensure care for his mourning mother.

Our trials will inevitably envelop those we love most. Let us resolve to fight the natural tendency to self-absorption and instead seek to envelop them with our love and care.

13

EVIL FROM GOD'S HAND

Read Job 2:10

When our eyes land on certain passages of Scripture, what they behold causes us to blink. Struck with the sense that things are out of focus, we stare at the text and find ourselves flustered. For we are prone to think of God differently than the words before us portray. "Shall we receive good from God, and shall we not receive evil?" Receive evil from God? Whoa! That can't be. Surely this is a poor translation, we think. But it is not. Therefore, we must pause and ponder.

Without doubt, many struggle with using the word "evil" to speak of anything that arises from God's hand. This discomfort is apparently felt by deeply devoted and talented translators of the Old Testament. Thus, many modern English translations deviate from the precedent of the King James Version—wherein *evil* is used—and elect to use words like *adversity, bad,* or *trouble*. While such alternatives may be technically acceptable, it seems that the English Standard Version (ESV) use of *evil* retains a force many modern translations do not. A leaking pipe in your home is trouble. Losing your wallet is bad. Driving in a blizzard is adversity. But the death of all your children, the robbery of most of your possessions, and then being struck with boils from head to toe—that is evil. *Adversity, bad,* and *trouble* don't do justice to describing the disaster that descended on Job. Such words also ignore the ignoble intent of the instigator behind it.

Make no mistake about it, what Job experienced *was* evil. No shading of words can hide this fact. The penultimate cause

74

of his calamities was evil in intent. Satan was not trying to test Job; he was seeking to turn him from God. It was moral evil in the truest sense—evil of the kind that eviscerated innocence from Eden. The marauding invaders who killed Job's servants and took his stuff were also carrying out acts of moral evil. They took what was not theirs and extinguished the light of fellow image-bearers. That's violating at least two of the Ten Commandments. What Job experienced can only be described as evil upon evil upon evil. Evil propagated by men and evil propagated by Satan. You cannot dress it up and make it appear differently. The terrible nature of what happened is visible through the transparent narrative.

But it was not unrestrained evil. It was permitted evil—for it was God who withdrew the protective hedge that enabled such evil to be executed. First, God shrunk the fence and limited the "no entry" space to Job's skin and all therein. He did so knowing full well what Satan intended to do with his newfound freedom. In round two, he protected only Job's pulse—allowing disease but not death. You see, Lucifer is not some lunatic running loose with abandon. He only touches what God permits. He is a restrained rebel. And God knows what will happen when he loosens the bonds of restraint. Not just generally, but explicitly. Thus, he only does so when it serves his purposes.

And herein lies the dilemma, the troubling truth. It defies what we want to believe. If Satan only penetrates where the Father permits, and our Omniscient Lord knows in advance what this lecherous leech will do, doesn't that mean evil is—in the end—brought by God? Does not responsibility lie at his doorstep? The story of Job answers this with a resounding yes. Unqualified and with no hesitation. Job called his experience what it was—evil. Specifically, evil from God's hand.

The events Job experienced are so bound to God's sovereign control that they are ascribed to God himself. Even Satan knows this. He challenged the Lord of heaven to "stretch out *your* hand and touch all that he has, and he will curse you to your face" (emphasis mine). Who does the reaching out and touching? During the second recorded meeting of the Divine Council, the Lord says to Satan, "[Y]ou incited me against him to destroy him without reason." God charges the Adversary with inciting him to do something to Job. Satan once more retorts, "[S]tretch out *your* hand and touch his bone and his flesh, and he will curse you to your face" (emphasis mine). The meaning is unmistakable.

It is true that the penultimate work of undoing Job was Satan's doing. The Lord declared, "Behold, he is in your hand." But he really wasn't—not ultimately at least. Even Satan knew this. So did Job. Which is why he spoke of evil as coming from God's hand. In doing so, "Job did not sin with his lips." His characterization was correct. He understood the source. But how can a good God bring evil into the lives of his children—especially one who is blameless?

This is where many students of Scripture make sausage. They try to harmonize seemingly irreconcilable truths by grinding them up and blending them together in such a way that the core ingredients are no longer recognizable. Such a sausage-making approach may make varied animal parts more palatable, but it tends to mask the meaning of biblical truth. In the early centuries of the church, this approach was tried with the Trinity and with the Incarnation—with disastrous deviations from Scripture. That's why creeds were created, to clear the confusion and express fundamental truths in easily memorized form. Though it may create tension, seemingly irreconcilable truths can stand arm in arm. Indeed, they must when they are both taught in Scripture. Trying to reconcile them removes the power of both, leaving us with a less potent faith.

Perhaps we can best make peace with this theological tension by recognizing that our greatest good came from the greatest evil ever perpetrated on this earth. Yes, I mean the cross upon which the Eternal Son was nailed and died. This was an act of great moral evil.

It began with a treacherous plot—an act of evil if there ever was one. It continued with an illegal trial based on lies. Deeper evil. Jesus was then condemned to death by a judge who publicly acknowledged that he found no fault in him. Tremendous evil. Ultimately, he was "crucified and killed by the hands of lawless men" (Acts 2:23). A final act of indescribable evil. Yet this was all accomplished "according to the definite plan and foreknowledge of God" (Acts 2:23). This was his plan. It was from his hand. The Father killed his Son.

It is nonsensical to try to nuance the words of Peter recorded in Acts to make them mean something different, because this plan of God is all over Scripture. From the curse pronounced upon the serpent in Genesis 3, to the portrait of the suffering servant in Psalm 22, to the One who bears the iniquity of sinners in Isaiah 53—the plan of God to offer his Son permeates the Old Testament. John the Baptist pronounced it powerfully: "Behold, the Lamb of God" (John 1:29). This was God's offering who would "take away the sin of the world." If you reject the truth that it was God's hand that was behind the death of his Son, you may as well donate your Bible to Goodwill.

Perchance we are inclined to think Jesus is an exception. He is unique, after all. One of a kind, incomparable. "Yes," we might agree, "God was behind this dreadful deed in Jesus' life. But does that mean he is behind evil that befalls mine?" In other words, Jesus' life shows the possibility, but is it really a pattern also true in our lives? For there were other things uniquely experienced by the Incarnate Son (virgin birth, angelic announcement of his arrival, etc.). Fair question, and one easily answered.

We should remember the fella with a fabulously colored coat. Joseph's jealous siblings sold him into slavery. Surely evil. He was falsely accused when he declined the solicitation of a seductress. More moral evil. He was imprisoned, even though the plaintiff didn't really believe the pleas of his seducing wife (hence, sparing the life of this falsely accused slave). Evil upon evil. Then a broken promise left him pining in prison for years. Evil piling on. But in the end, this was how Joseph characterized it when his brothers pled for forgiveness: "[Y]ou meant evil against me, but God meant it for good" (Genesis 50:20). There you have it. God was ultimately behind the evil of his brothers. And he is behind the evil that may befall you, though his intent is not evil.

Job seems to have known nothing of substitutionary death, imputed righteousness, or the promised Messiah. The core belief of Job was simple. He believed the God of heaven was in control of all things—even evil. Moreover, this God makes no mistakes. I decided long ago, come what may, to live by this same conviction. I encourage you to emulate Job as well.

14

TRUE FRIENDS

Read Job 2:11-13

Eliphaz, Bildad, and Zophar were friends, not frauds. Often skewered in sermons, they have been called out for their glaring errors about Job's character. It is true that their train of thought jumped the track and led to error about Job and God. But that is not how the journey started. We must see that the conflict in their hearts and minds—though not their bodies—was close to what Job experienced. His perplexity became their perplexity, as they shared in his anguish for seven days. Just as a clock that doesn't work is right twice a day, there are moments from these guys that are insightful. And we should remember that, like Job, they did not know the backstory of Job's suffering.

We should set the stage for their arrival. It is clear Job was not just a local hero. Wealth in those days was gained much like today, through commerce. Surely he was well traveled in name and perhaps in person. While the locations of these friends cannot be known with certainty, most scholars concur that they came from a distance—perhaps hundreds of miles. This implies significant time transpired between the onset of Job's trouble and his friends' appearance. Job's later statement, "I am allotted months of emptiness" (7:3), also suggests that the duration of his affliction before their arrival was months.

Today, we are rather loose with our use of the word *friend*, but this does not appear to be the case among the ancients. These were not mere acquaintances. Since Job was among the elite of his day, it is likely this trio of friends were noted men in their own right. Hearing of Job's undoing, they set a date to meet together to "show him sympathy and comfort him." These were honorable men. The trio shared a mutual admiration for this man from the land of Uz. They came with good purpose. Moved by the evil that befell their friend, they sought to help. Soon, however, their sorrow turned to shock:

> [W]hen they saw him from a distance, they did not recognize him. And they raised their voices and wept, and they tore their robes and sprinkled dust on their heads toward heaven.

The apparition they beheld was appalling. Their disfigured friend was as unrecognizable as he was pitiful. But it was him. This man of men, this most highly esteemed of citizens, was a mere shadow of his former self. What depth of disaster so changes a man? The shock of his appearance evoked expressions of deep anguish and the tearing of their robes and dusting themselves with dirt. Oh, the horror of it all!

It would be hard to sensationalize the scene. Job was a man who had it all. But he was not like the bombastic elites so common in our day. No, he was a blameless man whose possessions did not hold his soul. He was the portrait of prosperity *and* the definition of decency. To see him reduced to his desperate condition was beyond shocking. It was incomprehensible. His affliction unraveled these friends' notions of how the world operated. They were overwhelmed by it. As a consequence, Eliphaz, Bildad, and Zophar sat in somber silence mourning with their friend for seven days.

While the subsequent conversation of these friends criticized Job, we should not miss their care. It was no small effort to travel in those days. They set aside their schedules and personal comfort to be with their friend in his time of need. They inconvenienced themselves for his benefit. And they were deeply moved by Job's lot in life. That's what true friends do. They go out of their way to help their friends in need. They do not ignore the disaster that unsettles others.

They don't marginalize friends because things have become messy. They enter into their sorrow and pain.

But where were Job's other friends? What of those who also lived in the land of Uz? Why was Job alone in his sorrow when these friends from afar arrived? Job was a man who was generous in spirit, reaching out to help those in need:

> *I delivered the poor who cried for help,*
>   *and the fatherless who had none to help him.*
> *The blessing of him who was about to perish came*
>   *upon me,*
>   *and I caused the widow's heart to sing for joy.*
>   *Job 29:12-13*

Were there none he had helped in their time of need available to help Job in his? And where was his extended family?

The picture given to us is that Job is suffering in isolation. I don't want to read too much into the blank spaces, but in their seven days of collective mourning, it seems there were no others to join them until the final day when Elihu appears unannounced. Apparently, those closest to Job had tired of his trouble. When disaster fell, they turned on Job. Later, he declares, "I am a laughingstock to my friends" (12:4). Ouch. You can feel his pain when he states, "My relatives have failed me, my close friends have forgotten me" (19:14). How could you forget a man who once was the most prominent in the east? But they have not just forgotten him. "All my intimate friends abhor me" (19:19). Pretty strong words. To them, he has become as loathsome as the sores on his skin.

There is something important here that should cause us to pause before joining the chorus of boos that often rain down on Eliphaz, Bildad, and Zophar. These men of renown came to their friend who was now despised by others. Not just abandoned, but abhorred. These well-connected men surely knew not only of his calamity but also how others had turned on him. Despite his ruined standing before others, they came. They were faithful friends. They stuck with him when others did not. There is much to commend in that.

The Bible warns us that some people are fair-weather friends. They care not for us, but rather what they can gain from us. Calamity reveals their true colors.

Wealth brings many new friends,
but a poor man is deserted by his friend.

Proverbs 19:4

It takes a true friend to stick with you through times of suffering and sorrow—especially in the long haul. Perhaps few will actually abhor sufferers, but many will abandon friends when trouble comes. Most often, when friends disappear, it is because life is busy for them. Other priorities demand attention. They don't mean to abandon us. We are simply out of sight and out of mind.

I have heard numerous widows state: "No one calls or remembers anymore. The first few weeks after my husband's death, lots of people showed their care and concern. But now, they seem to have forgotten." It pains me to hear such words, for I am guilty of such neglect. People struck with injury leading to disability often experience the same. Early on, attention is high. But as time goes on, people drift away. Persistent suffering often lands one on a lonely road.

Jesus knows what it is like to be abandoned by friends. On the night of his arrest, every one of them fled for their own well-being. Not a single one was willing to stand by his side. Indeed, it was a friend who betrayed him to those who sought to destroy him. When his suffering was the deepest, he suffered alone. For over two thousand years, uncounted "friends" have denied him when the going got rough. Others just drift away because they prioritize the things of this world. We have a Friend who knows what it feels like to be abandoned by others.

Here is a challenge to us. Are we faithful friends? Trouble never comes when it is convenient. Needs rarely present themselves when we have extra time. Like the disaster itself, being there for others is always inconvenient. It inevitably costs us something.

The point is priorities. Is loving others a priority for us? It was for Jesus. He served when he desired solitude. He reached out when he needed rest. He filled others when hungry himself. Jesus knew nothing of the common call of today to take care of yourself first. This is because he had a food that others did not understand. He was most nourished by doing his Father's will.

May God help us to be true friends—friends that remain for the long haul, and who stick around, even when things get messy.

15

SUFFERING WITH OTHERS

Read Job 2:13

Nothing is more times opened by mistake than the mouth. The latter actions of Job's three friends admittedly affirm this adage. But their subsequent failure should not cause us to forget their gracious solicitude. Seven days they sat in silence with Job. When was the last time you spent seven days in silence? Their silence shows their empathy— they entered into his agony. They shared his pain like no other. They encountered his grief by grieving themselves.

Some commentators criticize Job's friends, asserting that their silence added to his anguish. I respectfully disagree. The text tells us nothing of the sort. Indeed, what it does tell us is that they remained silent because "they saw that his suffering was very great." Very great indeed. This was not your run-of-the-mill affliction. Job was suffering with an intensity rarely seen. And so, they sat in silence. They shared in his sorrow—an expression of sympathy in itself. Just being there is meaningful in a time of suffering.[15] If nothing else, it wards off the dangers of solitude for the suffering soul.

Two days after my son's tragic death, a dear friend came and sat with me for a while. We barely spoke a word. But the presence of my friend of deep faith helped anchor my soul in the present. In a very real way, he helped prevent me from being engulfed by darkness. When I spoke, he just listened— occasionally affirming. His prior nearness as a friend

---

15 Author and pastor David T. Furman, who suffers from a chronic nerve disease, has written a helpful book on this subject entitled *Being There: How to Love Those Who Are Hurting* (Crossway, 2016). I highly recommend it.

allowed him to be near in my frailty. Not just anyone could be there in this time of disorienting grief. This experience helped me realize that we have a special role to play in the lives of close friends. When trouble brings turmoil into their lives, we can be there in a way that others cannot. We should not miss the privilege to do so.

Two days later, one of our young pastors stopped by. Words escaped him as he stood with my wife and me in our foyer. He did not try to speak when he did not know what was proper to say. The three of us just cried together. That was one of the most meaningful moments in our time of grieving. He left us with no memorable words, but I will never forget his tears. They said all that needed to be said.

We should not underestimate the value of just being there for someone in a time of sorrow or suffering. I do not want to imply that silence is always the best response. Wisdom must be our guide on when to speak and when to know that silence is golden. But we don't have to know what to say to minister meaningfully. Our simple presence can be a balm to a pained soul.

Yet we can be there without really being there. If our emotional state doesn't fit the circumstances, our presence will bring little help—and possibly added hurt. I have heard many patients speak of the callousness of physicians toward their suffering. While sometimes an unfair judgment, their sense that their attending physician is unmoved by their suffering is very real. That perception only adds to their suffering. I have also heard believers who were aggrieved by a visit from a pastor who showed no compassion for their trial. The inability to enter into the suffering of another is a barrier to bringing them comfort. If you have been called to shepherd a flock, you must learn how to enter into the suffering of people in the midst of their trials. A detached deacon or preoccupied pastor will not help the hurting.

The trio who visited Job were not just present; they were pained by his anguish. This was shown in their countenance and actions when they drew near. We are told "they raised their voices and wept," as well as tearing their robes and sprinkling themselves with dust. Their conduct may seem strange to us, but it fit the context of their culture. Their shared anguish was visible to Job. They grasped the gravity of his tragedy. He knew they cared. He was not alone in his sorrow. These were friends indeed. They were a gift in his time of loss.

We should not be afraid to express heartfelt sorrow at the suffering of another. Don't be troubled by letting your own tears fall. After all, we are exhorted to "weep with those who weep" (Romans 12:15). It's biblical to cry with others; in fact, it is commanded. Our Lord Jesus wept over Jerusalem and at the tomb of Lazarus—making his compassion for both clear to all. Crying shows care. Shared emotions, whether joy or sorrow, can bring us closer to others. Tears can bring us together in times of sorrow.

But Job's friends' example also warns us that coming close in times of great tragedy can confuse us. Seeing people suffer is unsettling to the heart. This is why health professionals working in especially taxing settings, such as trauma units and oncology wards, often seem aloof. It can be a protective mechanism to deal with the emotional trauma of observing so much suffering day in and day out. Their detachment is a defense to protect their own heart. What would you do in that setting?

Job's friends could relate. Sitting with Job, observing the pitiful sight of this man's incessant scraping of his skin, dusting himself with ashes, and warding off flies attracted to his loathsome sores was harrowing. The retreat of light each night gave relief from the sight. Nonetheless, hour after hour through the dark they heard his moans and confronted their helplessness to lessen his agony. By the end of a week, his friends would have been worn down themselves. Why is this godly man suffering so? Why? Why? Why?

Trouble came when they moved from sorrow to trying to understand the cause of his suffering. Their arguments that follow reveal they spent too much time in their own heads. They lost track of why they were there. Good intentions often dissolve in the face of calamity. These friends came "to show him sympathy and comfort him." In the end, they fell into unhelpful debate. Their words brought added pain rather than healing. How quickly good intentions can vanish.

Truth be told, as consoling friends we are frail and prone to fail—unless we point others to Jesus. Job did not know the Friend of sinners. We who know Jesus are never alone. He will not leave nor forsake us in our time of trouble. We *never* walk alone. In this sense, our experience differs greatly from Job's. And you can see this by the examples of suffering in the New Testament.

Perhaps, then, we should just stay away and allow the sufferer to see Jesus. Let him come to them rather than us. After all, we don't want to make things worse by saying or doing the wrong thing. But that would be a terrible strategy, an unbiblical approach. Here is a truth we must not miss: Jesus is embodied in his church—the people of his church. We are his hands and feet, not just to a watching world but also to suffering saints. We *must* draw near. For we in whom the Spirit of Christ lives can help them see and remember Jesus, the founder and perfecter of our faith. We can remind them of the One "who for the joy that was set before him endured the cross" (Hebrews 12:2).

We who have lived through trials and experienced his comfort ourselves have a special responsibility in this regard. The Apostle Paul, a man much acquainted with suffering of various sorts, declared:

> *Blessed be the God and Father of our Lord Jesus Christ, the Father of mercies and God of all comfort,*

who comforts us in all our affliction, so that we may
be able to comfort those who are in any affliction,
with the comfort with which we ourselves are
comforted by God.

2 Corinthians 1:3-4

A key purpose in the comfort we receive in affliction is to be equipped to assist others in their affliction. Can we bless God for comfort we receive and then not share it? By sharing God's comfort with fellow pilgrims, we actually serve Jesus himself. In talking of the last days and the time of final judgment, Jesus speaks of those rewarded because they fed him when he was hungry, gave him a drink when he was thirsty, visited him when he was sick, and came to him in prison. Not knowing how they did this, we are told the righteous will ask when these things happened. "Truly, I say to you, as you did it to one of the least of these my brothers, you did it to me" (Matthew 25:40).

Do you see the implication of these words? Being there for others in their time of affliction is being there for Jesus. Wow! I want that privilege. How about you?

16

WHEN DARKNESS DESCENDS

Read Job 3:1-19

At times, life deposits you alone in the depths of an inescapable cavern. The days are cold, dark, and foreboding. Try as you may, you cannot find a source of light. You grope at the darkness trying to find a path to escape the gloom and doom. But none is to be found. For some, such seasons are brief—even momentary. For others, they seem interminable. There are people who experience times of darkness periodically across their span of life. When such darkness descends, it is deeply disorienting. Such was the experience of Job, as revealed by the volcanic eruption of his first words in the company of his friends.

Chapter 3 represents a major transition in the book of Job. Fail to recognize this and you will get lost in a labyrinth of words. The text moves from narrative to poetry—a genre representing a road less traveled by most modern readers. I have primed the pump for this pivot by occasionally inserting poetry among prose in previous meditations. Admittedly, my efforts are feeble and amateurish compared to the profound words that lie ahead in Job.

Hebrew poetry is meatier material than "roses are red and violets are blue." It follows no linear path to a foregone conclusion. This is evident in the vast majority of Psalms. It takes time to untangle word pictures spoken through ancient eyes and identify the point of a passage. If roses ever become extinct, the little ditty previously quoted will become obscure. So it is with ancient poetry. Some words picture things unseen by modern eyes—clouding their message to present-day readers. Thus, in the dense dialogue of Job and his friends, some puzzles will remain unsolved. Their meaning has been lost with the passing of time. In such instances, it is best that we acknowledge ignorance rather than assert insight that is tenuous.

The impenetrable darkness that engulfed Job is revealed in the prelude to his poem: "After this Job opened his mouth and cursed the day of his birth." Talk about despair. When we last heard from Job he was the model of steadfast confidence in the sovereign choices of God. But the pain has persisted and sorrow now overwhelms his heart. There is no end in sight. Misery is his close and unfailing companion. And it is wearing him down.

We should not underestimate the destructive power of persistent suffering—whether it be physical or otherwise. But I do believe chronic pain, or other physical suffering, is especially taxing in the long term. Unfortunately, chronic pain is widely misunderstood. This is because most people only experience acute pain. Pain is usually most intense when an injury is inflicted, then regresses with healing. But this is not the experience of those with chronic pain year after year. It waxes and wanes over time, within days and between days. It never goes away, but the degree of impairment may vary over time.

Likewise, those whose trials have been brief—regardless of intensity—may fail to understand the experience of those whose testing lingers. There are days when faith is strong, and days when it is weak. Present steadfastness does not shield one from future despair. The weariness of getting repeatedly hit with affliction sometimes causes you to waver in your faith. Such was the experience of Job. Far too many students of Scripture skip this scene from Job's story. But it is his state of being for most of the dialogue.

Job may represent mountaintop faith, but it's windy at the top of a mountain—making it hard to stand tall all the time. Job was not unwavering in the face of affliction, nor will most of us stand unmoved in every moment of anguish. So, we need something to hold on to when the winds of adversity blow strong. To find that anchor, Job had to experience the whirlwind in its full force. But that's getting ahead of the story.

At this moment, Job has been overtaken by despair. His suffering has consumed him. He has, so to speak, lost his way. His experience reminds us that even those of deep faith can fall into darkness. Let us be careful how we judge those in the grip of despair. Don't chastise the confused. Console them. Treat them gently. Don't break them further.

For Job, life had become so dark that he wished he had never seen the light of day. He cursed the day of his birth. What does that mean? Job shows us. It is poetic, but not pretty.

Let the day perish on which I was born,
and the night that said,
"A man is conceived."
Let that day be darkness!
May God above not seek it,
nor light shine upon it.

In Job's mind, his pain has erased every meaningful experience that preceded it. He has discarded the joy his birth brought to his parents. He has forgotten the years of enjoyment his marriage provided. He has erased the bountiful blessings he experienced with his children. Every delight has been forgotten and every blessing vanished. All the good has been subtracted as his affliction has multiplied. Job has been confounded by his affliction and is now exasperated with his condition.

Cursing the day you were born is a sorry state. But Job does not stop there. He questions why. Why was he given life? "Why did I not die at birth, come out from the womb and expire?" If the day was not blotted out, why not his very life? If his birth could not be prevented, why could it not have ended then and there?

For then I would have lain down and been quiet;
I would have slept; then I would have been at rest.

Can you hear his desperation? Do you sense his loss of perspective? Suffering has so deeply penetrated his soul that Job wishes all his days were cancelled. No good he has experienced in this life is worth the suffering he now endures. Yet that period of his trial has been only months at most. Talk about despair. How did he get there?

Physical suffering is disorienting. It can overtake you like nothing else. I have seen patients do things and say things completely out of character when suffering intense acute pain. I have known people who believe in the sanctity of life turn and take their own when the pain wouldn't stop. People in persistent pain sometimes speak nonsense. Their thinking becomes clouded. We should see it for what it is— the darkness of despair. Oh the trouble that can come when darkness engulfs us!

In his humanity, even our Savior experienced the disorienting darkness of pain and isolation. The night he was betrayed, he pled for the cup of wrath to pass. But it came nonetheless. As the world darkened, when his pain was at its height, he felt abandoned. Thus, he cried out: "My God, my God, why have you forsaken me?" What anguish! The Father never truly forsook his Son. But it felt that way. In that moment Jesus knew an unmatched darkness. He knows what darkness is like.

It is frightening when you become clothed in darkness. It is unsettling to watch another gripped by darkness. We want so badly to lift them out. But we cannot do it. We cannot reach that far. There is only one way through the darkness: to see light in the midst of the darkness, the True Light. David, the Singer of Israel, knew and experienced this:

Even though I walk through the valley of the shadow
    of death,
    I will fear no evil,
for you are with me;
    Your rod and your staff,
    they comfort me.

Psalm 23:4

Do you see it there? It is not being lifted out of the valley. Rather, it is seeing our Shepherd from within the depths of the valley. It is seeing he is *there*, in the valley with us. If we would see the darkness lifted, we must see God. It is not a change in circumstance or an end to the pain that will bring what we need. No, we must see him—as Job will do when the whirlwind appears. And when we care for another in despair, we must see this is their true need. So, we pray. Pray that God will come to them. That they will see him. For only he can lift the darkness.

17

A DESIRE FOR DEATH

Read Job 3:20-26

Life is not always worth fighting for—at least, that is the conclusion Job draws in his despair. In this moment of the drama, Job desires death. In truth, what he really desires is the relief he is certain death will bring. I have sat with others, including two very dear to me, whose physical suffering provoked the same longing. Misery robbed them of the desire to live. It was hard to hear them say death is better, and it is hard to read Job say the same.

Why is light given to him who is in misery,
*   and life to the bitter in soul,*
who long for death, but it comes not,
*   and dig for it more than for hidden treasures*

These are dark words. They picture the anxious desire for the end of his days—days that have of late been filled with suffering. This not the detached thinking of a philosopher. It is the painful pleading of a wounded soul. The text expresses the depth of despair that has overtaken Job. Robbed of all joy, he sees only one way for its recovery:

who rejoice exceedingly
*   and are glad when they find the grave*

Rejoicing at death? Gladness in finding the grave? Isn't death our enemy? Yes, it is. But when your lot in life is loathsome, your view of life—and death—can become distorted. As your world is turned upside down through suffering, so is your thinking. So, we should consider what leads to this state of mind and how one can recover.

Admittedly, this is a subject most of us would rather avoid. Lingering with others in darkness can be troubling. Hence, we tend to avoid it. But the text demands our attention. Yet there is another reason we should consider with care this troubling subject. For these words of Job draw us into a state of mind common in our day. On an average day in the United States, about 125 people take their own life—more than the number dying from breast cancer or auto accidents. Globally, one person dies by suicide every forty seconds. For every successful suicide there are twenty-five attempts. Some are surprised to learn that the highest frequency of suicide occurs among people in their fifth decade of life and beyond—often people who are living with incessant pain. The point is that this longing for death is not just an ancient desire. Chances are that everyone reading these words has rubbed, are rubbing, or will rub shoulders with someone longing for death. Thus, it is good to ask what Job can teach us about this dark desire.

First, do not miss the glimmer of light in the midst of Job's despondency. He cursed the day of his birth and longs for the sweet relief of death, but he shows no inclination to take matters into his own hands. Though he expresses a death wish, he is not suicidal. It defies credulity to assert, as some have, that he lacked the means to do so. No, he lacked the desire to do so. Do not miss this point. And the reason is plain through the record of his words. He believed God was sovereign in all things. His faith that God was in control remained unshaken. He questioned the why behind his excruciating trial, but he never doubted who was behind it all. And he was not about to try to usurp God's decision that he live. Question it? Yes. Overrule it? No.

Do you believe that faith in God's sovereignty is a guard against taking matters into your own hands and ending your days? The despair of Job was profound, but it did not lead to this defiant act. And yes, I do mean defiant. For suicide is denying that the number of our days is in God's hands. It is seeking to take what is not rightfully ours to grab. We are not the captain of our own destiny. There is Another who charts that course.

So where did Job go wrong? If he held strong in his belief in God's unmitigated control, then what led to his dark descent into a desire for death? The answer is quite simple, though Job can be readily forgiven for not seeing it: he did not have the treasure of Scripture we have that allows us to see what was blurred for him. The problem is that Job could see no purpose for his suffering:

Why is light given to a man whose way is hidden,
    whom God has hedged in?

Asking why is the understandable wail of an anguished soul, but it is not the path to peace. It is not wrong to ask why, but if the answer is not obvious, we should move on. For the why question can rarely be answered. The whys of God's ways are mysterious, in the sense that they cannot be discovered by reasoning with our minds. Our understanding is finite. As described in previous meditations, there is a spiritual world of goings-on of which we know next to nothing. The drama of Job exemplifies this. This dear man did not know about the cosmic conflict in which he was a key character. Apart from God directly revealing these facts to him, it was undiscoverable. To be sure, there was a why behind his awful trial. But it remained unknown to him.

Persisting in asking why only leads to frustration and confusion. Continually reaching for the unreachable is a waste of energy and time. Grabbing for something I cannot have serves no useful purpose. Even worse, it can be harmful when we embrace false notions of why a trial has come, especially a trial that persists. Some who cannot understand why God is allowing a trial find themselves seeking a human cause for their ongoing suffering. Too many counselors have led people suffering with anxiety, fear, anger, or other troubles to blame others for their ongoing internal problems. Assigning blame often leads to bitterness—a destructive force that will gnaw at the soul.

Yet Job shows us that simply *believing* in God's sovereignty is not a guard against despair. Embracing his sovereignty must be joined with *trusting* his sovereignty. God is not only in control, but he also has a purpose in the suffering of his people. There is always a purpose behind suffering. Always. Knowing this, I can turn from asking why to asking what— what can God accomplish in me through this trial? And here is where we who live on this side of the cross have wisdom that Job did not possess. James, the brother of our Lord, had some of the most helpful words on this topic:

> *Count it all joy, my brothers, when you meet trials of various kinds, for you know that the testing of your faith produces steadfastness. And let steadfastness have its full effect, that you may be perfect and complete, lacking in nothing.*
>
> James 1:2-4

At its root, every trial is a test of faith. Such testing is designed to produce steadfastness. It is intended to make us perfect and complete. Trials make us more like Jesus. They mold us into his image that we might be better used for his kingdom purposes.

Job did not see this in his own experience of suffering. That the purpose was hidden from him did not mean there was none. What if God granted his desire for death? We would have been robbed of the consolation of the book of Job. He and his wife would have been robbed of the restoration that followed his misery. What if Joseph gave up while a slave or while rotting in prison? He would not have experienced the elevation to the right hand of Pharaoh and being the deliverer for Israel.

How many, like Job, have desired death in the early stages of suffering—only to find purpose and joy in the years ahead?

As she lay in the trauma unit where I would later experience part of my clinical training, Joni Eareckson Tada longed for the sweet relief of death. A diving accident had left her a quadriplegic. Life seemed to promise nothing but perpetual misery. Yet, at her fiftieth anniversary in a wheelchair, she could beam of the God-ordained blessing her life has known.

To those who find themselves in the deepest crucible of affliction, I plead, "Hold on." Because you cannot see purpose in your suffering does not mean there is none. Because you feel you cannot endure does not mean you won't—in the strength the Lord provides. The absence of joy in the moment does not mean joy will not come in the morning. So, hold on. Wait for the Lord. He will come. And he will accomplish his good purposes in and through you.

18

WHEN COUNSELORS NEED HELP

Read Job 4:1-5

Health professionals often make poor patients. Accustomed to helping others, they find it hard to seek and receive help for themselves. Confident they know what is wrong and how to proceed, they unwisely become their own physician. Pastors and biblical counselors can struggle in a similar fashion. They may find it difficult to acknowledge their own spiritual needs. Overconfidence can blind them to their need for help. It appears Job may have fallen into this very trap himself.

Job's friends sat with him in silence for seven days. From the subsequent dialogue, it is clear this provided time to ponder Job's predicament. For an entire week, they ruminated on his ruin. Then they were ready to declare their thoughts and counsel to their friend. Job's outburst of distress opened the door to release their pent-up thoughts. One can picture them on the edge of their seats, so to speak, waiting for their turn to pronounce their judgment on the matter. Given the opportunity, they unleashed a torrent of largely errant theology sprinkled with ill-founded accusations.

Anyone who knows the story of Job knows his friends erred in their explanations. But that does not mean everything they said was wrong. Their exhaustive discourse has not been preserved in Scripture only to be summarily dismissed by subsequent generations. There is a reason this lengthy dialogue has been captured, and we do well to mine it for nuggets of truth. Even words that miss the mark can be instructive. If nothing else, they reveal erroneous ways of thinking that we should avoid.

As we read through the dialogue, it is imperative to remember these words are spoken by friends. They have sacrificed much to be with Job, with the goal of showing sympathy and bringing comfort. There is no malicious intent here. Though their words reveal frustration at both his plight and impetuous outbursts, this man is dear to them. Their deepest desire is to help.

At its core, there is a glaring error in their view of God's ways in the world. And that error has compounded their own perplexity at Job's plight. They are themselves troubled souls. Their weeklong entering into Job's mourning has left them an emotional mess. Their nerves are frayed, their patience has worn thin, and they are surely physically exhausted. As a consequence, they failed to help their friend in his time of need. But their failure is simply a reflection of their own deep needs—spiritually, emotionally, and physically. We should not fool ourselves into thinking we would do better were we in their shoes.

Eliphaz the Temanite is the first to speak. That he goes first, and that the Lord later speaks to him as the representative of the trio (42:7), implies he is the elder among the friends. Despite his stature, you can sense the trepidation in his opening words:

If one ventures a word with you, will you be impatient?

Do you feel the distinctly possible pregnant pause after this question? Though anxious to speak, he is hesitant. Eliphaz fears his counsel will not be received well. The reasoning for this fear is opaque but not hard to deduce. Men of prominence are not used to receiving counsel from others. A man who is head and shoulders above his fellows is not readily rebuked by "lesser" men. People of unusual wisdom are not easily challenged.

There is a lesson here for those who serve as pastors, teachers, and biblical counselors. Do others see you as approachable? Is the door open to challenge your thinking and acting? A place of prominence can be dangerous. Intended or not, prominence can make others hesitate to fulfill their spiritual obligations toward you in terms of exhorting, reproving, and rebuking. All of us need others in the body of Christ to serve this role in our lives. Even unintentionally creating barriers to this service will be detrimental to our spiritual well-being. A prominent position should not shield a person from others' words of wisdom. So, take stock of your life. Have you done what you can to open the door to reproof when and if it is needed? Have you made it clear that godly counsel is welcome? The clearest signal you can give in this regard is by receiving it humbly when it is given. In contrast, defensiveness creates a barrier not easily removed.

Job is in trouble. His anguish has distorted his view of things. He is unable to see beyond his pain. His calamity has consumed him. He needs one who will come alongside him and help him blow away the clouds of despair so that he might see the light of truth. This great man is in great need.

Though unsure of how it will be received, Eliphaz cannot suppress the urge to speak. He defends his decision by declaring, "Yet who can keep from speaking?" Silence, in his mind, is no longer justified. Job's words must not go unchallenged. While his moaning was tolerated, his muttered death wish demands a response. But how to proceed? How do you challenge a man who is without equal in the land? You tread gently. Before giving counsel, you remind him of what he knows—that there is value in the counsel of others.

Behold, you have instructed many,
and you have strengthened the weak hands.
Your words have upheld him who was stumbling,
and you have made firm the feeble knees.

While there is much sarcasm in the later retorts between Job and his friends, I see no reason to read the words of Eliphaz here as anything less than sincere. Too many Bible students perceive the errors in his friends' theology and conclude there is a critical spirit behind all that these men say. No, I believe Eliphaz is here reminding, not reprimanding, his friend.

Job was not aloof in response to the affliction of others. He served the role of comforter and counselor. He came alongside those who were weak and strengthened them. Eliphaz reminds Job that the afflicted benefit from the counsel of those who care. Job had watched others nearly stumble when afflicted. He helped restore their footing on steady ground. But he needs that help now.

But now it has come to you, and you are impatient;
It touches you, and you are dismayed.

Words on a page do not communicate tone. But the tone Eliphaz used would definitely have revealed the intent with these words. Spoken sarcastically, the words would convey a different meaning from the same words spoken in compassion. It is best to assume the tone reflected their friendship and expressed his care. "Oh, Job, my friend. Can you not see what has happened? What you have seen in others has overtaken you. You are stumbling. Dismay has you in its grip. You need help." While acknowledging that numerous commentators interpret this verse as a cutting remark, I read this as an affectionate appeal. He wants to woo his friend into humble acceptance of his help. This man who counseled others so well is now destitute in spirit.

It's hard to see that you are not seeing clearly. If we are honest, we will readily admit we often lie to ourselves. I lie to myself more often than anyone else. I tell lies to myself about God and about myself. And I believe those lies wholeheartedly. I think I am better than I am. I think I am wiser than evidence supports. I think I can do things in my own strength and don't need help. I think less of God than I ought. I question whether his promises apply to me. Sadly, I could go on. I doubt that I am an anomaly among Christians. That is why it is healthy not to "lean on your own understanding."

But there is good news. We who follow Jesus are part of a living organism—the Body of Christ. We need one another as much as we need our various physical body parts. You can reveal blind spots in me that I do not see. You can check my errant thinking and strengthen my weak hands. You can steady me when I stumble. And I can do the same for you. This is what the "one anothers" of the New Testament are all about. We are called to care for one another, comfort one another, serve one another, bear with one another, forgive one another, submit to one another, admonish one another, encourage one another, and—most importantly—love one another.

Let us not be so proud as to think we don't need such help. If a blameless man such as Job needed help, then surely we all do—no matter how prominent we may be in the eyes of others.

19

THE COMPOUNDING ERROR

Read Job 4:6-7

Compounding interest is a good thing. It means your savings feeds itself, yielding greater profit as you gain interest on your interest. It is the principle through which retirement savings are built. But compounding error is bad. Really bad. Because it means an error is like a snowball rolling downhill—it builds on itself and ends up being a really big error when things come to a halt. This analogy explains why Job's three friends went so wrong so quickly, and why they ended up in such a terrible state. Indeed, it led them to misrepresent God and his doings on this earth. For that, they required Job to intercede with sacrifice on their behalf (see 42:7-9). Thus, we must dissect this error from the start. Miss the problematic reasoning here, and we are easily led astray throughout their protracted polemic. So much of what they say sounds reasonable, but it is built on a faulty foundation.

After seeking to woo Job into embracing the counsel that is to come, Eliphaz lays out the belief that underpins the following arguments. The superstructure each of the friends will subsequently build differs a bit in appearance, but all three are erected on the same unsound footing.

Is not your fear of God your confidence,
and the integrity of your ways your hope?

The Hebrew word translated "integrity" in verse 6 is the same root as that which is translated "blameless" in the first and second chapters to describe Job's character. Eliphaz is, in effect, saying, "You know how this works, Job. You have counted on your blameless character to continue the flow of God's blessing. Your life revolves around the knowledge that integrity incurs reward." But here's where things get confrontational. The opposing corollary must also be true.

Remember: who that was innocent ever perished?
Or where were the upright cut off?

"Job, you know that evil receives its just desserts. Innocent people do not suffer, for God is not unjust to bring trouble to the upright." Eliphaz is not trying to convince Job of something he does not believe, though he has perhaps forgotten. This is simply the way things work in the world. His words imply that everyone knows this—it is axiomatic, a self-evident truth. Meditate on this for a moment. It may seem he has woven a tight argument, but there are some loose threads underneath it all.

Their thinking, which seemed common among the ancients, is rooted in the belief that God is sovereign over everything. Good theology so far. Since this is true, all that comes into our lives is determined by God. Job has stated as much earlier in the drama. In addition, though, they firmly believe the realm of men to be governed by justice—which means God acts justly. But here is where things begin to go astray. Since this principle is true, the outflow is that goodness is rewarded and evil is punished. God blesses the righteous and exacts retribution from the wicked. And here's where things get really dicey: blessing must affirm one's righteousness and affliction reveals one's evil. In their minds, trouble in this world is a sign of God exacting retribution. After all, he controls where, when, and how affliction comes. Since God is just, he must bring affliction on those who deserve it. This is where Eliphaz wandered into error.

The subtlety of the error is easy to miss. On the surface, their belief is certainly true. God does punish evil, including evil people. The Lord Jesus made clear that at the end of the age men will give account for their deeds. The unrighteous will experience everlasting retribution. And those made righteous by his shed blood will receive eternal blessing. But the timing of reward and retribution is critical. Miss this and you wander through a maze of errant views of life's experience.

God is in complete control and will exact justice. However, the fulfilment of justice is delayed. It is currently withheld for a simple reason: "The Lord is not slow to fulfill his promise as some count slowness, but is patient toward you, not wishing that any should perish, but that all should reach repentance" (2 Peter 3:9). God continues to call people to himself, redeeming them through faith in his Son. Until all he has chosen have come, full justice is delayed.

You see, Eliphaz and his companions confused the truth of ultimate justice with current conditions. Understanding the experience of a person in a given moment is more complicated than they think. The calculus of the final judgment does not provide the formula for interpreting present experience. Both Job and his friends erred on this same point, though for different reasons. Job's friends thought they saw things clearly. In their framework, Job's trouble is evidence of personal guilt. Thus, his only way out is to repent of the hidden sin. "Come clean, confess your sin, and all will be restored." Eliphaz began down this road by reminding Job of their common belief—a truth he asserts all will acknowledge.

Can you see where applying this reward-retribution paradigm to our present experience readily leads? It means I can judge your true character by what you experience. If you are prosperous, you must be blessed by God because of your goodness. If afflicted, you need to come clean with your hidden sin. That is where Job's friends will take their arguments. Certain that their diagnosis is accurate, they end up falsely accusing God of doing something he is not doing and charging Job with something he did not do. They will compound error upon error.

Privileged with the backstory, we can see these friends are wrong. Job's calamity is not tied to personal sin. He has done nothing deserving of retribution. God himself makes that clear. Sin is not the cause of Job's calamity. Yet this notion of reward-retribution in the present refuses to die. In John's gospel, Jesus tells the account of a man blind from birth (9:1-40). The disciples thought surely this was the result of his or his parents' sin. The Pharisees believed the same—seen by their disdainful dismissal of the man by saying, "You were born in utter sin, and you would teach us?"

This mistaken belief continues into our day. The heralds of the prosperity gospel declare that reward is unequivocally promised to the faithful. There is no place in their theology for suffering saints. Their malicious lies have deceived many—while making themselves filthy rich. But unjust gain has its own reward and sure retribution will one day come upon them. Others declare, "You have not been healed of your disease because you are holding on to unconfessed sin." So certain that righteousness is always rewarded with good health, they conclude continued illness is rooted in faithlessness. But these are also liars.

Still others are subtler in their views. "Surely," they say, "God has brought this affliction to humble you and enable you to see sin in your life that needs to be addressed." Such an argument can sound persuasive. After all, none are wholly innocent. On any day of the week, I can unearth sin in my heart that needs to be killed. I just need to look for it. Can't you do the same? So, if affliction comes, it will not be hard to find sin to address. There you go, we may think—principle proven. But the presence of sin and affliction at the same time in the same life does not mean the sin has brought the affliction. Causation is not determined by their mutual presence. Tribulation has many purposes, and we err if we assume it is tethered to sin.

I do not read Paul's repeated recounting of his many afflictions as having the purpose of rooting out sin in his life. Nor was such the purpose of the trials experienced by Joseph, Ruth, Jeremiah, or others. Can affliction expose sin in the life of a believer? Absolutely. But it is erroneous to conclude, therefore, that every trial has as its purpose the exposure of sin. The book of Job tells us otherwise. And on this point Jesus and the Apostles agree.

So be careful, my friends. Let's not repeat the error of Job's would-be comforters. We cannot know the unknowable. We must not judge our brethren based on their experience of affliction in this life. We cannot assume it is tied to sin. The Bible makes clear that God has various purposes for the trials and tribulations he brings into the lives of those who belong to him. If we fail to recognize this, we can end up like Eliphaz, Bildad, and Zophar: falsely judging God by ascribing to him something he has not done. That's an error I don't want to repeat. Do you?

20

WHEN DREAMERS DREAM

Read Job 4:8-21

Dreams are mysterious things. Sometimes scary, while at other times bizarre, the what and why behind our dreams continues to baffle neuroscientists. Yet, from time immemorial, people have sought meaning behind their nocturnal musings. Eliphaz was convinced that his midnight madness enabled him to see the why behind Job's trouble.

After a hesitant start, Eliphaz reminded Job of the way things work in this world. Integrity is rewarded and retribution is unleashed on evil. Job knows this and Eliphaz affirms it to be supported by his own experience: "As I have seen, those who plow iniquity and sow trouble reap the same." And this reaping is not the fruit of impersonal forces. No, "by the breath of God they perish." Then, with poetic power, he assures Job that fierce forces of wickedness are smashed in the mouth—like lions losing their teeth. They will not persist. Retribution always comes and their evil thereby exposed. But here is when things take a weird turn.

"Now a word was brought to me stealthily,
my ear received the whisper of it.
Amid thoughts from visions of the night,
when deep sleep falls on men."

And then, things get downright spooky.

"A spirit glided past my face;
the hair of my flesh stood up."

What do we do with that? We may be inclined to rush through these verses. "Move on, nothing to see here, folks." It is best to resist this urge. We are better served to slow down and think about what they tell us—as well as their implication and application for today. For the truth is, many who live with persistent affliction will testify of numerous instances where they have encountered their own Eliphaz. Some dreamers are subtler, others equally bold in their claims. They profess to see what we do not, to have insight into our personal trouble. Thus, we must know what to think about and how to deal with such dreamers, because they will appear. I know firsthand. Some have confronted me with their "visions."

Perhaps it is easiest to dismiss the notion of visions altogether. All such claims are false. End of discussion. Next topic. But this terse verdict leaves us in troubled territory. For God *has* communicated to his people in times past through visions. And not just Daniel, Ezekiel, and others who held the prophetic office in the Old Testament era. There was also Peter, Paul, and John. Numerous allusions exist in Acts to suggest such occurrences were not limited to the Apostles. Other believers saw visions.

It is, I suppose, comfortable to claim that such means of communication ended with the closing of the New Testament canon. That's a tidy response. It is true that John closed the book of Revelation with a warning about adding to "the words of the prophecy of this book." But it is a stretch to see this as referring to the entire New Testament (which had not yet been compiled), let alone a vision meant for a specific person in a given time.

Far be it from me to assert how God can and cannot communicate to his people in our day. The testimony of numerous recent converts out of Islam suggests God may yet speak through visions when it serves his purposes. Accounts of some missionaries also suggest God is not done with this means of getting his point across to people in special times of need. That possibility may make us uncomfortable, but when is anything about our awesome God "comfortable"?

Theologians better equipped than I have addressed the issue of how God speaks today and how to discern his voice. But in the present context, we turn to consider claims of insight into personal suffering—those who claim to possess special knowledge into our affliction that we have not seen.

It will help to step back from the details of the dream and peer into the central claim Eliphaz makes—for this is what ties it most to current-day experiences. Something has come to him, uniquely him, that enables Eliphaz to speak to Job's dilemma with uncommon insight. Like the Gnostics of later years, Eliphaz claims something for himself that sets him apart from others. He thinks he has what Job does not: insight, wisdom, knowledge, revelation. Hence, he speaks for God—or at least purports to comprehend what God is doing in a way Job does not. While it is true Eliphaz never identifies the source of his vision, the Lord's judgment on the entirety of Eliphaz's polemic (42:7) makes it clear he was misrepresenting what God was doing in Job's affliction. That alone should serve as a warning to those who would diagnose the cause of disorder in others' lives. Claiming to know just what God is doing in a particular affliction is dangerous.

I presume there are few reading this who claim a dream in the night has provided them insight into another person's problems. But it does happen. I will spare the guilty and not recount specific instances from my own life. Suffice it to say, would-be prophets still make their pronouncements. I have always found the preposterous nature of the claims to be self-evident. The unsoundness of what they profess to have seen or heard is easily demonstrated by applying biblical truth. I hesitate to assert one could *never* bring me a word from God through such means, but I've heard none that withstood the scrutiny of Scripture.

More common, and subtle, are those who claim insight into what God is doing in the lives of others based on their specialized training. Such claims are not entirely unreasonable. Experience and education can provide important insight into many things, including those helpful to people in times of affliction. But we can be misled into thinking such insight gives us an unerring understanding of the human heart or the ways of God in specific circumstances. It takes wisdom not to tread into this territory.

The error of Eliphaz should serve as special warning for those who counsel others. Some are trained in the field of human psychology, leading them to believe they can understand the heart and mind of people in ways others cannot. Psychology is inclined to label people, putting people into different boxes that can give false confidence that you know exactly what is going on in their heads. "Ah, he's a narcissist," as though such a label lets you read the mind of others and provides the power to predict their future responses. Psychology can give insight into patterns of human behavior and practices that can help some people change, but it provides no inerrant way of getting to the root of people's problems.

Using Scripture as their guide, biblical counselors have better insight into the working of the human heart— though not infallible perception. The Bible does not reveal with certainty the why behind a specific person's struggle in the present moment. I have seen biblical counselors overconfident in their ability to read the human heart and wrongly deduce the cause of a problem, causing them to bring unmerited guilt upon a counselee and unnecessary fracturing of family relationships. Some have led to disastrous consequences. Biblical counselors can do and have done much good, but knowing one's limitations is critical to avoiding errors like that of Eliphaz.

So, where does all this leave us when someone comes to us confident they bring insight into our affliction that we do not possess? First, be like the noble Bereans. Test to see if what they say is consistent with the Word of God. Second, ask if they are claiming unerring insight into something man cannot possess. If they claim to be able to accurately read your heart or the why behind God's doings in your life right now, head for the hills. Men may tell us things to look for in our heart. They may warn us of patterns they have seen in others and that we should look for in ourselves. But a true reading of my heart is held by the Almighty alone. And the ways of God are far too complex for anyone to give a sure answer to the why behind what he has brought into my life.

21

NO ROOM FOR MYSTERY

Read Job 5:1-27

The unexplained makes us uncomfortable. Mystery is maddening. We want to know the why, how, when, where, and who. We prefer tight theology that leaves no loose strings or gaps in the fabric of life. But such is not to be had. Our transcendent God will not fit into our carefully constructed boxes—though we are inclined to try to force him in anyway. This was the error of Eliphaz.

Eliphaz has a well-crafted view of the world that serves as a paradigm by which to judge all things. He does not appear to lack self-confidence. He believes he sees the matter at hand with great clarity. The basis for this confidence is plain. He says he has searched and discovered the truth.

Behold, this we have searched out; it is true.

Hear, and know it for your good.

Job may wonder what is going on, but Eliphaz does not. Seven days of silent vigil have provided ample time for him and his companions to "search out" the answer. He has discovered the why, and if Job would just listen, he too will be enlightened. Much of what he says would be uncontested. Errant theology is commonly mixed with grains of truth. Eliphaz affirms that God is sovereign. God's justice is also indisputable, as shown by the examples he provides. Yet his false step arises in the pivot point of this chapter—as he completes his reminder of the inevitable affliction of the foolish and moves to rehearse the sovereignty of God. And, in his sovereignty, God accomplishes his work of chastening. Eliphaz declares that God

does great things and unsearchable,
marvelous things without number

His view of God is high. But perhaps not high enough. Do you see how close he comes to acknowledging the limits of his understanding of God's ways? If they are unsearchable and without number, surely Eliphaz cannot know or understand them all. It's right there. But alas, he slides past this reality and rehearses a series of truisms about the God who controls all things.

[H]e gives rain on the earth
and sends waters on the fields;
He sets on high those who are lowly,
and those who mourn are lifted to safety.
He frustrates the devices of the crafty,
so that their hands achieve no success.

If only he would pause and back up a bit. What he needs to hear was spoken from his own lips: "unsearchable," "without number." Eliphaz is too confident of his own understanding. As a consequence, he cannot admit that Job's predicament is beyond his ability to explain. In his mind, he has it all figured out. Too many have followed in his footsteps.

During my clinical training, our department chairman would put us through a tension-filled exercise via the Socratic method—aggressive questioning intended to test the limits of our knowledge. Standing in the hall of the internal medicine ward, he would pepper one of us with questions about a complex patient in a nearby room. The questions began simply but soon left us squirming. He would intentionally force us to the limits of what we knew to see if we would admit what we did not know or, at least, could not be expected to know. He was trying to guard us against professional arrogance. He wanted us to be willing to admit the limits of our understanding—to say so when we didn't know. Apparently, Eliphaz had no such mentor.

The Bible is filled with reminders—both by explicit statements and by exemplar stories—that there is much about God and his ways that are simply beyond our discernment.

> *For my thoughts are not your thoughts,*
> *neither are your ways my ways, declares the Lord.*
> *For as the heavens are higher than the earth,*
> *so are my ways higher than your ways*
> *and my thoughts than your thoughts.*
>
> *Isaiah 55:8-9*

This does not mean God is unknowable. After all,

> *Long ago, at many times and in many ways, God spoke to our fathers by the prophets, but in these last days he has spoken to us by his Son, whom he appointed the heir of all things, through whom also he created the world.*
>
> *Hebrews 1:1-2*

God has spoken. In doing so, he has revealed much about his person and his plan. But there is also much he has not revealed, including the specific why behind one's affliction. This means we must learn to live with mystery.

Accepting mystery acknowledges the inability to know some things, things held in the mind of God alone. Failure to accept the reality of mystery leads people to try to fill in the white spaces of Scripture—to say what is left unsaid by the text itself. The inability of Eliphaz to admit the limits of his understanding led to words that border on heartless:

> *You shall know that your tent is at peace,*
> *and you shall inspect your fold and miss nothing.*
> *You shall know also that your offspring shall be many,*
> *and your descendants as the grass of the earth.*

Talk about insensitive counsel. Nothing missing from your fold? Has he forgotten Job lost all his livestock? Why would you tell a man who just lost all ten children that his offspring shall be many? How does a friend who has come to help end up saying things so hurtful? It seems Eliphaz has strung his theology so tight he can play no other tune. He cannot discern that his ideas are discordant with the circumstances at hand. Job is a blameless man who has lost everything.

Eliphaz earlier urged Job to humbly submit to the chastening that has come from the Lord. Yet it is Eliphaz who needs humility. He is so sure of his understanding of God's ways that he leaves no room for not understanding—and thereby runs afoul of truth. It is an ailment that remains common in our day.

Perhaps it takes the experience of affliction to come to grips with the truth that we cannot fully grasp the ways of the uncontainable God. Hymn writer William Cowper learned this through his own trials. He experienced dreadful periods of deep, dark depression throughout his life. Though he tried through various means, every time he sought escape through suicide, some unexplainable force stayed his hand. The tide was too low when he prepared to cast himself into a turbulent sea. He could not garner the strength to lift the bottle and pour the poison he obtained over his lips. The rope he sought to hang himself with snapped the moment his weight put tension on it. Finally, he gave up—concluding that perpetual despair was his lot in life.

Soon, he found a dwelling place next door to the writer of *Amazing Grace*, John Newton. The latter taught Cowper to bear the darkness by putting light on paper with a pen. The hymns this exercise produced have ministered to people for generations. The why behind his persistent periods of darkness that would not lift remains unknown. Nonetheless, what was produced through them has been of immeasurable benefit to Christians around the world. In the words of his hymn *Light Shining Out of Darkness*, he reveals his appreciation for the mystery of the God he loved:

God moves in a mysterious way,
  his wonders to perform;

He plants his footsteps in the sea,
*   and rides upon the storm.*

Cowper was humble enough to understand what he could not understand. He learned to be at peace with mystery. His assertion of the mystery in God's ways expresses faith, not fear. He knew behind the dark clouds was a God who loved him. In his hymn, Cowper continued:

Judge not the Lord by feeble sense,
*   but trust him for his grace.*
Behind a frowning providence
*   he hides a smiling face.*

Human sense cannot comprehend all that God is doing, so it is foolish to judge our circumstances through our cerebral capacity. Cowper knew some things were best left with God. For

God is his own interpreter,
*   and he will make it plain.*

Only God can tell us why. There are things men cannot tell us, things too wonderful for feeble men to discern. But what Cowper discerned was very true. Behind whatever dark clouds may surround us, there is a God who loves us. And one day, we will see his smiling face. With this knowledge, we can find peace in our present afflictions.

22

IS GOD AGAINST ME?

Read Job 6:1-13

At the age of twelve, I fell backward off a diving platform. It was a surreal experience. As time seemed to slow, I was engulfed by a strange sense of my life flashing before me. Nevertheless, I anticipated the thud that would mark my arrival on the concrete pad below. Just as expected, moments later I made a rather abrupt and painful crash landing. In contrast, Job expected no end to his free fall. To him, it felt like an unending injurious descent. Though he longed to hit bottom, the pit into which he fell appeared bottomless. So, as he falls, he grasps at anything to break his descent. He mostly grabs nonsense notions that will not help. As the fall continues, he is desperate for the conclusion—however devastating that final impact may be. He just wants the fall to end. This expressed desire will only further confound his friends.

Job begins his reply to Eliphaz by silencing his friend's arrogant slander:

Oh that my vexation were weighed,
and all my calamity laid in the balances!
For then it would be heavier than the sand of the sea;
therefore my words have been rash.

The reason he is repulsed by Job's lament is because Eliphaz does not realize the weight of his friend's affliction. The burden Job bears is greater than the collective sand of the sea! Massive. Immeasurable. More than his friends have ever borne. They just don't understand the incomprehensibleness of the weight

119

that has fallen on Job. Hence, the rashness of his words. And herein lies a helpful warning. Be careful about judging people walking through trials the likes of which you have never known. Do not minimize the challenge they face when you don't really have a basis to judge the weight they bear.

While young in the faith, I struggled with the depth of grief I saw in the lives of fellow Christians who lost a loved one who was a believer. I could not grasp why they became undone when they knew their loved one was safe in the arms of Jesus. Then my own mother died. I was grateful that her years of suffering from a disease that assaulted her body one organ at a time was over. I knew her longing to go home to the Lord was now fulfilled. But the depth of grief that gripped me was unsettling. It took a special work of grace for the darkness that nearly paralyzed me to lift. It was a humbling experience that revealed the arrogance and error of my earlier view of others. I just didn't understand what depth of grief comes upon you when one you dearly love dies. And so, I judged others. Thankfully, I had not voiced that judgment to those in despair, but I thought it nonetheless. It took bearing that trial myself to understand. I urge you not to repeat my folly, nor that of Eliphaz.

This chapter also reveals to us Job's state of mind as his pain persists. He knows his free fall is no accident. It is from the hand of God. That knowledge leads to a frightful, though false, conclusion: God has turned against him. He was probably not the first, and certainly not the last, to see affliction as the anger of God against him. The depth of his vexation on this matter is pointedly pronounced:

For the arrows of the Almighty are in me;
> *my spirit drinks their poison;*
> *the terrors of God are arrayed against me.*

Absorb that for a moment. Don't miss what Job is saying. One of the troubling notions he lays hold of as he continues his dark journey through affliction is that God is against him—a thought which terrifies him. And if this is so, there is no escape. Thus, it would be best for this drama to end.

> *Oh that I might have my request,*
>> *and that God would fulfill my hope,*
> *that it would please God to crush me,*
>> *that he would let loose his hand and cut me off!*

"Just let me hit bottom and end this tragic journey." At this moment, Job's perspective is pitiful. His perception of his state is tragic, though not entirely unreasonable.

Consider Job's conclusion carefully. If God is sovereign in all things, if his ways cannot possibly be thwarted, if no power can withstand him, then what hope do you have if he is against you? Of course, all these things are true. So, if God is indeed against you, your future holds nothing but ruin. And terror is the right response.

This is a needed warning. If you live your life in defiance of God, your life will end in ruin. That is the clear message of the Bible. Jesus' warnings on this are more pointed than anywhere else in Scripture. He warned of a punishment where "the fire is not quenched" (Mark 9:48). A judgment by God upon sinners is coming. His judgment will not be frustrated. Your sin will find you out and you will deservedly experience his wrath. No merit of yours will forestall the anger of God against sin. If you persist in your sin, you should live life in terror of the judgment to come. For "[i]t is a fearful thing to fall into the hands of the living God" (Hebrews 10:31).

But the good news is that Jesus came to rescue us from the wrath of God. Through his death on the cross, he paid the debt we owe so that we might gain the heaven we cannot earn. The Apostle Paul speaks of this great exchange:

> *For our sake he made him to be sin who knew no sin, so that in him we might become the righteousness of God.*
>> *2 Corinthians 5:21*

Through his death on the cross, Jesus provides the path to reconciliation—peace with God through the shed blood of the Lamb of God. We experience this reconciliation when we place our faith in Jesus. Elsewhere, Paul puts it this way:

> *Therefore, since we have been justified by faith, we have peace with God through our Lord Jesus Christ.*
>
> *Romans 5:1*

Here is the assurance that Job lacked. It is an assurance that all who live this side of Calvary should cling to. When Jesus brings peace, God is no longer against us. When Jesus becomes your supreme pleasure, God is forever for you.

Many of the epistles of the New Testament were written to people who were suffering. It is not surprising, then, that we find many words of assurance that God will not forsake his own. Emotionally, we can feel forsaken in the midst of suffering. Like Job, we know God controls all things. So, if affliction has come upon us, we might conclude God has turned against us. Nonetheless, God's word to us is that this will never happen. Never! Did he not say, "I will never leave you nor forsake you" (Hebrews 13:5)? The Apostle Paul was encouraged by this assurance through his own experiences of suffering:

> *But we have this treasure in jars of clay, to show that the surpassing power belongs to God and not to us. We are afflicted in every way, but not crushed; perplexed, but not driven to despair; persecuted, but not forsaken; struck down, but not destroyed; always carrying in the body the death of Jesus, so that the life of Jesus may also be manifested in our bodies.*
>
> *2 Corinthians 4:7-10*

Affliction need not crush us. It should not leave us perplexed nor driven to despair, because we have God's promises that we are not forsaken. The simple truth is that "A disciple is not above his teacher" (Matthew 10:24). Jesus suffered, he was sorely afflicted—by God's hand no less. We know God did not turn against him. Why should we see our affliction as evidence that God has turned against us?

Oh, my suffering Christian friends, please hear these words. I cannot tell you the why behind your affliction. I do not know the reason this sore trial has come upon you. But if you live by faith in Jesus, I can tell you what it is not. It is not a sign that God is against you. He has not turned from you. He has not become your opponent. Do not embrace the baffling notion that gripped Job. God never forsakes those who belong to him. Do not let your feelings mislead you. You may feel like God has turned against you, but you are being lied to by your own heart. Reject such nonsense. Rehearse biblical truth to steady your soul. Feast on his precious promises to you. God *cannot* be against you. Because *Jesus* is for you!

23

WHY FRIENDS MAY FAIL IN TROUBLED TIMES

Read Job 6:14-30

Have you ever walked away from an encounter with someone muttering to yourself about their stupidity? You're not talking to anyone in particular, just privately murmuring your grievances. It seems this may have been the scenario we are privileged to listen in on as the second half of chapter 6 begins. Job is muttering—to no one in particular—about his disappointment in his friends.

He who withholds kindness from a friend
    forsakes the fear of the Almighty.
My brothers are treacherous as a torrent-bed,
    as torrential streams that pass away

In other words, "When a man's friends come to him in a time of trouble, he expects them to bring kindness." This implies Job welcomed the arrival of this out-of-town trio. He anticipated their compassion. But as his words here show, his expectation was not met.

Kindness is a rather mushy word in English. But the Hebrew translation conveys a sense of a covenant obligation. It speaks of a serious responsibility arising from a relationship. In fact, Job states that one who fails to live up to that obligation "forsakes the fear of the Almighty." Why? Because the Lord will hold him accountable for his words to his friend.

Do you see kindness as an *obligation* toward others? The great call of the Christian life is to love God and love others. As the Apostle Paul reminds us, "Love is patient and kind" (1 Corinthians 13:4). He reminded his son in the faith, Timothy, that "the Lord's servant must not be quarrelsome but kind to everyone" (2 Timothy 2:24). Indeed, kindness is a fruit of the Spirit (Galatians 5:22). Kindness is bound to our obligation to love others. But it seems to be in short supply today.

Eliphaz failed in this obligation. He did not refresh his parched friend. Instead, his words deepened the wounds. As a consequence, Job compares his friends to a torrent-bed. A torrent-bed is a *wadi*—a dry riverbed that does not deliver the water expected. When you see the riverbanks from a distance, like approaching friends in a time of trouble, you anticipate refreshment. There must be water there. But when you arrive at the edge, you find it to be dry. Disappointment descends. It would have been better that you had never seen it, for it built a false hope. This is what Job feels as his friends have turned on him. He then extends the *wadi* image—picturing his expectation for help to be like that of a caravan searching the length of a riverbed for its expected source. Like them, he is disappointed to find no help or relief from his friends.

For you have now become nothing;
  you see my calamity and are afraid.

His hoped is dashed; they are good for nothing. In other words, better that they stayed home. But why are they afraid? Quite simple. If Job's suffering is unexplainable, if nothing merits retribution from God, then they are likewise susceptible to such tragedy. But if they can come up with a logical cause for his ruin, they can feel safe from such harm. I suspect that some people with an overconfident ability to explain the why behind things have a similar motive. They are only fooling themselves. Time and trials will teach them truth. They are not safe from calamity.

Job then moves to identify their error with precision. He does so with an open challenge to these would-be counselors:

Teach me, and I will be silent;
  make me understand how I have gone astray.

How forceful are upright words!
But what does reproof from you reprove?

Can you see why these friends failed? They reproved a man undeserving of their reproof. In their self-righteousness, they laid guilt upon a guiltless man. In particular, they reproved him but could not name the sin for which he deserved their reproof. They put themselves in the place of Job's judge when what he needed was the kindness of a friend.

Ultimately, these friends failed because they lost track of themselves. They lost their place and their purpose. They forgot why they had come. They forgot the role a friend should play to help in a time of grieving. Instead of comforting, they chastised. They delivered unmerited and unkind reproof. If my experience and that of some of my friends is an accurate barometer, there are many in our day like Job's three friends. They don't seem to know what to say and what not to say in response to another's loss. They end up being like a *wadi*.

My wife and I were dumbfounded by things Christians said to us after our son's tragic death. Some took affront to our lament that our son, to the best of our knowledge, had died without faith in Christ. For reasons unclear to us, hearing our lament provoked anger within them. So, they turned on us with their self-righteous reproofs. Some did so based on a dream they claimed to have had that they were certain was meant for us. Others did so with wishful thinking they were confident represented rock-solid truth. Still others brought reproof by misapplying passages of Scripture. All of it was painful to endure, but it gave us a better sense of what Job experienced. Numerous friends have shared similar painful experiences—unfathomable words from "friends" in their times of loss. Thankfully, we and they also experienced words and acts of kindness from wiser friends.

My scholarly research and writing in the area of living with chronic illness reveals this problem of judging the suffering of others to be widespread. In conversations with patients with chronic illnesses, as well as from reading memoirs and essays from such patients, I found that one of the most common complaints is the hurtful things other people say. These words reveal that others do not understand what these patients are experiencing. Patients say that the responses of others to their suffering is one of the hardest parts about living with chronic illness. Apparently, the "spirit" of Job's friends lives on.

I don't want to be like Eliphaz, and I assume you don't either. Yet, as I look back on my experiences as a health professional and in ministry, there are instances where I have. My reading of Job and my own errors challenge me to ask how I can avoid such unkindness and stupidity in the future. I believe this section of Job provides the key. If we will listen well to Job's lament in these verses, we will find a guide to help us. But we must listen and meditate on what he says.

It begins by realizing that our first obligation to a person in the midst of affliction, whatever the source, is kindness. We should be a source of refreshing, not of further pain. Don't pour salt on their wounds. If we encountered a parched soul lost in a desert, would we chastise him for getting lost? I hope not. What we should do is refresh him with water, cover his head to protect him from the sun, and assure him we are there to help. He is no longer alone in this. Perhaps sometime in the future we might gently broach the subject of how he had gotten lost in the desert. But a troubled soul in a turbulent state needs relief, not reprimand.

Even if a person has brought their suffering upon themselves through sinful actions, there is no place for us assuming the role of judge. That responsibility belongs to another. We must fight the inclination to judge others. But what if they haven't yet repented? In such instances, we do well to remember the words of the Apostle Paul, who reminds us that "God's kindness is meant to lead you to repentance"

(Romans 2:4). Do you realize that the kindness of God can be shown through believers, and used by him to bring repentance? Let us not fall into the trap of thinking sinners bearing the consequences of their sin are not deserving of our kindness. After all, "God shows his love for us in that while we were still sinners, Christ died for us" (Romans 5:8). The kindness of God came to us, "while we were still sinners." How can we withhold it from others when it is within our ability to give it?

Let us "put on then, as God's chosen ones ...kindness" (Colossians 3:12).

24

THE SPEECH OF A DESPAIRING MAN IS WIND

Read Job 6:26

Gems are magnificent minerals. Often encrusted in drab-looking rock, their beauty shines when they are removed from their dull surroundings. Isolated and polished, they sparkle. So it is with an important statement by Job. There is a helpful gem hidden in the crust of his complaint, one worth isolating and contemplating.

Do you think that you can reprove words,
 when the speech of a despairing man is wind?

Here is some of the wisest counsel in the entire book of Job. It provides a warning of monumental proportion—a warning often unheard and unheeded. If you are a counselor to others, I urge you to memorize this verse. I promise it will serve you and others well.

Job has broken the silence by vocalizing his complaint. He has openly shared his despair with his three friends. At this, they pounce. They proclaim him guilty of sin and sharply reprove his words. Sadly, they continue in this same vein throughout the unfolding drama of their encounter with this pitiful man. But, as God himself will later declare, they acted wrongly. The deepest problem is that they misrepresented God, which led them to falsely accuse their blameless friend. An additional error was how they responded to Job's words of complaint.

Even if some of Job's words were nonsense, they should have heard it for what it was—the meaningless rambling of a man sifting through the rubble of a ruined life. They should

129

not have put much weight on his thoughtless words, for "the speech of a despairing man is wind." Wind comes from out of nowhere and just as quickly disappears. It has no root in the present. So it is with the words of a man in despair. There is no need to shore up a person's theology based on the gusts of lament that flow forth in his darkest hours.

Perhaps Job's friends should be excused for this error. They did not possess the poignant examples of lament we find in the book of Psalms, a rich tapestry of beauty and bare expressions of human anguish. They contain some very disturbing complaints, ideas every bit wrongheaded as Job's.

> *Why, O Lord, do you stand far away?*
> *Why do you hide yourself in times of trouble?*
>
> *Psalm 10:1*

> *My God, my God, why have you forsaken me?*
> *Why are you so far from saving me, from the words of my groaning?*
> *O my God, I cry by day, but you do not answer, and by night, but I find no rest.*
>
> *Psalm 22:1-2*

Of course, God is never far away. He does not hide himself in our times of trouble. And he certainly does not forsake his own. Though it may feel that way at times, none of these things is ever true. Never. Such words from the psalmists do, however, remind us that feelings can mislead. In our pain, what we sense turns out to be nonsense. And truth be told, we know it to be so. But calamity clouds our vision, and what is actually near seems so far away.

So why are words of nonsense spoken by people in their times of confusion recorded in God's perfect word? Well, like most why questions, we'll have to wait to hear from God for the answer. But the benefit we gain from their inclusion is bountiful. Primarily, they tell us it is okay to voice our feelings to God. The words of the psalmists are often raw and real. Like the psalmists, we have an open door to talk to God about our feelings. And—here is a critical point—we should not be disturbed when we hear others do so. As a faithful Father, he welcomes our deepest expressions of anguish. We can feel free to openly express the agony of our souls. Did not our Savior choose the words of the psalmist to express his agony on the cross?

Moreover, the psalms containing the pained expression of an anguished soul also show us the path to dealing with our struggle—how to move from frustration to faith, from turmoil to trust. Perhaps none is more illustrative than Psalm 42, a psalm from the sons of Korah—those who led Israel in worship. The scene is of them being taken away from Israel into the Babylonian captivity. Apparently written at the edge of the Jordan while the hills of Jerusalem remain a distant sight, they express anguish at the longing to fulfill their role of temple worship once again.

As a deer pants for flowing streams,
so pants my soul for you, O God.
My soul thirsts for God,
for the living God.
When shall I come and appear before God?
My tears have been my food
day and night,
while they say to me all the day long,
"Where is your God?"

Then, the psalm moves to sweet remembrance of what once was, the role they played in worship.

These things I remember,
as I pour out my soul:
how I would go with the throng
and lead them in procession to the house of God
with glad shouts and songs of praise,
a multitude keeping festival.

Can you sense the depth of longing for what has been lost? And then we hear where this all leads:

I say to God, my rock:
  "Why have you forgotten me?
Why do I go mourning
  because of the oppression of the enemy?"
As with a deadly wound in my bones,
  my adversaries taunt me,
while they say to me all the day long,
  "Where is your God?"

Yet this is not where the psalm ends. Following the basic pattern of lament, having talked to God about his feelings, now he talks to his feelings about God.

Why are you cast down, O my soul,
  and why are you in turmoil within me?
Hope in God; for I shall again praise him,
  my salvation and my God.

Both in the middle and at the end of his lament, the psalmist preaches to himself. He steadies his soul with truth and resolves to trust. That is where lament is meant to lead.

What do you do when a sufferer stops with complaint? They express their anguish but do not seem to move to trust. They are tossed to and fro, lost in the tempest of their trial. It is important to realize the psalmists were not likely recording a moment-by-moment experience in real time. They are recording their experience after the fact. We do not know how long it took David, for example, to move from a tortured complaint to a trusting confession. Minutes? Hours? Days? Weeks? Most likely there was a gap between his complaint and his subsequent expression of trust.

We need to give the Holy Spirit time to work in people's hearts. We cannot do his work for him. It may be unrealistic to expect a seamless transition from turmoil to trust. In the meantime, we can model the process of lament for them. As you pray audibly in their presence, model the steps of lament. Begin by empathetically expressing anguish at their suffering. Be real and raw, like the psalmists. You may even be well served to borrow their words. Then move to expressing timeless truths that express trust in God's control and goodness. Rehearse his faithfulness in times past. As you take them with you to the throne of grace, you are helping the sufferer see the fruitful pattern of biblical lament. Some things are better caught than taught.

What should we take from Job's warnings that the speech of a despairing man is wind? We should be careful not to overanalyze what a troubled soul says. People traumatized by affliction are vocalizing their turmoil, not their theology. Those who are sorely afflicted should not be expected to, in the midst of their agony, provide a coherent analysis of the situation. The Psalms give many examples of wrongheaded thinking, foggy notions about God, that were patently mistaken. But the fog clears as the psalm progresses and their view of things lands where it should. Give space for those in turmoil to work through their lament. Like the psalmists, most will end up in a safe harbor. Let God do the work lament is intended to accomplish. And come alongside as modelers, not maligners.

25

WHEN PAIN STEALS YOUR HOPE

Read Job 7:1-21

A scan of the landscape of Job's life reveals that it is dry and dreary, with no oasis to break the barrenness. It has been reduced to heart-crushing, mind-torturing misery. This is the portrait provided in Job 7. While there is much that could be dissected in Job's discourse in this chapter, the deduction from his words is undeniable—Job has lost all hope. In fact, Job is living proof that "hope deferred makes the heart sick" (Proverbs 13:12).

I say he lost hope because before his calamity, Job lived with hope. Job made sacrifices for his children in case they had cursed God. He obviously did so with the confidence that God would accept the sacrifice and their offense would be cleared. The anger of God could be forestalled, retribution averted. But there is no sacrifice to make for one who is suffering innocently, as Job knows to be his case. If there is nothing to atone for, how will the suffering ever end? What will stop the torment God has brought? Can anything stay his hand? It is a woeful state.

Nothing will crush a person into dust more effectively than the loss of hope. Those who live without hope represent the true walking dead. There are tragic stories from Nazi concentration camp survivors that graphically tell what happens to people when hope is lost. The picture painted by those who persevered is grim to the extreme. Yet there are also compelling stories from some people in those same camps who were empowered by hope to endure

134

unthinkable misery. Extreme experiences don't always bring the death of hope.

Equally compelling, and perhaps more aligned with Job's experience, are accounts of people who bear protracted pain from disease. Some, like Job, succumb to hopelessness. Others soar with hope in the midst of physical misery. What provides this hope is important to consider, because mankind has waged a highly successful battle against diseases that steal life quickly—especially heart attacks, strokes, and even traumatic injury. As a consequence, more people face their final years in a slow, pain-racked march toward death. The fraction of people living with chronic illnesses that bring persistent suffering increases each year. The likelihood that you, my dear reader, will live a portion of your life with an affliction that causes you daily suffering is high. Are you prepared for that? Hence, it will serve us well to allow Job to teach us how hope is lost, and how the gospel brings hope to the darkest landscape—the valley of protracted physical pain.

We should recognize that Job's persistent physical misery eclipsed the loss of his children and possessions. Throughout his laments and responses to his friends, he mentions children only once, and never his possessions. But his laments are filled with dark poetic descriptions of his bodily misery. His words describing the dermatologic disease and penetrating agony it produced are vivid. This persistent pain has led to mental torture—turmoil in his soul because of the injustice of it all. The daily drip of loathsome sores floods him with a sense that God has treated him unfairly. Indeed, as we journey with Job, I believe you will see that his sense of an injustice being done to him overtakes even the physical agony, though the two are tightly tethered. The loss of his children and possessions was unquestionably a dreadful blow. But the daily drum of his misery was pounded out by physical pain. The devil devised this disease for his undoing. And it nearly did. Listen to the weariness he feels:

Has not man a hard service on earth,
and are not his days like the days of a hired hand?
Like a slave who longs for the shadow,
and like a hired hand who looks for his wages,
so I am allotted months of emptiness,
and nights of misery are apportioned to me.

Job feels like a slave-laborer, whose daily backbreaking, mind-numbing toil never allows him to experience the fruit of his labor. As he toils each day, he can only long for the shadow of dusk, which marks the close of yet another day of work. Still, the night brings no respite.

When I lie down I say, "When shall I arise?"
But the night is long,
and I am full of tossing till the dawn.

There is no nocturnal comfort, as night brings its own form of torment. So, what does he see ahead?

My days are swifter than a weaver's shuttle
and come to their end without hope.

There you have it—no hope. And so it will be until the end of his days, or so he presumes. Days and nights of misery, though only months long at this point, have worn him down. Job has become weary with the protracted journey and landed in the desolate desert of hopelessness. You can almost hear the whisper of his despondent soul.

Where does a person go from here? Where Job went is clear, for now he turns and voices his complaint about and to God. It is, in Job's mind, all his fault. God has turned against him.

Am I the sea, or a sea monster,
that you set a guard over me?

In other words, "What threat do I pose to men or you that you would hem me in like this?" And so, he seeks to distance himself from the Almighty.

I loathe my life; I would not live forever.
Leave me alone, for my days are a breath.

"Why do you bother me with your tortures? My life is so brief, I'll be gone in a flash. I am no danger to you. Just let me be!" Do you see what Job is doing here? He is pushing away his only source of hope. He is, rather ridiculously, dismissing the One who can bring light to the darkness. For him, the chasm between them seems unbridgeable.

But let us not judge Job too harshly. He lived without much, if any, knowledge of what gives us our greatest hope. It takes a textual Sherlock Holmes to find evidence for the hope of heaven in Job's lament. If he had a sense of this promised haven of rest, he has hidden it well in his plaintive poems. The absence of this hope leads to understandable despair in the face of continual suffering. It should be with eternal gratitude that you and I journey through this life *after* the terrible yet wonderful events on Golgotha were completed. We have clarity and certainty that Job lacked.

Our Lord Jesus made it clear that his resurrection was not the completion of his work on our behalf. Amazingly, he had work remaining to prepare for our homecoming.

> *Let not your hearts be troubled. Believe in God; believe also in me. In my Father's house are many rooms. If it were not so, would I have told you that I go to prepare a place for you? And if I go and prepare a place for you, I will come again and will take you to myself, that where I am you may be also.*
>
> *John 14:1-3*

Don't read these words too quickly. They are intended by Jesus to comfort troubled souls. This is a mind-boggling, hope-filled promise. Jesus left this earth to prepare a place for those who are his. He does not occupy himself with this task on the off chance that we might find our way there. No, he is coming to get us to take us there so that we may be with him. That, my friends, is the assurance of every follower of Jesus. And it is this eternal hope that forestalls the crushing weight of affliction in this life—because there is hope for relief and more:

> *So we do not lose heart. Though our outer self is wasting away, our inner self is being renewed day by day. For this light momentary affliction is preparing for us an eternal weight of glory beyond all comparison, as we look not to the things that are seen but to the things that are unseen. For the things that are seen are transient, but the things that are unseen are eternal.*
>
> *2 Corinthians 4:16-18*

Paul was not denying the real agony earthly affliction brings, for he experienced far more than his fair share of that. But he knew it was light and momentary in view of the eternal glory that is ours in Jesus. No affliction nor adversary can rob us of this hope. It is a sure thing.

On this bedrock of truth, I say to those bearing sore affliction: don't lose hope. Set your mind on heaven. For when you arrive there, God will do something marvelous. He will wipe away every tear, he will remove every pain, he will lift every burden. Knowing this, on the darkest days, you can join with the Apostle John and say: "Come, Lord Jesus!" And come he will.

26

THE CRUELTY OF WRONGFUL JUDGMENT

Read Job 8:1-22

Long ago, in a land far away, a man complained to God. He felt God had mistreated him. But God had done him no wrong. Indeed, if he would turn from his error, all would go well for him. I speak here not of Job, but of Cain—the firstborn of Adam and Eve. When his sacrifice was not accepted, though his brother's was, he felt aggrieved. But he was wrong.

> *The Lord said to Cain, "Why are you angry, and why has your face fallen? If you do well, will you not be accepted?"*
>
> *Genesis 4:6-7a*

Is Job, through his complaint, repeating the error of Cain? He feels himself aggrieved, but has he misread things? It appears that Bildad, the next of his friends to speak, believes this to be the case. Like Eliphaz, he believes that the catastrophe Job's life has become is sufficient evidence to show that all is not right in Job's life—nor was it in the lives of his late children. And his conclusion leads to verbal cruelty.

> *How long will you say these things,*
> *and the words of your mouth be a great wind?*

Bildad apparently slept through Biblical Counseling 101. Why he thought he would gain a hearing with such a beginning is hard to fathom. It is unthinkable that he felt this would open the door to help his friend. Perhaps that's part of the lesson for us from his speech. Like Eliphaz before him, the grind of hearing Job's wailing and the whisk of the potsherd perpetually plowing his friend's skin has gotten to him. These maddening forces coalesce into volcanic fury in his inner being, which now erupts with a tongue lashing.

So, be careful as you seek to help sufferers. Realize that the prolonged pain and exasperated explosions of others can produce impatience in us. Their mindless ramblings can be maddening over the long haul. As we seek to help them, we must be wary of our own frailty. We must control our own emotions. It is amazing how quickly sympathy dissolves and gives way to scolding.

For Bildad, what comes out is cruelty produced by anger. And terribly cruel it is.

Does God pervert justice?
Or does the Almighty pervert the right?
If your children have sinned against him,
he has delivered them into the hand of their transgression.

Why would you say such a thing to a man who has lost ten children in the blink of an eye? Why not just kick him in the gut and smack him upside the head? Talk about pouring salt on someone's wounds. But this is not simply thoughtless taunting. This is deeply rooted in the bedrock of his worldview. And this view is not based solely on his personal reasoning; he commands the collective wisdom of the ancients for support:

For inquire, please, of bygone ages,
and consider what the fathers have searched out.
For we are but of yesterday and know nothing,
for our days on earth are a shadow.
Will they not teach you and tell you
and utter words out of their understanding?

Bildad believes he stands on the cumulative wisdom of the ages. With false humility, he confesses the limits of his own wisdom and invokes that of those who have gone before. Like Eliphaz, he knows that God rewards the blameless and exacts retribution from the guilty. Thus, Job's lot in life shows him to be guilty. Isn't it obvious? After all,

Behold, God will not reject a blameless man,
    nor take the hand of evildoers.

Right there you hear the ignorance of Bildad. He sees Job's tragedy as evidence that he is not blameless. Bewildered he may be, but blameless he is not. Yet we in the audience watching this drama unfold know that God has declared Job to be exactly that. Indeed, it is God's assertion of Job's blameless character that has gotten this poor man into this mess. Bildad, lacking any evidence and driven by his errant theological presuppositions, has brought false judgment on his friend.

There is absurdity in Bildad's accusation. Job was so conscientious about sin that he continually offered sacrifices for his children *in case* they had sinned in their hearts. Would such a man leave sin in his own life unaddressed? It is illogical to think Job is suffering because of unconfessed sin. Yet that is his friend's charge—and he calls the wisdom of the ancient fathers to bolster his case. It only adds pain to Job's predicament, for fewer things are more crushing to the human spirit than wrongful judgment. It is the height of injustice. And injustice is a cruel burden to bear.

We live in an era that shows little concern about wrongly judging others. People are frequently tried and condemned in the court of public opinion based on little more than sound bites. Words are taken out of context, tone of voice is unknown, events leading up to the moment are omitted, and photos are even altered—but these are deemed sufficient to pass judgment. We are so sure of our ability to determine someone's guilt. When a jury or judge that has spent weeks listening to a mountain of evidence declares "not guilty," we have no hesitancy refuting their verdict and decrying that an injustice has occurred. Though far removed from the details of the case, we are quick to pass judgment on the accused and jurists. We condemn people on the flimsiest of circumstantial evidence.

141

In contrast, the Bible sets a high bar for declaring people guilty. The Mosaic law commanded a minimum of two witnesses to find a man guilty for any offense (Deuteronomy 19:15). A similar requirement is made by our Lord for acting in the course of church discipline (Matthew 18:16), something repeatedly emphasized by the Apostle Paul (2 Corinthians 13:1; 1 Timothy 5:19). Circumstantial evidence is not sufficient, biblically, to declare a person guilty.

Bildad's error warns us: don't judge others based on circumstantial evidence. The Bible warns against this repeatedly. It is obvious that Bildad allowed his neatly mapped-out theology of life to lead him down the road to injustice. Based on Job's circumstances, and those alone, he declared Job guilty. And many follow that pattern in our day.

One of the ways this is manifested is by judging parents based on their children's choices. Wanting to believe they can ensure their own children's spiritual fidelity, many Christians pull an ace card out of their packet of Scripture verses: "Train up a child in the way he should go; even when he is old he will not depart from it" (Proverbs 22:6). So, if your child rebels, it must mean you did not train them properly. It's all your fault. But the totality of Scripture and centuries of Christian experience demonstrate that this view is as errant as Bildad's simplistic reward-retribution paradigm.

Another sad example of this occurs when pastors are determined to be unsuitable leaders because attendance is not growing. Based on the belief that the Lord always blesses faithfulness with numerical growth, pastors are ejected from their pulpits by congregational leaders when the numbers go south. Evidence of faithfulness to their calling is discounted and the census is determinant. How quickly people forget that many turned from Jesus when he began to speak uncomfortable truth.

Perhaps the most common forms of wrongly judging others today occur on social media. I confess that I've never sent a tweet, I don't have a Facebook page, I don't know how to post on Instagram, and I'm old enough to recall when TikTok was the sound of a clock. But Christian writing today is filled with those who decry the toxic environment Christians have contributed to on social media. Apparently, many people feel comfortable judging others based on the evidence of 140 characters or less.

The point is this: there is too much of Bildad in all of us. We are so prone to judge others, often as a way of inflating or comforting ourselves. In doing so, we compound the pain of others and violate biblical precepts. We often forget the words of Jesus, who said, "Do not judge by appearances, but judge with right judgment" (John 7:24). There is a place for judgment. But when we do it, we better get it right—lest we pronounce wrongful judgment and thereby repeat the error of Bildad.

27

WE NEED A MEDIATOR

Read Job 9:1-35

My granddaughters enjoy playing hide-and-seek, but they prefer hints as they search for what's hidden. "You're getting warmer," I tell them as they draw close to the hiding spot. "Now you're getting colder," I inform them as they wander away. Often, they oscillate between getting warmer and getting colder as they search. Back and forth they go. Despite coming close, sometimes they are unable to find the hidden object on their own, my hints notwithstanding.

There is a sense that Job does the same through his lengthy laments. He takes no logical path to finding the truth. In the end, he can't find it on his own. Through the protracted process, sometimes he wanders so far from what is really happening that the glow of truth is nowhere to be found in his words. Other times, he comes so close that a glimmer of the light of truth sneaks into his complaint. Chapter 9 is one of those ramblings when he seems to draw close, only to meander away again in chapter 10.

Readers of the book of Job are often confounded by the incoherent soliloquies of Job and his friends. But the incoherence is actually part of the drama; it helps us enter into what is going on. These poetic discursions are not coming from armchair philosophers detached from the hard facts of life. They are not discourses shared over their favorite warm beverage in the local café. No, these are men whose view of the way things work in the world has been turned upside down through Job's calamity.

Job is both crushed and confused. His suffering makes no sense to him. His trials also unsettle his three friends. For seven silent days they considered the perplexing problem of deep affliction in a man of unparalleled character. They have been grasping in the dark for something to steady themselves in their unsettled state. The four of them are on edge, exhausted, and emotionally spent. This is not a situation for carefully reasoned or expressed ideas. What you would expect to hear in this setting is a flurry of feelings, ideas couched in dubious arguments, and misapplied truths—all expressed without sufficient care. Frustration, dismay, and anger would flavor their speech. And that is exactly what we find. This may annoy those who like to outline the text into orderly segments, but the dissonance effectively draws the reader into the tension of drama. It is important to not just hear what is said but also to feel it. Only then can you grasp the full message of Job. Because a suffering life is a drama filled with feelings.

Bildad challenged Job to realize things are not right between him and God—and that this is at the root of his suffering. Job appears to agree, at least with the first part of Bildad's conclusion:

Truly I know that it is so:
But how can a man be in the right before God?

Job acknowledges that his life gives evidence that God is no longer for him, though he continues to disagree about the why. But therein lies the true dilemma: "How can a man be in the right before God?" The real problem facing Job is that no one can contend with the transcendent God.

If one wished to contend with him,
one could not answer him once in a thousand times.
He is wise in heart and mighty in strength
—who has hardened himself against him, and succeeded?

This God with whom Job struggles is wiser and more powerful than man. One cannot succeed in a contest of the wills against him. To make that clear, Job rehearses elements of God's creative power. He can flip mountains on their head. He shakes the very foundation of the earth—probably a reference to earthquakes. Indeed, he can turn off the lights of heaven if he so desires. This God is one

who does great things beyond searching out,
and marvelous things beyond number.

Since this is so, how can anyone contend with him? You cannot answer him; you cannot refute what he chooses.

If it is a contest of strength, behold, he is mighty!
If it is a matter of justice, who can summon him?

Though Job appeals to argue his case before God, he knows such a wish is futile. He would not prevail.

For he is not a man, as I am, that I might answer him,
that we should come to trial together.
There is no arbiter between us,
who might lay his hand on us both.

Job longs to stand before the court of God, to argue his case before the Divine Council. But alas, there is none to argue on his behalf—none to grab his hand and God's, that they might be brought together. Did you catch that? Job comes within a cat's whisker of the ultimate truth he needs. He needs a mediator, one who will bring him and God together—one who will bring peace between them.

I take in those words and sit back with a sigh. Poor Job. If only he knew of the promised Messiah. Oh, that he was aware of the arbiter that God would send one day. This is one of the passages in Scripture that makes me ponder why God waited so long to send his Son. No sooner do I think such thoughts than Paul's words come to mind:

But when the fullness of time had come, God sent
forth his Son, born of woman, born under the law.

Galatians 4:4

Jesus came at exactly the right time in God's plan. That plan may be inscrutable this side of heaven, but the timing

146

fulfilled God's purposes. He came neither too early nor too late. But praise be to God, come he did. Because of his incarnation, his death on the cross, his resurrection, and his ongoing intercession, he brings peace with God.

> *Therefore, since we have been justified by faith, we have peace with God through our Lord Jesus Christ.*
>
> *Romans 5:1*

Peace with God. How Job longed to know that. One has grabbed the hand of this God "who made the Bear and Orion, the Pleiades and the chambers of the south" and the hand of man, bringing them together. The One who has done this is the Lord Jesus Christ. He gives a hope that Job did not know.

Job did see what many fail to see today: our God is awesome and, apart from a mediator, unapproachable. People today are so flippant in their view of God. They talk about him as the big guy upstairs or speak of him with the brazen familiarity of a fraternity brother. No, a true vision of God should make us shudder. When the prophet Isaiah, the most righteous man in Israel of his day, was brought into the presence of God, he declared,

> *Woe is me! For I am lost; for I am a man of unclean lips, and I dwell in the midst of a people of unclean lips; for my eyes have seen the King, the Lord of hosts!*
>
> *Isaiah 6:5*

Isaiah penetrated the truth even more deeply than Job. He knew there was none righteous but the God of heaven. He felt the need for a savior with great intensity—one to save him from the wrath of this awesome God. And the great news for you and me is that this mediator has come:

> *For there is one God, and there is one mediator between God and men, the man Christ Jesus.*
>
> *1 Timothy 2:5*

There you have the solution to Job's dilemma and ours. There is a redeemer who lays hold of our hand and God's, bringing us together. He has brought peace through his blood. That is why, unlike Job, we come with confidence into his presence.

> Let us then with confidence draw near to the throne of grace, that we may receive mercy and find grace to help in time of need.
>
> Hebrews 4:16

My suffering Christian friend, there is no chasm between you and God—though you may feel like it in your affliction. But Jesus, our mediator, bridged that abyss on Calvary. So, go. Go to the throne of grace. Go confidently. There you will find help in your time of need.

28

TRUST FOR TROUBLED TIMES

Read Job 10:1-22

Sometimes the most important thing to see about a person is what you can't see—what is not there, but ought to be. Seeing what is missing can be momentous in our effort to help. Priscilla and Aquila demonstrate this in their encounter with Apollos.

> *Now a Jew named Apollos, a native of Alexandria, came to Ephesus. He was an eloquent man, competent in the Scriptures. He had been instructed in the way of the Lord. And being fervent in spirit, he spoke and taught accurately the things concerning Jesus, though he knew only the baptism of John. He began to speak boldly in the synagogue, but when Priscilla and Aquila heard him, they took him aside and explained to him the way of God more accurately.*
>
> *Acts 18:24-26*

Though Apollos "taught accurately the things concerning Jesus," something was missing. His understanding was true yet incomplete. Priscilla and Aquila identified the gap and filled it—making Apollos a more effective servant of the Lord.

Chapter 10 reveals what is missing in Job's life. This battered beacon of light in the land of Uz says much that is true. But what is missing is monumental. In fact, it is at the root of why his view of God has become distorted and has left his heart drowning in despair.

Having brushed near the truth of his great need for a mediator, Job turns from speaking to the air to airing his complaint to God. Scholars debate whether his words are more expressive of agony or anger. The former is more likely since God, when he appears, does not condemn Job's words.

I loathe my life;
I will give free utterance to my complaint;
    I will speak in the bitterness of my soul.
I will say to God, Do not condemn me;
    let me know why you contend against me.

And then come a series of questions, rhetorical inquiries that are both absurd and acrimonious. Suddenly, as though struck by the folly of his own words, he sees through the haze of his anguish and acknowledges God's intimate role in his creation.

Your hands fashioned and made me...
Remember that you have made me like clay...
Did you not pour me out like milk
    and curdle me like cheese?
You clothed me with skin and flesh,
    and knit me together with bones and sinews.

Job reminds the Lord—and in doing so, himself—of the Creator's intimate role in bringing him to life. Job knows his being on this earth is no mistake. His God is no blind watchmaker, one who winds up his creation and then leaves it to run on its own. No, he brought Job specifically into being. He molded him like clay, formed his most necessary parts. And the Lord's work did not end there.

You have granted me life and steadfast love,
    and your care has preserved my spirit.

These words speak of God's intimate knowledge of and involvement in the life of Job. It is to God that Job owes his preservation. This insight seems incongruent with the charges Job intertwines with his utterances about God's role in his life.

Does it seem good to you to oppress,
    to despise the work of your hands

and favor the designs of the wicked?
...and now you have destroyed me altogether.
...and will you return me to the dust?

How does Job dance between speaking of God's intimate formation of his being, as well as his sustaining work, and accusing God of seeking to destroy him? Why would he interject these incompatible ideas? If he knows God made him, why does he think his calamity means God is now against him? Because he is missing something really important: *trust*. Without it, Job sees his trouble as evidence of egregious actions by the hand of God.

Trust is an expression of confidence in someone. Confidence that they will do what is good and right. It is a settled assurance that they will be there when you need them. Whether you really believe that's true about someone is best demonstrated when trust is tested. That is why confidence is strengthened through testing. Remember when David stood before Goliath, the champion of the Philistines? This scrawny runt of Jesse's clan looked at the mammoth monster that paralyzed the army of Israel and told King Saul, "The Lord who delivered me from the paw of the lion and from the paw of the bear will deliver me from the hand of this Philistine" (1 Samuel 17:37). And with that confidence, he struck dead the giant who struck terror in Saul's men. He trusted God to empower him to prevail, for God had done so in past trials of danger.

Job apparently lacked experiences of testing that would lead to confidence in God's love and care for him. Untested, his faith was shaken in the face of enormous adversity. He also seems to have lacked the reservoir of Scripture recounting God's faithfulness to his children over the years. Israel's ceremonial celebrations were a tapestry of practices woven with reminders of what God had done in times past—reminders that should build confidence for his care in the future. Sadly, it appears Job lacked this historical record

151

that would have guided him in these hard moments.

Yet there is something even deeper missing in Job's understanding of God, something our Lord Jesus emphasized—a view of God that forms the bedrock for our trust. Job gives no evidence of seeing God as his *Father*. He did not grasp that God is not simply the giver of life and controller of all things. He is all those things that Job acknowledges. But he is also our Father.

There are whispers of the fatherhood of God as far back as Deuteronomy:

> *Do you thus repay the Lord,*
> *   you foolish and senseless people?*
> *Is not he your father, who created you,*
> *   Who made you and established you?*
>
> Deuteronomy 32:6

David and the prophets also provide glimpses of this truth. But it is Jesus who most clearly invites us to understand the intimacy of the fatherhood of God. Indeed, his most common way of referring to God is as our Father. And this is not just an expression of Jesus' own relationship to him as the Father's only begotten Son. No, he also uses this endearing title to refer to every believer's relationship to God. He encourages us to come to him with the open appeal "Our Father in heaven."

Nowhere is the understanding of God as our Father and trust more tightly tethered than in Jesus' teaching about why we should not be anxious in this world.

> *Look at the birds of the air: they neither sow nor reap nor gather into barns, and yet your heavenly Father feeds them. Are you not of more value than they? ...Therefore do not be anxious, saying, "What shall we eat?" or "What shall we drink?" or "What shall we wear?" For the Gentiles seek after all these things, and your heavenly Father knows that you*

need them all. But seek first the kingdom of God and his righteousness, and all these things will be added to you.

Matthew 6:26, 31-33

Our heavenly Father, who feeds the lowliest of birds, will care for us—like a good father should. Jesus appeals to us to recognize that God is not merely the sovereign king. He is also our gracious, loving Father. His tender love and care should banish anxiety from our hearts, because we trust him.

When a person places their faith in Jesus, they are adopted into God's forever family. We have become joint heirs with Christ. That, the Apostle Paul tells us, should cast out fear.

For you did not receive the spirit of slavery to fall back into fear, but you have received the Spirit of adoption as sons, by whom we cry, "Abba! Father!"

Romans 8:15

Like Job, the suffering Christian may not understand the why behind their terrible trial. But, unlike Job, we know that we rest safely in the hands of a Father who loves us. When in anguish, we can cry, "Papa! Father!" In doing so, we rest assured that in him we will find the comfort that only a Heavenly Father can give.

29

THE RELIEF OF REPENTANCE

Read Job 11:1-20

Have you ever spoken harshly in haste? Are you glad your words were not recorded for posterity's sake? Zophar was not so fortunate. Thus, his unseemly outburst has brought the frown of generations upon him. To him, the words of Job have been like the sound of an out-of-tune violin, or the scratching of nails on a chalkboard. He's had enough of Job's complaints, so he explodes. In doing so, he leaves no doubt as to how he measures Job in the moment.

Should a multitude of words go unanswered,
and a man full of talk be judged right?
Should your babble silence men,
and when you mock, shall no one shame you?

No mincing of words here. It sounds like he has been resisting the urge to physically slap Job, so he does so verbally. Job was sadly mistaken if he thought his words would forestall yet another speech. In fact, Zophar is the most brazen and in-your-face of the trio. He believes someone needs to put Job to shame, and he's glad to go toe to toe with him. He is appalled by Job's claim to blamelessness.

For you say, "My doctrine is pure,
and I am clean in God's eyes."
But oh, that God would speak
and open his lips to you,
and that he would tell you the secrets of wisdom!
For he is manifold in understanding.

Rather testy, isn't he? He'd quite enjoy seeing God speak and deliver Job a smackdown. And then, Zophar delivers his own sucker punch:

Know then that God exacts of you less than your guilt deserves.

Cruel and condemnatory. No other way to describe Zophar's words. This is a crushing blow from one who traveled far planning to bring sympathy and comfort. Maybe it would have been more tolerable if he had physically slapped Job. Why would he say this to a man who is deeply suffering? Job has pled for the relief of death, and his "friend" tells him he deserves worse? Seriously?

But here's the real kicker—neither Zophar nor his sidekicks ever successfully exposed what Job was guilty of to deserve such suffering. If his sin was so bad it merits worse than Job has received, how could such a trespass remain hidden? How can they be so sure if they don't even know what it is? These guys are miles off the mark, and they don't even realize it. They are walking in greater ignorance than Job himself, though they think the opposite is true.

I suppose at this point it would be understandable to just brush off everything Zophar says and move on. Perhaps he's not worth listening to. Nevertheless, sometimes our critics can provide constructive help. Even though their words are unnecessarily harsh, perhaps even spoken with ill intent, they may point us to a greater truth—a truth we do well to catch and contemplate. Such is the case with Zophar; so, let's stay with him for a bit. Because he actually stumbles into something beautiful—misapplied to Job, but a wonderful truth nonetheless.

After letting his zinger fly, Zophar catches his breath. Having given way to his pent-up emotions, he turns to a more rational tone. Now he points Job to the mystery and grandeur of our God. For it truly is beyond man's ability to comprehend him.

Can you find out the deep things of God?
Can you find out the limit of the Almighty?
It is higher than heaven—what can you do?
Deeper than Sheol—what can you know?

Absolute truth from the lips of Zophar! Neither Job, nor his friends, nor anyone else can discover the deep things of God. We cannot know what God has not revealed. Though God is inscrutable, his judgment is impeccable. He is never wrong, and no evil hides from him.

If he passes through and imprisons
and summons the court, who can turn him back?
For he knows worthless men;
when he sees iniquity, will he not consider it?

Zophar has steadied himself on solid ground. For it is true—God neither misses nor ignores iniquity. And when he judges the sinner, no one will turn back his hand of judgment. Judgment can only be forestalled if God chooses to withdraw it. And this leads to Zophar's cure for Job's calamity.

Convinced Job is guilty of sin, as evidenced by the supposed retribution God has brought, he calls on Job to repent. But it isn't a harsh "repent or else." No, it is a winsome presentation of the relief repentance provides. Unfortunately, he is mistaken in seeing this as Job's need. The misapplication may make us cringe, but the message should be celebrated. It would be our loss if his errant diagnosis caused us to ignore his description of repentance. For it really is a beautiful thing, this repentance of which he speaks. It will do us good to ponder it.

If you prepare your heart,
you will stretch out your hands toward him.

Zophar calls for Job to assume a posture of prayer, which always begins with preparing the heart. And he is right. The first step we need to take when confronted with our sin is to turn our hearts from ourselves to God. Though inclined to run *from* the One we have offended, we should set our heart *toward* him and stretch out our hands toward him; come before him with open hands ready to receive the forgiveness he has promised. Come as one who needs what only he can give.

If iniquity is in your hand, put it far away,
    and let not injustice dwell in your tents.

Repentance is more than just sorrow over sin. It is a turning from that sin. It is the determination to, in the words of Zophar, "put it far away." One reason we may struggle with besetting sins is that we experience sorrow but lack this key element of true repentance. We hate the consequences but not the sin itself. True repentance includes a determination to kill the sin within us, to resolve to give in to it no more—even if that requires drastic measures in our lives, like gouging out an eye or cutting off a hand (Matthew 5:29-30). This admittedly calls for a special work of grace through the Holy Spirit. Yet it is essential. We must, in the words of Colossians 3:5, "put to death" the sin that entangles us. But when it is done, oh the blessing!

Surely then you will lift up your face without blemish;
    you will be secure and will not fear.
You will forget your misery;
    you will remember it as waters that have passed away.
And your life will be brighter than the noonday;
    its darkness will be like the morning.

What joy, peace, and blessing there is in experiencing forgiveness in response to repentance. For then, we can face God securely, with no fear. The misery that guilt brought is banished, like water long passed downstream. The darkness of soul is removed with the restoration of the joy of our salvation, like the dawn of morning (Psalm 51:12).

And you will feel secure, because there is hope;
    you will look around and take your rest in security.
You will lie down, and none will make you afraid;
    many will court your favor.

When we have repented, we can breathe in the fresh air that forgiveness brings. The foul smell of guilt is gone, and hope reigns. The fear of condemnation due to guilt is replaced with "rest in security." The nighttime will no longer be haunted by shame and fear. What a marvelous picture of the relief that repentance brings.

Do you know this relief that repentance provides? Your affliction may not be due to sin, but if it has persisted, it is likely the enemy has used it to provoke sin in you—anger, impatience, selfishness, and more. Are you quick to turn your face toward God with open hands of repentance? Do you renounce and earnestly seek to turn from your sin? My Christian friend, something beautiful happens when we repent. Don't miss the relief it will bring to your life. Go now. Don't wait.

30

WHEN THE WORLD TURNS ON YOU

Read Job 12:1-10, 14-25

The edge of my backyard is scattered with nut trees: walnut, chestnut, and pignut hickory. The random descent of the nuts to the ground leaves them mixed together. If we wanted to make a tasty recipe, we'd have to separate the hodgepodge into their specific kinds first. Only by separation could we enjoy the distinctive flavor of each. So it often is with Hebrew poetry. Without a more familiar linear arrangement of thought, we must tease out similar portions to savor the richness of the whole. This concept will serve us well as we consider the lengthiest of Job's replies to the initial responses of his friends who have turned into tormentors.

With the last of the three having now spoken, it is clear all of them have turned against Job. They each doubt his claims to innocence and are certain that he is hiding something. Even worse, they see his suffering as justified, the deserved agony of the guilty. Moreover, they are tired of hearing his complaints. More than tired—annoyed, aggrieved, and angered. They'd rather not hear any more of his whining. So, Job begins his reply in cutting fashion:

No doubt you are the people,
and wisdom will die with you.

When sarcasm surfaces, things have gone sour. Like curdled milk, the words of his friends disgust him, as does their arrogance. They are so sure of themselves, certain that they have insight into what Job lacks. He dismisses their arguments with words of derision. In essence, "The arrogance of these simpletons!" And the monologue goes south from here.

But I have understanding as well as you;
I am not inferior to you.
Who does not know such things as these?

Job mocks the "wisdom" parroted by his friends. They think they've brought great insight into the discussion, but their knowledge is known by all. They have added nothing to the situation, provided no insight into his dilemma. They have simply joined others in turning on him. And that adds to his pain.

I am a laughingstock to my friends;
I, who called to God and he answered me,
a just and blameless man, am a laughingstock.

Don't miss who has turned on him: "my friends." It is painful when the people closest to you turn on you. They doubt, dismiss, and sometimes even denounce you—all of which adds to the suffering. It is painful to watch, even more painful to bear. Where do you turn when the world has turned on you? What do you do when unjustly treated by others? Imperfectly, Job shows us the way.

One of the most common ways this happens today is when people doubt the physical complaints of others. Many people live with undefined ailments that meet no definition of disease. Over the course of years, they visit a variety of physicians seeking answers. The differing opinions lead to discordant diagnoses. As a consequence, their complaints of pain, fatigue, dizziness, and other symptoms are sometimes seen as contrived to gain attention or avoid responsibilities. The doubt of others only adds to their suffering. Some have had spouses denounce their wedding vows, unwilling to remain bound to someone who is always feeling unwell. Friends and family withdraw, weary of hearing the complaints of the sick. As Job declares, those free from the daily toil of a trial are often dismissive of those who suffer:

In the thought of one who is at ease there is contempt
  for misfortune;
it is ready for those whose feet slip.

Those who are free of misfortune often have no patience for those struck by trouble. Indeed, their absence of trials can lead to an arrogant contempt for the suffering of others. There is a warning here. If you have been spared much hardship, realize man tends to have no compassion for others' trials. You must be aware of this common weakness and not fall prey to it. Perhaps this also provides a special call to those who have suffered in particular ways. You will have an understanding others lack. You can play a special role in encouraging those going through similar trials. Most people won't understand what they are going through. You do, and that can be of great help when you apply that experience wisely.

But there are other ways, besides physical ailments, that people experience the indignity of doubt and dismissive reactions toward their suffering. For example, some live with the terror of an abusive spouse or parent who is skilled at hiding the physical, verbal, or emotional injuries they inflict. When the abused person gains the courage to tell another, their claims are dismissed because the confidant has not observed anything themselves. They see the accusation as inconsistent with what they know. Far too many live with the pain of abuse *and* the unwillingness of others to believe what is happening to them. It leaves them feeling very alone in their anguish.

I recently listened to a man who spent nearly thirty years in prison for a crime he did not commit. Think of that. Thirty years of your life locked in prison knowing you are innocent. Day after day you bear the oppressive environment of prison, with all its threats to your life and degradation unimaginable to most of us. As you awake each morning, you face anew the painful injustice of an innocent man declared guilty. No one believes you. "Sure you are," is the reply of the guards when you tell them you are innocent. "Aren't we all?" is the retort of fellow prisoners when they hear your claim. When asked how he bore this burden for three decades, the man declared that God knew he was innocent and one day, all would be set right. His relief of belief from others was nearly inexpressible when he was declared innocent and released.

So where do you turn when others have turned on you? You turn to the only one you can turn to, and the only one who really matters anyway. You turn to God. And, however imperfectly, that is what Job does.

Who among all these does not know
    That the hand of the Lord has done this?
In his hand is the life of every living thing
    and the breath of all mankind.

What has happened to Job is truly awful. Yet this does not change this simple fact: God governs the universe in every detail. Even the beasts and birds know this. Friends may have abandoned him, but they have not plucked him out of the hand of God. Moreover, the lives of those who have turned against Job lie in the Lord's hands as well.

He deprives of speech those who are trusted
    and takes away the discernment of the elders....
He takes away understanding from the chiefs of the people of
    the earth
    And makes them wander in a trackless waste.
They grope in the dark without light,
    and he makes them stagger like a drunken man.

Do you realize what Job has just said in these verses? In essence, God even controls the blindness of those who have turned against him. It is he who takes away discernment and understanding. He makes them grope in the dark, like those without light. This may be hard to accept when people have turned against you, but God is in control of their betrayal. The One who brings calamity into our lives for his sovereign purposes also brings those who turn against us. What? you ask. Why would he do that? How could that lead to any good?

Remember the disciple Judas? For three years he was in the intimate circle of Jesus' closest disciples. He was trusted with the money bag. In the end, he did not just turn away from Jesus; he turned on Jesus. This traitor of traitors gave him up to the wicked rulers of Israel—leading to his crucifixion. Yet this greatest betrayal of all time led to the greatest blessing of all time. This one who turned on Jesus was a part of God's plan through which the grace of eternal life entered the world.

Yes, God can even use the turning of the world against us for his good purposes. So, when the world turns on you, trust Him. He is still in control and worthy of your trust.

31

WISDOM FOR TIMES OF TROUBLE

Read Job 12:11-13, 13:1-12

The turmoil of trials can be confusing. As we seek to understand the why behind what is happening to us and what we should do, things are further confounded by the varied voices who add their own version of "truth." It is a time when wisdom is needed, but it may be in short supply. Alas, this was Job's experience. Wisdom was not his friends' forte, but Job—despite his desperate state—was wise enough to discern this. And in his response, he shows us the critical need for wisdom and its source. It is a message we do well to heed.

Think for a moment about Job's predicament. In the midst of his agony, three friends from afar arrive. They graciously mourn with him in silence for seven days. These guys really care; they empathize with their unfortunate friend. But when Job breaks the silence with his complaint, they unleash a torrent of accusations. How would you respond to three prominent friends assaulting you with the same arguments: "You are guilty of sin, so repent and all will be well!"? What if Job had given in and followed their counsel?

First, he would have been burdened with unjustified guilt that could find no relief—for he was not guilty. How would this have tormented his mind, as he searched for some hidden sin that was not there? Falsely conjuring up some sinful cause for his affliction, however well intended, would have led him astray. Second, he would have gone down a pointless path, repenting and expecting restoration. Yet since sin was not the cause, repentance would not have cured him. His suffering would not have been taken away through repentance, for that was not the purpose behind his affliction. But Job was not misled. He did not heed unwise advice. Why?

Does not the ear test words
as the palate tastes food?

Our taste buds are both a signal of delight and a source of discernment. Tasty food is enjoyed, bad food is rejected. At times, rejection prompts ejection from our mouths, preventing us from getting seriously sick. Likewise, a discriminating ear detects unsound advice. Discerning ears, like a discerning palate, can save us from trouble. Indeed, if we do not have discerning ears, we can mistake foolishness for wisdom. Job did not simply listen and comply; he tested the words. And he could see they brought no insight.

Behold, my eye has seen all this,
my ear has heard and understood it.
What you know, I also know;
I am not inferior to you.

Job's words may sound ill-tempered, but his friends' words were ill-conceived. They have battered him with false accusations. They needed to be brought down a notch or two, so he does the honor. In fact, their counsel is worthless, and it were better had they kept silent.

As for you, you whitewash with lies;
worthless physicians are you all.
Oh that you would keep silent,
and it would be your wisdom!

Sometimes wisdom is best displayed through silence. Those are words to remember. Indeed, "Even a fool who keeps silent is considered wise" (Proverbs 17:28). In contrast, Job's friends presumed to speak for God.

Will you speak falsely for God
and speak deceitfully for him?
Will you show partiality toward him?

Will you plead the case for God?

As we have seen before, the problem was that these friends thought they could know what only God can know. So, their "wisdom" failed to deliver.

Your maxims are proverbs of ashes;
your defenses are defenses of clay.

Job summarily dismisses their dictums as nothing but ashes. He had the discernment to see that their words missed the mark—by a long shot. But if he is going to reject the words of his "worthless physicians," where will he turn?

Wisdom is with the aged,
and understanding in length of days.

The gray hair on my head might make this sound self-serving, but Job declares something really important here—something often rejected, or at least ignored, in our day. We like to speak of some young people as being wise beyond their age, but true wisdom requires a combination of knowledge and experience. And experience comes with time. Not all older people are wise, but there is no substitute for length of days. For the aged have seen how the vicissitudes of life play out. Experience alone does not bring wisdom, but it is an essential ingredient. We do well to treasure the aged among us who have demonstrated wisdom. We are wise when we seek their counsel.

Yet even the aged are limited. Their wisdom is not fail-safe, nor even boundless, as Elihu will point out when he appears on the scene. Job knows this as well. And as an aged one himself, he seeks a higher wisdom than flesh can provide.

With God are wisdom and might;
he has counsel and understanding.

This is true wisdom indeed. It is not merely a declaration of irrefutable truth, though true it is. His words are a recognition that the why behind his horrendous trial is beyond the ability of human wisdom to comprehend. And it is to God that Job must turn to get this understanding.

But I would speak to the Almighty,
and I desire to argue my case with God.

So, he does. He turns from talking to his friends to talking to God—making his case before the Almighty.

But we do well to pause before proceeding. For something is missing here. Something Job really needs. He needs to hear from God. He does not need to hear from himself anymore, nor his friends and their folly, but he desperately needs to hear from God.

Thanks be to God, you and I have what Job did not—what he needed most. We have heard from God, for God has already spoken. That Word can do what the wisdom of man cannot.

> *For the word of God is living and active, sharper than any two-edged sword, piercing to the division of soul and of spirit, of joints and of marrow, and discerning the thoughts and intentions of the heart.*
> *Hebrews 4:12*

We have a grid for discernment that Job lacked—a means to "test words" by wisdom from above. Luke's account of the response of the Bereans when they heard wisdom from Paul shows us the way:

> *Now these Jews were more noble than those in Thessalonica; they received the word with all eagerness, examining the Scriptures daily to see if these things were so.*
> *Acts 17:11*

They did not just hear with eagerness. They heard and then evaluated what was said by testing it against God's sure word already revealed—determining if Paul's words aligned with God's.

My Christian friend, make sure you test the words of advice you get from others. First, test them through the grid of Scripture. Be like the noble Bereans: compare the words of men to the words of God. Second, seek the counsel of the aged, who have proven themselves wise through their knowledge and application of God's Word—those who can rightly combine experience with knowledge to apply truth to life. A discerning ear finds and clings to words to wisdom. And it also knows where true wisdom is found.

32

A DANGEROUS APPEAL

Read Job 13:13-27

Chapter 13 represents a watershed moment in Job's journey through suffering. It reveals a decision he already alluded to, but now is the moment for decisive action. Rebuked by his three friends, and a laughingstock in the eyes of others, he makes a dangerous appeal. But it isn't really dangerous; he just thinks that way. His misconception of his suffering has distorted his view of God. Job has come to see God as his tormentor. The pressure this all-powerful, all-knowing, ever-present God is applying on him will kill Job—or, so he thinks. "So be it," he declares, "but at least tell me why!" Thus, he appeals for an audience with God, an encounter sure to lead to his demise.

The gospel enables us to think more clearly about our suffering than Job could. Thus, we should not see his example in this chapter as one to be followed. We should interpret neither our suffering nor God's actions in the manner of Job. But before we get to that, we must dive back into the drama of Job's dilemma through the words of Job himself.

Let me have silence, and I will speak,
and let come on me what may.

Job wants to hear no more from his unhelpful friends. He is about to take bold action through a brash appeal. He knows it is risky, but "let come on me what may." Why does he say that? Because he knows his determined action is likely to turn out badly.

Why should I take my flesh in my teeth

and put my life in my hand?

In other words, "why should I risk my life by taking such bold action?"

Behold, he will slay me; I have no hope.
Yet I will argue my ways to his face.

Job is saying, "God is killing me through his torment anyway. I have no chance of surviving, no hope. So why not make my appeal to him face-to-face? What have I got to lose?"

It is likely your Bible version translates verse 15 differently than I quoted above, though it may have a footnote that includes this as an alternate translation (as does the ESV). The common translation, "Though he slay me, I will hope in him," is one of the most widely quoted verses from Job; even the inspiration for songs. But it is a poor translation and misses the context of Job's words.

When you step back and look at the overall message of chapter 13, it becomes clear that Job expresses resignation, not hope. Job is done with the nonsense his friends have shared. Instead, he wants an audience with God. Yet that prospect is terrifying. After all, he is God. How could Job survive such an encounter? But his affliction will not abate. As he looks over the horizon of time, he sees that his scourge—brought by this God he wishes to speak to—will kill him. Only death will bring relief, so what has he got to lose? Why not get it over with and get his answer to his suffering?

Having chosen this dangerous course, Job turns from talking to his friends to talking to the God he seeks an encounter with.

Only grant me two things,
then I will not hide myself from your face:
withdraw your hand far from me,
and let not dread of you terrify me.
Then call, and I will answer;
or let me speak, and you reply to me.

170

Job wants to speak with God but is terrified by the prospect. This audience can happen only if God will both withdraw the hand that harms him and overcome Job's innate dread of facing God. What Job expressed here, and in the verses that follow, is not a healthy awe of the holy. No, it is pure terror. He is afraid of God, this one he believes to be his tormentor.

> *How many are my iniquities and my sins?*
>> *Make me know my transgression and my sin.*
> *Why do you hide your face*
>> *And count me as your enemy?*
> *Will you frighten a driven leaf*
>> *and pursue dry chaff?*

So, he is caught between two states. On the one hand, he naturally withdraws—literally hides—from God in terror. On the other hand, he desperately wants to converse with the sovereign ruler of all things so that he might understand what sin, what grievance, has he committed that would bring this horrendous suffering into his life.

Here is where the gospel enlightens us, and makes clear that we should not be like Job with his tortured soul, not if we belong to Jesus. Reverence and awe are proper perspectives when we approach the One who is "holy, holy, holy." But terrified dread of God does not belong among us.

The writer of Hebrews reminds us of this truth—the reality that Jesus dramatically changed our approach to the living God:

> *For you have not come to what may be touched, a blazing fire and darkness and gloom and a tempest and the sound of a trumpet and a voice whose words made the hearers beg that no further messages be spoken to them. For they could not endure the order that was given, "If even a beast touches the mountain, it shall be stoned." Indeed, so terrifying was the sight that Moses said, "I tremble with fear." But you have come to Mount Zion and to the city*

of the living God, the heavenly Jerusalem, and to
innumerable angels in festal gathering, and to the
assembly of the firstborn who are enrolled in heaven,
and to God, the judge of all, and to the spirits of the
righteous made perfect, and to Jesus, the mediator
of a new covenant, and to the sprinkled blood that
speaks a better word than the blood of Abel.

Hebrews 12:18-24

We are not like those who came to Mt. Sinai, shaken with dread that one false move will bring our destruction. No, we come based on a better covenant, one for which Jesus is the mediator. His blood has been shed so that ours need not be. He died to set us free. Therefore, we come before him as a part of a festal gathering, a gathering of joyful worship to the One who is worthy.

Job lived in terror of judgment because he did not know the redeeming love of God in Jesus Christ. Indeed, we all once lived apart from God and would have rightly been in terror at the thought of coming into his presence. If we stood before God, our sin would have undone us. But why did this change the moment we were born again? Why should we not be struck with terror now? Because, as the Apostle Paul reminded the Corinthians (who had wicked pasts):

But you were washed, you were sanctified, you were
justified in the name of the Lord Jesus Christ and by
the Spirit of our God.

1 Corinthians 6:11

Therefore, we have no fear of being in his presence—for we have been washed and justified. Even when we suffer affliction in our own lives, we have this confident assurance:

So we have come to know and to believe the love
that God has for us. God is love, and whoever abides
in love abides in God, and God abides in him. By
this is love perfected with us, so that we may have

*confidence for the day of judgment, because as he is
so also are we in this world. There is no fear in love,
but perfect love casts out fear. For fear has to do
with punishment, and whoever fears has not been
perfected in love.*

1 John 4:16-18

The love of God in Jesus Christ removes the fear of
punishment—which is the cause of terror before God. For the
price has been paid and we have been perfected in love. The
Father poured his wrath upon the Son, placing on him the
punishment we would otherwise provoke in his presence.
Since the price has been paid, no punishment remains to be
borne. Thus, there is no reason for fear.

My suffering friend, there is no dread in our approach to
God in times of turmoil. Unlike Job, we should not be struck
with terror at the prospect of coming into the presence of
God. Instead of fearing he will pour his *wrath* upon us, we
rest in the assurance that he poured his *love* upon us through
his Son. And when we experience his perfect love, "it casts
out fear." Love forever banishes fear. Gone. Never to plague
us again. Don't be like Job. Let no thoughts of terror strike
you as you come to God. For every moment in his presence
will be full of delight, not dread.

33

DEATH COMES TO ALL

Read Job 13:28–14:22

Most people are apprehensive about death, but even more so when death seems imminent. At such moments, it is wise to ponder what death means and will bring. Thus, the turn in Job's speech should not surprise us. He has made a brazen decision that may cause his demise— for how can he survive an audience with this God who has become his tormentor? So, he turns to the topic of death. He poetically pictures what he knows to be certain *and* what he hopes for, though he seems to let go of that hope very quickly. For him, it is like grasping at smoke. But first, the certainty of death.

Man wastes away like a rotten thing,
like a garment that is moth-eaten.
Man who is born of a woman
is few of days and full of trouble.
He comes out like a flower and withers;
he flees like a shadow and continues not.

Job is certain that death will come, for it comes upon us all. As sure as the flower withers and the shadow disappears, man will die. Like the garments he wears, time consumes his body. In the grand scheme of things, his days are few. There is no escaping this reality. As the old nursery rhyme puts it, "we all fall down." Hence, it is good for us to ponder this from time to time. King David, a master in expressing deep truth, put it this way:

174

O Lord, make me know my end
  and what is the measure of my days;
  let me know how fleeting I am!
Behold, you have made my days a few handbreadths,
  and my lifetime is as nothing before you.
Surely all mankind stands as a mere breath!
                    Psalm 39:4-5

Do you live like you're going to die? Living with an awareness of the brevity of life keeps our priorities straight. It is a tonic against treasuring what is temporal. Jesus declared that a man unaware that death may overtake him at any moment is a fool (Luke 12:20). Let us not be fools. May we, like David, plead for the Lord to give us an awareness of the fleeting nature of life on this earth.

Job was certainly conscious of this truth. In fact, the brevity of man's life makes him wonder why God bothers to look upon or even judge him.

And do you open your eyes on such a one
  and bring me into judgment with you?

Why does God waste his time on man? Why exact retribution on one so quickly passing? Especially since God himself has set the limits of a man's days on this earth.

Since his days are determined,
  and the number of his months is with you,
  and you have appointed his limits that he cannot pass

These words are worth a pause. Death is never a surprise to God. Never. No one dies too soon or too late by God's reckoning. He numbers our days. We will not outlive, nor underlive, the days God has set for us. We cannot outsmart the meter of the time allotted to us. And, no one can short-circuit the length of days the Maker of man has given a person.

This truth has always comforted me, but never more so than upon the tragic death of my son. For a period after his death, I tormented myself with questions about what I might have done to prevent his passing. I found myself replaying moments from the weeks before his death and was haunted by the question, "What if I had...?" Graciously, the Lord brought this truth to my mind—reminding me that he controls the timing of our departure from this earth. That does not make our decisions meaningless, for our actions are often how his will is accomplished. But God's providence sets the span of our life, as well as the lives of those we love.

Perhaps you have been similarly haunted, worried that a medical decision or another decision may have led to a different outcome for a loved one. Don't assault your mind with such questions. God has determined every person's days and has "appointed his limits that he cannot pass." That limit is decided by God, not your actions. This truth is not a call to reckless living, but it is a cause to rest in his sovereign choices.

So, death will come. Then what? Job seems ...uncertain. He vacillates between despair and hope, though that hope is like life itself—fleeting.

> For there is hope for a tree,
>> if it be cut down, that it will sprout again,
>> and that its shoots will not cease.
> Though its root grow old in the earth,
>> and its stump die in the soil,
> yet at the scent of water it will bud
>> and put out branches like a young plant.

Job, as he frequently does, shows himself to be a careful contemplator of creation. A tree may be cut down, yet its roots spring to life again. The woodsman's axe does not remove its life from the soil. Yet it is not so with man.

> But a man dies and is laid low;
>> man breathes his last, and where is he?
> As waters fail from a lake
>> and a river wastes away and dries up,
> so a man lies down and rises not again;
>> till the heavens are no more he will not awake
>> or be roused out of his sleep.

A man cut down is not like a tree felled. When a man dies, he has no root on this earth to spring from again. Life is simply over. Done. Never to be seen again. If those words seem to suggest life is pointless, Job's words at the end of the chapter make it more painful.

His sons come to honor, and he does not know it;
they are brought low, and he perceives it not.
He feels only the pain of his own body,
and he mourns only for himself.

That is as bleak a view of death as you could get. Not only will man not rise again, but his post-death existence will be one of suffering. All he senses is his own pain and loss. Yet between these bookends of futility, Job reveals why he sees death this way and shows the only basis for hope.

Oh that you would hide me in Sheol,
that you would conceal me until your wrath be past,
that you would appoint me a set time, and remember me!
If a man dies, shall he live again?
All the days of my service I would wait,
till my renewal should come.
You would call, and I would answer you;
you would long for the work of your hands.
For then you would number my steps;
you would not keep watch over my sin;
my transgression would be sealed up in a bag,
and you would cover over my iniquity.

Job knows his only hope is if by some means he could be protected from the wrath of God until it has passed. If he could be concealed from this time of judgment, so that he could live through it, God might remember him—he who is "the work of [God's] hands." But for this to be so, God would somehow need to "cover over [his] iniquity." His repeated phrase "that you would" suggests what little hope he has hangs by a thread. Not so for you and me. We know that God has done what Job hoped for through the gift of his Son. Job wanted to hide in Sheol; we are "hidden with Christ in God" (Colossians 3:3). Indeed, we shall "be saved by him from the wrath of God" (Romans 5:9).

We may experience times of intense suffering on this earth—physical, spiritual, and emotional. When we do, let it remind us that we have been saved from the most intense suffering possible: eternal suffering. For God has covered our iniquity with the blood of his Son. Because of this, we are hidden from his wrath and will rise again! And that gives us hope in the face of death. Hold to that hope and don't let go— for "death is swallowed up in victory" (1 Corinthians 15:54).

34

THE BLINDNESS OF LEGALISM

Read Job 15:1-35

Legalism has persistently presented a distorted view of God. It is a mindset that refuses to die. The Lord Jesus reserved his harshest words for the religious legalists of his day, the scribes and Pharisees. The Apostle Paul, himself long trapped in works-righteousness, repeatedly exposed its damning teaching. Legalism not only warps a person's view of God; it also blinds one to the true nature of human suffering. Mark these words: you can't grasp the causes of misfortune while shackled in the chains of legalism. In his second speech, Eliphaz shows us why this is true.

Should a wise man answer with windy knowledge,
and fill his belly with the east wind?
Should he argue in unprofitable talk,
or in words with which he can do no good?

Eliphaz has moved from arrogance to anger. In his first speech, he carefully, but piously, asserted that he had successfully untangled the cause of Job's calamity. Now, he is spitting mad. In his mind, the words of Job are not just scandalous, they are dangerous.

But you are doing away with the fear of God
and hindering meditation before God.

This is a serious charge leveled against a man God commends before the Divine Council. On what basis does he conclude Job's words "are doing away with the fear of God"? In each of his orations, it is obvious that Eliphaz holds a legalist's view of God and his dealings with man. Goodness is rewarded and sin brings retribution. Therefore, suffering must be evidence of sin. The reason calamity descends on men is that God is exacting retribution for their transgressions.

But Job aggressively claims his innocence. Yet if even the innocent suffer, the legalist's view of life is turned topsy-turvy. If calamity falls upon the blameless, how will suffering serve as a warning? Trouble, in their minds, is meant to strike terror in men—fear that keeps them from evil lest they be similarly stricken. Job's view of things will remove the fear of God from men, at least the fear that the legalist's thinking motivates people to avoid sin.

For your iniquity teaches your mouth,
and you choose the tongue of the crafty.
Your own mouth condemns you, and not I;
your own lips testify against you.

Eliphaz has become agitated in his anger. He cannot tolerate how Job has thrown a wrench into his "wisdom" about the way the world works. He believes Job's sin has corrupted his speech as well as his heart. In the heat of his fury, he goes on to accuse Job of assertions the latter has not made.

Are you the first man who was born?
Or were you brought forth before the hills?
Have you listened in the council of God?
And do you limit wisdom to yourself?

Job has claimed no unique knowledge, except to the state of his own heart. Poor Eliphaz has worked himself up to the point that rational thinking is beyond reach. He is just one of a long line of legalists who respond in self-righteous rage when their finely tuned view of things is challenged. The scribes and Pharisees responded with violent anger when Jesus challenged the legalistic burdens they put on people. Their anger was so intense that they sought to destroy him, not realizing that in doing so they destroyed their own distorted system.

As Eliphaz continues his verbal assault, he does what legalists often do. He makes an irrelevant generalization. The claim is true but does not inform the dilemma facing Job: Why this terrible trial?

What is man, that he can be pure?
   Or he who is born of a woman, that he can be righteous?
Behold, God puts no trust in his holy ones,
   and the heavens are not pure in his sight;
how much less one who is abominable and corrupt,
   a man who drinks injustice like water!

The inherent depravity of the human heart, which Eliphaz here asserts, is certainly taught throughout Scripture. It is true that "all have sinned and fallen short of the glory of God." Job knows this too. Recall from chapter 1 that he regularly made sacrifices. His being blameless does not mean he never fell short. But it does mean that when he did, he dealt with it as God had prescribed—through offerings that appeased the God he had offended. He, therefore, had a clear conscience. There was no undealt-with sin in his heart. His assertion of being blameless was not a claim to sinlessness.

More importantly, the fact that no one is inherently righteous does not mean Job's calamity was caused by specific sin in his life—which is the basis of his three friends' accusations. Legalists always want to work backward and judge things by circumstances. When things turn out well for them, they congratulate themselves in their self-righteousness. They think they earned it. When they see others in trouble, they pronounce it as the just desserts of the guilty. And they are blind to evidence to the contrary. Eliphaz shows this in the remainder of his speech.

The wicked man writhes in pain all his days,
   through all the years that are laid up for the ruthless....
he will not be rich, and his wealth will not endure,
   nor will his possessions spread over the earth

No, Eliphaz, evidence refutes your neat formula—though you seem blind to it. The hard truth is that things often go well in this world for the wicked. Many unrighteous men have gone to their graves after long lives and without ever having to "wander abroad for bread." Psalm 73:3-12 reminds us of this truth. But the blindness of the legalists blocks their view of reality. They cannot see that the innocent often suffer and the wicked often prosper.

We may be inclined to readily dismiss Eliphaz's error with the confidence that we have embraced God's righteousness through faith in Jesus. "Legalism is not among my problems," we may assure ourselves. Nonetheless, we are well served to recognize the insidiousness of legalism. It is persistent in corrupting the minds of men. It almost seems that we are hardwired to think this way. Traces of it often contaminate even those saved by grace. It is usually revealed by the way we judge others due to their circumstances.

I find that I must fight this tendency toward legalism in my work with the homeless in our community. There are certainly many who are homeless because of destructive choices they have made. But not everyone who is homeless falls in that category. I was confronted with this truth nearly a decade ago. Leah was a woman who seemed a bit out of place with the rest of the homeless. Foul language never flowed from her mouth, and she was always courteous and helpful to others. After getting to know her over several months, she confided in my wife the reason for her homelessness. She was hiding for her life—literally. She had a husband who she was certain would kill her if he found her. Anonymity was the only place of safety. But you cannot own a home or car, rent an apartment, or be employed without leaving traces for people to find you. She felt the only way for her to remain hidden was to do so within the homeless community in a city far away from her husband. She was homeless to flee violence, not to escape responsibility. We've met young people whose journey into homelessness is rooted in fleeing abusive parents. Despite hearing these kinds of stories time and again across the years, I still fight the tendency to immediately assume homelessness is the just outcome of destructive choices.

Perhaps there is a bit of Pharisee in you as well? I dare you to look carefully, for I am confident you will find traces linked to your judgment of others. Eliphaz's error captured in this chapter can help challenge our hearts. Legalism blinds us to truth and binds us to errant judgment. The harsh words of Jesus to the legalists of his day show his utter disdain for Eliphaz's mindset. May the Holy Spirit convict us of our error, and keep us on the path of grace. In his grace, God often brings good into the lives of the wicked. And that same grace also brings trials upon the innocent.

35

MISERABLE COMFORTERS

Read Job 16:1–17:16

Did tears swell into your eyes as you read these two chapters? If not, please go back and read them again—slowly and out loud. Try to feel what you hear. Let Job's groans grip your soul. The next paragraph I have written can wait.

When I read these chapters, I find myself wanting to hold Job in my arms and cry with him. This poor, blameless man is in such a pitiful state. Surely he can fall no deeper into despair. I have never known nor seen the depth of darkness engulf a person in the way Job describes. But here's the real tragedy: his friends have pressed him deeper into the mire of his misery. Their words have increased his torture.

I have heard many such things;
  miserable comforters are you all.
Shall windy words have an end?
  Or what provokes you that you answer?

Job's charge reminds me of the first principle I discuss when lecturing students on medical ethics: *Primum non nocere*—Latin for "First do no harm." This principle should be embraced by all who seek to counsel those who are suffering. Above all, don't make things worse. Sadly, some would-be counselors do exactly that. Job knew this firsthand. In chapter 13 he pled for their silence, but they do not pause their slander. Their "windy words" have no end.

But you, come on again, all of you,
  and I shall not find a wise man among you.

184

As the audience, it is hard to watch things go so wrong with Job's friends. We see their arrival as a welcome balm to his soul. For seven days they join him in silent mourning. But the moment Job vocalizes his agony, they turn on him. Stuff flows out of their mouths unfiltered by the ways of wisdom. When he begs them to cease, they continue. They seem unable to stop themselves. They simply have to have the last word, so they ramble on. Perhaps that is a key part of the problem. Insisting on having the last word in a disagreement usually perpetuates conflict. This trio have become more concerned with winning the argument than helping their friend. And because of that, they made themselves "miserable comforters." May the Lord keep us from going down the same path.

I also could speak as you do,
  if you were in my place;
I could join words together against you
  and shake my head at you.
I could strengthen you with my mouth,
  and the solace of my lips would assuage your pain.

These words are a stinging rebuke. If the table were turned, and any of his friends the one suffering, he could verbally turn on them. But he would not. No, Job would use words to strengthen them in their plight and bring solace in their pain. Sadly, he is receiving the opposite from them. Yet he needs their help. He needs the comfort only others can bring.

If I speak, my pain is not assuaged,
  and if I forbear, how much of it leaves me?

In essence, Job is saying he cannot comfort himself. His own words do not dull his pain. Gritting his teeth and bearing the load has not lightened the burden. Though he is desperate for help, he has never felt so alone. Why does he feel this way?

Surely now God has worn me out;
  he has made desolate all my company.

185

Seven sons, three daughters, and countless servants vanished in a flash. His wife just wants him to die and get it over with. His fellow citizens have all forsaken him. Now, his trio of distant friends have done the same. Truly, his calamity has "made desolate all my company." No wonder he feels worn out. But worst of all, he feels that even God has turned on him—actually torn him asunder. So, he moves to complain about his injury.

I was at ease, and he broke me apart;
   he seized me by the neck and dashed me to pieces;
he set me up as his target;
   his archers surround me.
He slashes open my kidneys and does not spare;
   he pours out my gall on the ground.
He breaks me with breach upon breach;
   he runs upon me like a warrior.

His words seem over the top, and they are. His suffering is great, but not to the degree he describes. Nonetheless, this is what persistent suffering can do to a person—they lose all sense of proportion. This is especially true when they sit and sulk, completely absorbed by their plight. It is one of the dangers of isolation. Spending hours on end focused on your trouble takes the rest of life out of focus. For Job, it ultimately led him to despair life itself.

My spirit is broken; my days are extinct;
   the graveyard is ready for me...
My days are past; my plans are broken off,
   the desires of my heart...
if I say to the pit, "You are my father,"
   and to the worm, "My mother," or "My sister,"
where then is my hope?
   Who will see my hope?
Will it go down to the bars of Sheol?
   Shall we descend together into the dust?

Shakespeare could not have imagined a greater tragedy. A blameless man brought to ruin longing for the pit of a grave—and descending with him into the grave is hope. These words should have stunned his friends into silence. Unfortunately, Bildad will waste no time jumping in for another go at Job in the next chapter.

How should we respond so that we do not fall into being miserable comforters ourselves? One thing is clear: their sitting in silence with Job for seven days made him willing to be vulnerable. After seven days of jointly mourning, he opened his mouth and shared the deepest pain of his heart. Their response shows that his trust was misplaced. Let us not be like them. When one in despair is willing to be vulnerable and show the otherwise hidden thoughts of their heart—don't panic and rebuke them if those thoughts are dark. Remember, their words are but wind.

Job gives us hints of how else to help, and the rest of Scripture gives guidance.[16] First, Job tells us that if he were in his friend's shoes, "the solace of my lips would assuage your pain." But what words could we say that would lessen another's pain? Perhaps Paul and Silas help us here. With arms and legs stretched in stocks in prison after a beating, they sang to one another (Acts 16:25). They encouraged one another in song. Great hymns of the faith and the words of the psalter can give us words when we don't know what to say. Perhaps, like me, your own voice would be more likely to add pain. If so, use your smartphone playlist and let someone with a more gifted voice cheer you together.

Second, Job expresses his feeling that God has abandoned him. This is a frequent response among those in the cauldron of tribulation. Scripture is filled with reminders that, even in hard times, God is still there. He will not forsake his own.

---

16 Some readers may have experience with terminal cancer patients in such pain that they scream uncontrollably, and the slightest touch produces agony. Proverbs 31:6, "Give strong drink to the one who is perishing," should be our guide to help patients with extreme physical suffering—though we have better medicinal options today.

Read these promises to them. They need to hear from God. Don't argue with them, don't cajole or confront—trust the Holy Spirit to use the Word.

Third, pray with and for them. Job himself longed for one who "would argue the case of a man with God, as a son of man does with his neighbor." Only God can bring a man or woman out of deep despair. It is our privilege to intercede for others in such times of need. Persistently pound the door of heaven on their behalf. Let them hear your prayers of earnest appeal while you are with them, and continue those prayers when you are absent.

We don't have to be at a loss about what to do when we encounter another in the depths of despair. Share songs and hymns, read the Word, and pray. Such words will bring solace to their souls.

36

TERROR UPON THE WICKED

Read Job 18:1-21

On an afternoon long ago, the nineteenth-century Scottish pastors Andrew Bonar and Robert Murray M'Cheyne were discussing their preaching. Bonar mentioned that he had preached a sermon on Psalm 9:17, "The wicked shall be turned into hell..." (KJV). M'Cheyne turned to his friend and said, "Were you able to preach it with tenderness?" What a pastoral heart.

Conviction compels us to warn those who are racing headlong into eternal ruin. But it must be done with tenderness. We should take no pleasure in the fate of those who are perishing. Yet those who do not understand the gospel of grace—but think they earn their righteousness—tend to take pleasure in the declared fate of the wicked. Bildad, in his second reply to Job, shows himself to be of this mindset. Though misapplied to Job, the hardness of his words warns believer and unbeliever alike. It benefits us to listen.

It would appear that Bildad begins with a retort to his two companions, expressing his frustration at the ineffectiveness of their responses to Job.

How long will you hunt for words?
Consider, and then we will speak.

The word *you* is plural, indicating he is most likely speaking to his friends, not Job. They have failed to silence Job, unable to find just the right words to refute his arguments. So, Bildad intends to show them how it is done.

Then, turning his attention to Job, he fumes about the latter's disdain for the words of his friends.

Why are we counted as cattle?

> *Why are we stupid in your sight?*

Bildad has taken personal affront to Job's answers. He feels belittled and betrayed by his friend. "Do our words carry no greater weight than the moaning of a cow?" He is appalled by Job's brashness in dismissing the order of the world, the way things work.

You who tear yourself in your anger,

> *shall the earth be forsaken for you,*
> *or the rock be removed out of its place?*

"Do you think your situation calls for overturning the very foundations on which the world operates?" Job's claim that innocent people can suffer, rather than their suffering revealing their guilt, baffles Bildad. How can Job declare such nonsense? In fact, Bildad is convinced that Job needs a strong reminder of the fate of the wicked—which will surely settle the matter. Understanding their terror should turn him from his endless claims of innocence. Hence, he launches into a poetic description of the fate of the wicked, reminding all who read his words of the fate of "him who knows not God."

Indeed, the light of the wicked is put out,

> *and the flame of his fire does not shine.*

The light is dark in his tent,

> *and his lamp above him is put out.*

The way of the wicked inevitably extinguishes light. They will dwell in a darkness that never lifts. No light will pierce their abode. And it is their own folly that leads to this destiny.

His strong steps are shortened,

> *and his own schemes throw him down.*

For he is cast into a net by his own feet,

> *and he walks on its mesh.*

A trap seizes him by the heel;

THE HUMBLING OF JOB

a snare lays hold of him.
A rope is hidden for him in the ground,
  a trap for him in the path.

Like an animal caught in a snare, the way of the wicked will catch them. As they proudly parade in their own schemes, they are ignorant of their fate until—like unsuspecting prey—they are pulled down. Their fate is sure. They will be seized. Their end is certain. And when it comes, terror will grip them.

Terrors frighten him on every side,
  and chase him at his heels.
His strength is famished,
  and calamity is ready for his stumbling.
It consumes the parts of his skin;
  the firstborn of death consumes his limbs.
He is torn from the tent in which he trusted
  and is brought to the king of terrors.

The wicked may cause terror on earth, but they will experience terror in death. Bildad's description is no less vivid than Jesus', who warned that in hell there will be "weeping and gnashing of teeth." The fate of the damned is a place "where the fire is not quenched." Hell will be the ultimate house of horror. In addition to their personal torment, their memory is blotted out forever.

His memory perishes from the earth,
  and he has no name in the street.
He is thrust from light into darkness,
  and driven out of the world.

They leave no legacy for others to hold, no lasting impact that continues beyond their years.

Surely such are the dwellings of the unrighteous,
  such is the place of him who knows not God.

What can we take from these words of Bildad? They seem so ...horrific. Truly they are. But no less so than the descriptions Jesus provided of the fate of those who perish without faith in God through him. Thus, we dare not dismiss them as an exaggerated invective from a disgruntled debater. No, they accurately warn of the terror that will come upon the wicked. If we have never been born again, never experienced that new birth Jesus spoke of, they should strike terror into our hearts. Terror enough to flee from the wrath to come and fly to Jesus—the only hope to escape the judgment we deserve from the hand of God.

These words should also pierce the heart of every believer in Jesus. They remind us what we have been rescued from. The fate of the wicked that Bildad described is the deserved end of us all. We must never forget why it is no longer our fate.

> *But God, being rich in mercy, because of the great love with which he loved us, even when we were dead in our trespasses, made us alive together with Christ—by grace you have been saved—and raised us up with him and seated us with him in the heavenly places in Christ Jesus, so that in the coming ages he might show the immeasurable riches of his grace in kindness toward us in Christ Jesus.*
>
> *Ephesians 2:4-7*

It is God's love, manifested in his rich mercy, that has saved us from the terror our wicked hearts merited. He made us alive in his Son, seating us with him in the heavenly places, so that we might know blessings—not terror—in the ages to come. For that we should give endless thanks.

This knowledge of his grace poured upon us should also create in us what Bildad lacked—tenderness toward those racing headlong into the terror of eternal punishment. In his declaration of the fate of the wicked, Bildad gives no appeal for repentance. He expresses no anguish over the suffering of the wicked. His is a cold indifference. How different is our Lord.

*Have I any pleasure in the death of the wicked,
declares the Lord God, and not rather that he should
turn from his way and live?*

Ezekiel 18:23

*Say to them, As I live, declares the Lord God, I have
no pleasure in the death of the wicked, but that the
wicked turn from his way and live; turn back, turn
back from your evil ways, for why will you die, O
house of Israel?*

Ezekiel 33:11

These words merit our careful consideration. It is clear
this disposition of the Lord is not just toward the wicked
in the house of Israel. It is toward people from every tribe,
nation, and tongue.

*The Lord is not slow to fulfill his promise as some
count slowness, but is patient toward you, not
wishing that any should perish, but that all should
reach repentance.*

2 Peter 3:9

Could it be more plainly stated? May we not be hardened
like Bildad. May the Lord grant us compassion toward sinners.
We *must* be about the business of rescuing the perishing. After
all, we were once on the path to perdition ourselves. Let us
be like Paul, who passionately declared, "We implore you on
behalf of Christ, be reconciled to God" (2 Corinthians 5:20).

37

FORSAKEN BY ALL

Read Job 19:1-29

Forsaken. A formidable word that expresses a sense of abandonment. It is more painful than simple solitude. To be forsaken is not simply to be forgotten by others; it is to have others turn from you. They have intentionally left you to face whatever may come on your own. Being alone in misery is hard, but to be forsaken is agony beyond measure. Yet that is precisely what Job feels. Not just feels—he truly has been abandoned by everyone. But even in the midst of an overwhelming feeling of abandonment, he expresses a confidence that is like some of the text itself—mind-boggling.

This chapter is one of the most problematic in the book of Job. The passage of time has obscured the meaning of portions of the text, especially the last few verses. There is much uncertainty among translators, leading to varied suggestions to retain the poetic impact and assumed purpose of the words. We are best served to focus on what is certain and not exercise ourselves over what is not. And here is what is incontestable: though Job feels completely abandoned, he possesses hope for his ultimate vindication. Though held together in his turmoil by just a thread, the nature of that thread is key. Job knows God is in control of all things. He never wavers from this truth. It is a truth that is weaved throughout every reply he gives to his friends. For the moment, all have turned against him—seemingly even God himself. But Job knows the truth will ultimately be revealed, and his vindication along with it.

How long will you torment me
  and break me in pieces with words?
These ten times you have cast reproach upon me;
  are you not ashamed to wrong me?

Words don't break bones, but they can break us emotionally. The words of Job's friends add to his torment and shatter him to pieces. There seems to be no end to the fiery darts they fling in his direction. There is no shame in them. And it makes no sense that they have taken offense.

And even if it be true that I have erred,
  my error remains with myself.
If indeed you magnify yourselves against me
  and make my disgrace an argument against me,
know then that God has put me in the wrong
  and closed his net about me.

Even if they believe him to be in the wrong, his error is not against them. So, why do "you magnify yourselves against me?" No, it is God he must deal with, not these friends turned foes.

Behold, I cry out, "Violence!" but I am not answered;
  I call for help, but there is no justice.
He has walled up my way, so that I cannot pass,
  and he has set darkness upon my paths.

Job feels like a man under assault who cried out for help, but none answered. Like a trapped animal, there is no escape. And the opposition he faces is unconquerable—for it is God himself.

He has kindled his wrath against me
  and counts me as his adversary.

Here's the real kicker: it is also God who has vanquished all who might stand with Job.

He has put my brothers far from me,
  and those who knew me are wholly estranged from me.
My relatives have failed me,
  my close friends have forgotten me...

195

My breath is strange to my wife,
and I am a stench to the children of my own mother...
All my intimate friends abhor me,
and those whom I loved have turned against me.

We have seen what Job poetically expresses—all have abandoned him. Everyone has turned from him and on him. But Job sees something deeper. It is God who is behind even this. It is God who "has put my brothers far from me." Does that thought trouble you? Set aside the questions it raises for a moment and consider this: God's absolute sovereignty in every detail is unassailable in Job's mind. Through the darkest times of his terrible affliction, it is a truth about which he never wavers. Never. I assert that this is the root of his steadfastness that James points to (James 5:11). Job's emotions roll like the waves of the sea. But his conviction about the sovereignty of God in all things is like the rock of Gibraltar. It is never shaken. And in this we find the source of steadfastness in the midst of trials.

The sovereignty of God is the secure anchor that will hold us through life's storms. Tethered to this truth, we can endure any tempest. Without it, we will be cut loose from the moorings of our faith and find ourselves tossed to and fro. From Genesis 1:1 to Revelation 22:21, the sovereignty of God in all things is the clearest and most persistent message of the Bible. Feeding our souls with this truth will empower us to face anything.

For preachers of the Word, the absolute sovereignty of God should be a thread weaved through every sermon. There is no better way to equip the saints than instilling within them the confidence Job constantly expressed—God is in control no matter what comes. It was in this confidence that the Apostle Paul declared,

> *And we know that for those who love God all*
> *things work together for good, for those who are*
> *called according to his purpose. For those whom*

he foreknew he also predestined to be conformed to
the image of his Son, in order that he might be the
firstborn among many brothers. And those whom he
predestined he also called, and those whom he called
he also justified, and those whom he justified he also
glorified.

Romans 8:28-30

The man who wrote these words faced opposition we have never experienced. He walked through unthinkable trials—physical, emotional, and spiritual. But he never wavered in his suffering. Why? He knew God's plan cannot be thwarted. God will accomplish his plan in his people. The end is sure, and all things work to that glorious end that he has determined. Because he is in control of all things. Through every trial and affliction, this was the steadfast truth to which Paul clung.

And, however dimly, Job also seems to see the certainty of his vindication—though this thought seems incongruent with his present circumstances.

Oh that my words were written!
Oh that they were inscribed in a book!
Oh that with an iron pen and lead
they were engraved in the rock forever!

Why does he wish for a permanent record of his words? So that in the day of vindication, they might be validated.

For I know that my Redeemer lives,
and at the last he will stand upon the earth.
And after my skin has been thus destroyed,
yet [without][17] *my flesh I shall see God*

Though abandoned at the moment, Job expresses the confidence that there is for him a redeemer. It is mind-boggling that in the midst of his appeals for mercy and profound sense of abandonment he would speak these words. It is a surprising turn in his complaint. But no matter

---

17   The alternate reading in the ESV is "without my flesh" as opposed to "in my flesh." The former fits the context and flows with the text better than the latter.

how battered he may be, this is the anchor of his soul. Even in the tempest, God is in control. "And after my skin has been thus destroyed," when this earthly body is gone, "I shall see God." And since God knows all, controls all, and is just beyond measure, his day of vindication will come. Come what may in the here and now, to this truth he holds.

My suffering Christian friend, at the moment you may be holding on by your fingernails. Your faith is being pulled apart by powerful forces. Everything about your circumstance cries "Injustice!" You are overwhelmed with a sense that you have been forsaken. If so, don't let go of this truth—God is in control. No one and no trial will pry you out of his sovereign hand. So much about your suffering may be mysterious, but this much is certain—God is in control, even in this. Cling to that truth and the certainty that his plans for you will be fulfilled. Let it be the anchor for your soul.

38

THE CRUELTY OF SELF-CENTEREDNESS

Read Job 20:1-29

What makes a man crush the heart of a friend with cruel words? What within a person moves them to plunder the poor? What defect of the soul allows one to take the roof from over another's head? Unintentionally, Zophar reveals that the sin delivering each of these evils is the same. It is the sin at the heart of the wicked man he condemns, as well as the sin in his own heart that has caused him to turn on Job with callousness. But it is also a sin believers in Jesus must battle with daily—including during times of suffering.

The overall theme of Zophar's reply to Job is a familiar tune. He asserts, yet again, that the wicked are judged by God with temporal loss. Thus, Job's true heart is revealed by his suffering. If we find Zophar's recurring argument vexing, imagine how Job felt. Over and over again he listens to his friends drone on with the same thesis. Like the endless pounding of waves on a rock, it wore him down. The repetition, though, is part of the drama. We are meant to feel it, just like Job.

Admittedly, it can be tedious to read the same arguments many times. We may find ourselves wondering why such repetitive rationalizations have been recorded in Scripture. Clearly, there is something in it for us to learn. "For whatever was written in former days was written for our instruction" (Romans 15:4). We should realize that our hearts are like hardwood—it often takes repeated pounding for the nail of truth to penetrate. Hence, we should receive the repetition in

Scripture as a gift, an opportunity to let needed truth sink in.

Zophar's scathing lecture is quite plain. He presents the course of the wicked in three stages. First, he declares that their prosperity is short lived. They may enjoy the fruit of their folly for a time, but that time is short. The evildoers' prosperity will disappear.

Do you not know this from of old,
*   since man was placed on earth,*
that the exulting of the wicked is short,
*   and the joy of the godless but for a moment?...*
He will fly away like a dream and not be found;
*   he will be chased away like a vision of the night.*

From an eternal perspective, this is true. The wicked only grip the goods they've obtained for a fleeting moment. Yet, as Job will assert in his subsequent response, that moment may represent an earthly lifetime. This can fool the wicked into thinking there will be no accounting for their folly. Lacking an eternal perspective, they may believe all is well. But they are blind to their fate. Their exulting in sin will not last forever. Like a nighttime vision, they "will be chased away."

This leads to Zophar's second point—their sin is self-destructive. Like a toxic substance, it will eat away at them from the inside. It may seem pleasant, but it is destructive.

Though evil is sweet in his mouth,
*   though he hides it under his tongue,*
though he is loath to let it go
*   and holds it in his mouth,*
yet his food is turned in his stomach;
*   it is the venom of cobras within him.*

A single bite from a cobra can kill an elephant, though it takes hours for its lethal venom to complete its fatal effects. So it is with sin. The impact of evil may not be seen at first, but it is the seed of the wicked man's demise. Men often overlook the self-destructive nature of sin. Yet Proverbs 6:27 asks, "Can a man carry fire next to his chest and his clothes not be burned?" Playing with sin is like holding fire to your chest. You will get burned. It is foolish to ignore this. Zophar's words should remind us that the delight of sin soon evaporates, but its destructive impact is enduring.

The third and final stage identifies the source of destruction. Their ultimate suffering comes from the hand of God—it is a manifestation of his wrath against them. He has not only built the principle of sowing and reaping into his creation, but he also actively brings judgment upon them.

...God will send his burning anger against him
and rain it upon him into his body....
The possessions of his house will be carried away,
dragged off in the day of God's wrath.
This is the wicked man's portion from God,
the heritage decreed for him by God.

Wrath upon the wicked is sure to come. He will not get away with his evil but will be called into account. He may be living in luxury now, but he will be "dragged off in the day of God's wrath." Wicked men may escape the justice of other men, but they will not hide from the Judge of all creation. Zophar's description of the fate of the wicked is true, but his application to Job is wrong. This is not why Job is suffering. Evil *is* behind his loss, but not *his* evil—rather, that of Satan. How cruel to misjudge Job in this way. Comparing this blameless man to the wicked is wicked.

What about this common sin I mentioned as afflicting both the wicked man he denounces and Zophar himself? That is exposed the moment he opens his mouth to reply to Job.

Therefore my thoughts answer me,
because of my haste within me.
I hear censure that insults me,
and out of my understanding a spirit answers me.

Notice the focus in these verses: "my ...me, my ...me, I ...me, my ...me." It's all about Zophar. His self-centeredness is self-evident. He feels insulted, and that has become the central issue. His personal affront is what drives him. Zophar completely sets aside his responsibility to comfort Job. Driven by his ego, he erred in his counsel to Job. More than erroneous, his counsel is evil. It is all because he is consumed with self-centeredness—the very thing motivating the wicked man he goes on to condemn.

For he has crushed and abandoned the poor;
he has seized a house that he did not build.
Because he knew no contentment in his belly,
he will not let anything in which he delights escape him.

What kind of man crushes the poor and leaves him more impoverished than before? Who would take another's home, leaving them without shelter? A man who "will not let anything in which he delights escape him." Only a man who is the center of his own world would do such things. A man who is devoted to his own comfort and pleasure above all things.

It is a self-centered man who pleases himself at the cost of others. It is what drives the megalomaniacs of Silicon Valley and the corrupt landlords that blight our cities. Self-centeredness is what drives men to abuse their wives and lash in anger at their children. It is at the root of those in positions of power who neglect and abuse those in their care. And it is the sin behind those who can think only of their own suffering and ignore the needs of those around them—even those most dear.

Of course, the gospel teaches us another way. The way of Jesus himself, the way we are called to emulate through his empowering Spirit.

> *Do nothing from selfish ambition or conceit, but in humility count others more significant than yourselves. Let each of you look not only to his own interests, but also to the interests of others. Have this mind among yourselves, which is yours in Christ Jesus...*
>
> *Philippians 2:3-5*

Living this truth is always hard. But it is especially difficult when you are suffering. When the siren of pain screams through your body and will not be silenced, it is easy to be self-focused. When fighting through discomfort is your daily experience, it is difficult to seek to comfort others. When the weight of sorrow weighs heavy on your shoulders, it seems beyond your ability to lift another's burden. In fact, it is beyond your ability. But the Lord does not ask us to live in our own power, does he?

> But the fruit of the Spirit is love, joy, peace, patience, kindness, goodness, faithfulness, gentleness, self-control; against such things there is no law. And those who belong to Christ Jesus have crucified the flesh with its passions and desires.
>
> *Galatians 5:22-24*

Do you see the counterweight to our self-centered inclinations? It is the work of the Spirit within us. So, we must pray and yield. In the midst of suffering, we must pray for the full measure of the Holy Spirit to be manifest in us—that the fruit of the Spirit would blossom in the soil of suffering and sorrow. And that the self-centered desires of our flesh would be put to death. This is a work he delights to do. For it makes us like the Savior who emptied himself for us.

39

BLIND COUNSELORS

Read Job 21:1-34

My infrequent excursions to the grocery store are a source of comedy and consternation. Inexplicably, a fog descends on me as soon as I walk through the doors. As I travel down the aisles, I exhibit a remarkable inability to see what is in front of my face. I have brought items home whose labels provide compelling evidence that they are not the product my wife requested. To say I am often an unhelpful shopper would be an understatement.

In a more serious vein, Job's three friends were overcome by a fog that blinded them to the obvious. It is evident from their words that they are not seeing things clearly. As a consequence, they have ended up hurting rather than helping their friend. The three had a neat paradigm by which they believed the world operated. But they failed to see the evidence that refuted their erroneous theology. Job, in response to Zophar's latest salvo, turns to help them see what should be plain for all to see.

This speech is unique among Job's responses. It is the only one in which he limits himself to directly refuting the words of his three companions. In other speeches, he often ignores what his friends say and simply complains to God or mumbles to himself. Sometimes he briefly dismisses their words and then moves on. But here, he takes their combined assertion that the wicked suffer loss and points to evidence to the contrary.

Keep listening to my words,
  and let this be your comfort.

Bear with me, and I will speak,
and after I have spoken, mock on.

Job begins by asking them to hear him out. They have mostly ignored his prior arguments, simply rehashing their view of life as rewards to the righteous and retribution to the wicked—implicating him with the latter. "Listen for a moment, then continue your mocking if you must." Then he moves to expose three areas where they are blind. The first is that his complaint is not against them; it is with God.

As for me, is my complaint against man?
Why should I not be impatient?

They continue to take personal affront at his words. But his complaint is not against them or any man. Is it unreasonable that he has grown inpatient in his search for an answer to why God has done this?

There is a caution here for those who would counsel others in times of trouble. It is an unspoken warning that arises repeatedly in this drama. Job's friends have taken his struggle with God personally. His perplexity at the ways of God pains them. But more than that, they are angered that he does not simply accept their pat answers at face value. Unable to see their own insufficiency for the matter at hand, they see his continued turmoil as an indictment against themselves. So, they lash out at him.

Regardless of the wisdom or experience we bring, it is God who must do the work in the hearts of those we seek to help. Only God can truly see their need. We have no microscope to peer into the heart of another. We have all been misjudged by others, so we should be hesitant in our confidence to read another person's heart. I'm not dismissing the need to confront obvious sin. But Job's frustration with his circumstances is not labeled by God as sin. His despair is not rooted in evil within his heart. He was, after all, a man labeled blameless by God. I fear we have become too quick to label spiritual weakness as sin, when it may simply be weakness. I am unconvinced by arguments that feeble faith flows from sin. Struggling through trials should not be equated with sin.

Perhaps more importantly, we must realize the Lord may or may not use us to help. But if he does, it will be in his timing, not ours. What if the Lord has lessons for us to learn in the struggle and not its resolution? If we become impatient when we think change is slow, are we not being impatient with God? Are we assuming a deeper knowledge than we possess? Does our impatience show we have forgotten our role? How easy it is to follow in the footsteps of Job's friends when trying to help those walking through protracted trials.

The second blind spot that Job's friends have developed is his need for compassion. He should be comforted, not confronted. But they have become blind to his pitiful state.

Look at me and be appalled,
and lay your hand over your mouth.
When I remember, I am dismayed,
and shuddering seizes my flesh.

Job's friends have become numb to his pain. When they first saw him, they were emotionally overwhelmed. They wept, tore their robes, and threw dust in the air. After sitting with him for seven days and more, they have lost their sensitivity toward his suffering. Their personal affront at his words has caused them to forget his persisting affliction.

Walking with someone through a protracted trial is hard. Family members easily get used to seeing their loved one's pain and can lose their compassion. Friends grow weary and disappear. Pastors feel drained by times of sitting with the suffering and, as a consequence, neglect the battered sheep. Whether it is an incurable illness, a wound of the soul that will never heal, or a weakness in the flesh that causes faith to falter, it is easy for others to lose compassion for those whose suffering does not subside. It takes a special work of grace to retain compassion and stay alongside the suffering for the long haul. Let us pray that God would make us such people.

The third area of blindness that Job confronts is that, contrary to his friends' assertions, the wicked often prosper.

Why do the wicked live,
reach old age, and grow mighty in power?...
Their houses are safe from fear,
and no rod of God is upon them....
They spend their days in prosperity,
and in peace they go down to Sheol.

Their tidy theology of the wicked's assured retribution that they have repeated several times already does not withstand scrutiny. The simple fact is that the wicked often prosper and do so until they reach the grave. "No, my friends, life is often unfair. The wicked prosper while the righteous suffer." This simple fact, which they have overlooked, is widely known.

Have you not asked those who travel the roads,
and do you not accept their testimony
that the evil man is spared in the day of calamity,
that he is rescued in the day of wrath?

Therefore, his assessment of their counsel should not surprise us.

How then will you comfort me with empty nothings?
There is nothing left of your answers but falsehood.

But we should take things a step further than where Job leaves us. What do we do when we think the counsel we have received from others is falsehood? We can see plainly that this is the case with Job's friends, for we know the backstory. Yet we are not detached observers in our own lives. Hence, our first step should be to check our own hearts. Are we rejecting counsel because it is not what we want to hear, or is it truly in error? Serious work with God in prayer is needed to discern truth in such cases. Second, we must confront the errant counsel (as Job did) if we are convinced that is what it is. Then we should listen humbly to the reply. We both may learn from the exchange. Third, we should continue seeking God. This is what Job did. He was convinced his friends were in error. So, he kept pleading with God. He did not give up but continued his cry toward heaven.

But there is another compelling call that arises from this chapter. It is one that will help us imitate Jesus. Unlike Job's friends, let us stick with those who suffer for the long haul. As they endure their persistent affliction, let us pray that God would empower us to persist in our compassion. Jesus never abandons those he loves in their time of affliction. May we never abandon them either.

40

THE SIN OF SLANDER

Read Job 22:1-30

The words of Eliphaz force us to think about a sin widely practiced yet repeatedly condemned in Scripture. Slander. To slander a person is to make false statements about them. In doing so, harm is brought to the target of the slander. It is ironic that the drama of Job opens with slanderous words about him from the chief of slanderers, but now Job's "friend" has picked up where Satan left off. It reminds us that slander is a contagious sin, one we too readily slip into. We must be wary of the risk. Watch how quickly it happens to Eliphaz.

Can a man be profitable to God?
  Surely he who is wise is profitable to himself.
Is it any pleasure to the Almighty if you are in the right,
  or is it gain to him if you make your ways blameless?

Eliphaz confronts what he believes to be Job's arrogance. In persisting in his claim of innocence, what is Job saying about God? If Job is in the right, is he not saying God is in the wrong? Is that pleasing to God? Does the Almighty gain from this claim by Job?

Is it for your fear of him that he reproves you
  and enters into judgment with you?

"God does not exact retribution on those who fear him. Your supposed piety did not cause your calamity." In the mind of Eliphaz, Job cannot see what should be obvious. His lack of fear of God has brought reproof in the form of judgment.

Is not your evil abundant?
    There is no end to your iniquities.

Eliphaz now ratchets things up a notch. He moves from his previous argument that Job must be hiding sin to alleging that Job's life is full of iniquity. And then, he slides into slander.

For you have exacted pledges of your brothers for nothing
    and stripped the naked of their clothing.
You have given no water to the weary to drink,
    and you have withheld bread from the hungry....
You have sent widows away empty,
    and the arms of the fatherless were crushed.

These are serious charges. He claims that Job strips the poor of their clothing. Eliphaz accuses him of neglecting the needy, holding his wealth tight to his vest instead of offering help. Worst of all, he says Job oppresses widows and orphans. How low can you get? But there's a problem with his indictment. We know that each of these accusations is false. God repeatedly declares Job to be blameless. The words of Eliphaz are slander, pure and simple. He's made this stuff up. He has accused Job of using his power and influence to crush the weak and downtrodden. Though Job may think God does not see his sin, Eliphaz says Job is following a well-worn path trod by the wicked from time immemorial.

Will you keep to the old way
    that wicked men have trod?

This man of sterling reputation is accused of aligning himself with the wicked men of the ages. But on what basis does Eliphaz make such outlandish accusations? Because of the calamity that has befallen Job. For, Eliphaz is certain, God always dashes the hopes of the wicked in the midst of their comfort. They get their just desserts.

They were snatched away before their time;
their foundation was washed away.

The fruit of the wicked is always plucked away before their time, or so Eliphaz believes. In the neat formula he has for the world, the loss of health and wealth proves the point. Job is clearly guilty. Why else would he be reduced to such a pitiful state? No one loses all Job has lost without the hand of God snatching it away. It is plain to see: Job is a guilty man, and his loss is the only evidence needed. Somehow, Eliphaz has convinced himself that Job's intransigence justifies his own fabrications.

The wickedness Eliphaz has wandered into is wretched. He has become a mouthpiece for Satan in his slander. It is, in fact, Eliphaz who now stands in danger of the swift hand of God falling upon him. While the arrival of affliction provides no diagnostic insight into a person's heart, the tongue that speaks slander reveals the wickedness of the heart it is spoken through.

> But what comes out of the mouth proceeds from the heart, and this defiles a person. For out of the heart come evil thoughts, murder, adultery, sexual immorality, theft, false witness, slander.
>
> Matthew 15:18-19

Slander is serious—not only is it destructive toward others, but it also reveals evil in the heart of the slanderer. Did you catch that? Slander provides a window into the heart. And what it reveals is evil. It should be obvious that slander has no place in the life of the Christian, a fact stated repeatedly in the New Testament.

> Let all bitterness and wrath and anger and clamor and slander be put away from you, along with all malice.
>
> Ephesians 4:31

> But now you must put them all away: anger, wrath, malice, slander, and obscene talk from your mouth.
>
> Colossians 3:8

*So put away all malice and all deceit and hypocrisy
and envy and all slander.*

1 Peter 2:1

These repeated warnings against slander should cause us to take notice. Apparently, sliding into slander was a common problem in the culture these readers were saved from. Not the only problem, of course, but one meriting repeated warnings not to bring it into their new life in Christ. It is a matter we need to take to heart as well.

Let's face it, trafficking in slander is a common pastime in our day. People get paid to do it. They work for newspapers, magazines, cable TV, syndicated radio, political campaigns, and the list goes on. Destroying the reputation of others through outright falsehoods or purposeful misrepresentation has become a form of entertainment. It is pervasive in our culture, especially through antisocial—I mean *social*—media. How easy for us to jump on to the bandwagon and join the "fun." But it is evil, through and through. We must think twice before we pass on the slander spoken by others. When we share slander posted by others, we partake in their evil. Instead, we must put it away from us. Its pervasiveness in our culture demands active avoidance by Christians. So, be cautious about sharing the words of others on social media. Don't share unless you know it is true, lest you become like Eliphaz.

There is also, I believe, a very applicable warning in this regard to those living with chronic suffering. If we don't watch our tongues, it is easy to let slander slip. How so? We tell others a particular physician is uncaring because they did not listen well during our visit, when they may have simply been distracted by the conundrum of the previous patient. But in denouncing them to others, we damage their reputation. We complain about the absence of a pastoral call, declaring it shows their neglect of the flock—when it may reflect they are overwhelmed and our expectations are unreasonable. Indeed, they may be unaware of our need. After all, it is hard for another to meet unspoken needs or expectations. But our complaint to others makes us complicit with Satan's schemes to sow disunity. The chief slanderer loves to have us aid his cause.

As James reminds us, the tongue can set the world on fire (James 3:5-6). This is especially so when it speaks slander. Our allegiance to Jesus demands that we forsake the path of the slanderer and speak truth. Only truth. That includes not saying things we are uncertain of or often cannot know, such as what is in the heart of another person. May we follow the way of Wisdom, who declared,

> *All the words of my mouth are righteous;*
> *there is nothing twisted or crooked in them.*
> *Proverbs 8:8*

Oh, that this could be said of us!

41

WHEN GOD IS HIDDEN

Read Job 23:1-17

Where is God when you need him most? Why does he seem to disappear in times of crisis? Such is often the cry of his children in times of affliction. It was a common complaint of David—especially during King Saul's lengthy pursuit of his rival for the throne of Israel. Even our Savior uttered words expressing a sense that God had left him: "My God, my God, why have you forsaken me?" Surely, there must be very few people who walk with God and never experience the feeling that he has hidden from them.

So, what do you do when you feel as though God is hiding from you—when you search in a time of need but cannot connect with him? Job, in his latest soliloquy, brings our focus to this critical subject. Perhaps most important, he helps us understand *why* we sometimes sense that God is unreachable. And through that, Job helps us find the hidden face of God.

Stepping into this chapter presents a profound shift in the drama. For Job stills the tempest that the dialogue with his friends has become. Eliphaz, the most recent to have spoken, turned up the heat with slanderous charges. Job, however, shows incredible restraint in his reply. Indeed, his last words to his friends at the end of chapter 21 have set the stage for his response: "There is nothing left of your answers but falsehood." He knows they merit no further hearing. There is no sense getting worked up over what they say. Their words are best ignored. So, he passes over them.

Today also my complaint is bitter;
my hand is heavy on account of my groaning.

You can almost hear the lowered voice of Job, as much of
a sigh as anything else. He has mentally left his friends and
speaks once again to the air. Today is like the many days that
have preceded it—he feels the barrenness of an unanswered
cry. It has left him with heavy hands. Have you ever been
there? Have you been so weighed down that the simple act
of lifting your hands seems too much? What help is there for
this poor, heavily burdened man?

Oh, that I knew where I might find him,
that I might come even to his seat!

With these words, Job reveals the deepest cause of his
agony. He cannot find God. This blameless man who walked
with God for so long no longer knows the path to find him,
though he has tried. He has looked every which way.

Behold, I go forward, but he is not there,
and backward, but I do not perceive him;
on the left hand when he is working, I do not behold him;
he turns to the right hand, but I do not see him.

No turn of his body has enabled him to catch a glimpse
of God. He has searched, but the Almighty is nowhere to be
found. It is all ...darkness. You know what that feels like,
don't you? Many of us have stood where Job found himself—
looking for but unable to find the only one who can help.

Yet what would Job do if he gained this audience he has
repeatedly requested? Has he not previously spoken of the
terror of coming into God's presence?

I would lay my case before him
and fill my mouth with arguments.
I would know what he would answer me
and understand what he would say to me.

There is a calmness in Job's declaration that was missing in
earlier appeals. His heart and mind have turned from his foolish
friends. He has set his face like a flint toward God, though he

is unsure where to find him. In fact, he now expresses his conviction that God would grant him a fair hearing.

Would he contend with me in the greatness of his power?
No; he would pay attention to me.
There an upright man could argue with him,
and I would be acquitted forever by my judge.

There is a confidence in Job that we have not heard since chapter 2. He has now come to see that the Lord would not crush him with his power. Granted a hearing, he knows God would listen, judge rightly, and acquit this blameless man. The upright *will* find justice before God. On this truth he stands. And then, Job makes a tremendous expression of trust:

But he knows the way that I take;
when he has tried me, I shall come out as gold.

I hope you did not read those words too quickly. These might be the most helpful words from Job to memorize. They will serve us well if we repeat them to ourselves in times of affliction. When affliction strikes, we must remember that God knows, he is working through it, and we will be the better for it. Job has steadied himself on an important truth—truth that will steady us as well in times of need. The Refiner's Fire both proves and purifies. As it did for Job, it can prove the blameless to be blameless. But if there is dross in our lives, it is removed and we shine more brightly for Jesus. That puts affliction in a very different light, one spoken of elsewhere in Scripture.

For you, O God, have tested us;
you have tried us as silver is tried.

Psalm 66:10

Behold, I have refined you, but not as silver;
I have tried you in the furnace of affliction.

Isaiah 48:10

In this you rejoice, though now for a little while, if necessary, you have been grieved by various trials,

so that the tested genuineness of your faith—more
precious than gold that perishes though it is tested
by fire—may be found to result in praise and glory
and honor at the revelation of Jesus Christ.

1 Peter 1:6-7

In truth, trials will make us either better or bitter. The outcome is determined by our response. Frankly, Job seemed dangerously close to the path toward bitterness. But he has taken a breath and settled his heart on the truth that his experience is actually the Refiner's Fire. Yes, God is trying him. But in the end, he will come forth refined like gold. And that seems to help Job sense what is really going on.

yet I am not silenced because of the darkness,
nor because thick darkness covers my face.

Job is unable to see because of a darkness that has descended. He thinks God is not there. But the One who seemed so far away was actually near. Job now realizes his cry is not silenced by distance. God saw and heard everything, from Job's affliction to his friends' accusations. He knew it all. He had not banished this faithful servant. In fact, he had boasted of Job's integrity before the Divine Council. No, God was nearer than Job ever realized. He had not moved away. The same is true in our lives. We are repeatedly reminded of this fact in Scripture.

> *The Lord is near to the brokenhearted*
> *and saves the crushed in spirit.*
>
> *Psalm 34:18*

The Lord is near in our times of affliction. And he is especially near when his children call to him.

> *The Lord is near to all who call on him,*
> *to all who call on him in truth.*
>
> *Psalm 145:18*

217

But if this is true, why does it so often seem that God is far away when I need him most? Because affliction often shrouds reality in darkness. And that darkness is disorienting. It was for Job, and it is for us. In such moments we grasp for what perhaps may not be gained—the why behind our suffering. Instead, when darkness descends, we need to orient ourselves with truth that is unmovable. That's what Job did. And so did David, with words often quoted from Psalm 23:

Even though I walk through the valley of the shadow of death,
I will fear no evil, for you are with me

Sometimes feelings mislead us. This is why we must rehearse for ourselves rock-solid truths in times of trouble. God is always with us, no matter how dark the valley. My Christian friend, have no fear, he is near. He is with you—always. Wait on him. The fog will clear, and in due time, you will again know the comfort of his nearness.

42

THE PERSISTENCE OF INJUSTICE

Read Job 24:1-25

There is, in our day, an almost fever pitch about injustice. It seems that the course of nations is often marked by periods of heightened awareness of injustice and protest against it. Indeed, movements against injustice have sometimes given birth to nations—such as the United States of America through the American Revolution or the rise of the French Republic as the fruit of the French Revolution. However errant their solution, the persistence of pervasive injustice has been at the heart of every Marxist revolution over the past century.

But the problem of injustice runs deeper than the course of nations. The human spirit has long been troubled by the injustice of the prosperity of the wicked, which is often gained and sustained by oppressing the poor. This dynamic has especially unsettled those who believe in a good and gracious God who rules in the affairs of men. Some, like Job's friends, seem blissfully ignorant of this injustice. They have created a worldview in which the wicked are always punished while the righteous prosper. Moreover, they are convinced they can separate the wheat from the chaff by whether a person is materially blessed or destitute. Job has repeatedly reminded them that their view of the world is contradicted by abundant evidence—if only they would open their eyes to see it.

In the twenty-fourth chapter, Job invites us to ponder this dynamic of the persistence of injustice in the world. He doesn't solve it for us, but he invites us to face its hard reality. For we who live in the affluent West, where the poor and wealthy are often separated into their own disparate worlds, it serves as a healthy reminder of a troubling truth. As though speaking to no one in particular, Job begins with the perplexity that often troubles the souls of men:

Why are not times of judgment kept by the Almighty,
and why do those who know him never see his days?

Having expressed his confidence that this God he cannot see is in control, Job naturally moves in his mind to the incongruence that should unsettle us all. Why does the God who is in control not bring judgment now? Why does he seem hidden from both those who are his and, frustratingly so, from the wicked as they prosper on earth? This is not the way we would run the show. So, why does God follow a different script?

Some move landmarks;
they seize flocks and pasture them.
They drive away the donkey of the fatherless;
they take the widow's ox for a pledge.
They thrust the poor off the road;
the poor of the earth all hide themselves.

The wicked take land and livestock. They steal from defenseless orphans and widows. They run roughshod over everyone to get their way, especially the vulnerable poor. They have no pity in their aggressive pursuit of wealth. They grab whatever they can get. And this leaves those already poor even more destitute.

Behold, like wild donkeys in the desert
the poor go out to their toil, seeking game;
the wasteland yields food for their children.
They gather their fodder in the field,
and they glean the vineyard of the wicked man.
They lie all night naked, without clothing,
and have no covering in the cold.
They are wet with the rain of the mountains
and cling to the rock for lack of shelter.

What makes their suffering even worse, is that relief is near at hand:

They go about naked, without clothing;
hungry, they carry the sheaves;
among the olive rows of the wicked they make oil;
they tread the winepresses, but suffer thirst.

The rich not only plunder the poor; they also enslave the oppressed as laborers without just compensation. The poor carry the bundles of grain (the sheaves) of the wicked while going hungry themselves. They tread the winepress of their oppressors yet suffer from unquenched thirst. The means of relief is there, but the wicked will not share. But even more painful is that their cry for relief goes unanswered ...from God himself.

From out of the city the dying groan,
and the soul of the wounded cries for help;
yet God charges no one with wrong.

If Job's description does not provoke pain in your heart, you have not read his words with the care they deserve. The injustice he portrays should provoke righteous indignation. How is it that God lets the wicked get away with this? But this is just one element of the evil of those who seemingly evade God's judgment. They also murder, steal, and commit adultery. And the wicked know they are doing wrong—which is why Job goes on to describe their deeds done in darkness, where things are hidden from sight.

While the remaining verses of this chapter present some challenges for translators, the central message is clear: the notion that the wicked suffer for their evil is not apparent when you observe their earthly lives. Indeed, they seem to prosper through their wickedness. Look for yourself—don't the wicked seem to get away with their abuse of others to feed their own greed?

If it is not so, who will prove me a liar
and show that there is nothing in what I say?

221

So, there you have it—injustice is there for all who are willing to see it. In every society throughout man's reign on this earth, injustice persists. No neat formula or worldview will make it disappear. Job challenges us to admit it. But what do we do with it then?

First, it is good to note that Job—despite the intensity of his own suffering and sense of injustice against him—has risen above self-pity. He has pondered the plight of the poor. And this is a healthy thing to do, to realize we are not the only people in the world facing affliction. Indeed, it is most likely that the lot of many others in this life is worse than ours. Far worse. This recognition brings balance. Job, through his example, invites us to consider the suffering of others.

Second, through his pondering of this perplexity, Job forces us to face the reality that all is not right in this world. When life is going well for us personally, it is easy to be blissfully ignorant of the injustice all around us. This is not the way of Christ—who came to preach good news to the poor and to proclaim liberty to the oppressed (Luke 4:18). If there is any group who should be moved by the suffering of the poor, it is we who follow Jesus.

Third, we should relieve suffering and rectify injustice whenever it is in our power to do so. When the church first spread among the Gentiles, the Jerusalem Council sent simple instructions: "remember the poor" (Galatians 2:10). As Scripture tells us, "Religion that is pure and undefiled before God the Father is this: to visit orphans and widows in their affliction, and to keep oneself unstained from the world" (James 1:27). Our brethren who lived centuries before us founded the first hospitals and orphanages. The leading abolitionists in England and America were followers of Jesus. The legacy of Christians relieving suffering and fighting injustice is long and deep.

Finally, remember the wicked are not getting away with anything. Justice will come.

Come now, you rich, weep and howl for the miseries that are coming upon you. Your riches have rotted and your garments are moth-eaten. Your gold and silver have corroded, and their corrosion will be evidence against you and will eat your flesh like fire. You have laid up treasure in the last days. Behold, the wages of the laborers who mowed your fields, which you kept back by fraud, are crying out against you, and the cries of the harvesters have reached the ears of the Lord of hosts. You have lived on the earth in luxury and in self-indulgence. You have fattened your hearts in a day of slaughter.

James 5:1-5

Don't be fooled by the apparent lack of consequences upon the wicked for their unjust deeds. James reminds us that judgment will fall. Do not envy them, do not be like them. And do not think injustice will prevail. No, "he has fixed a day on which he will judge the world" (Acts 17:31).

43

CAN A MAN BE RIGHT BEFORE GOD?

Read Job 25:1-6

The Apostle Paul reminds us that there are things that will remain unknown this side of heaven.

> *For we know in part and we prophesy in part, but when the perfect comes, the partial will pass away. When I was a child, I spoke like a child, I thought like a child, I reasoned like a child. When I became a man, I gave up childish ways. For now we see in a mirror dimly, but then face to face. Now I know in part; then I shall know fully, even as I have been fully known.*
>
> *1 Corinthians 13:9-12*

Even prophetic revelation is limited—there is much that has not been and will not be revealed until the consummation of all things. Yet it is also true that God's revelation to man has been progressive across the span of human history. There are things David knew that Abraham did not. Daniel understood things Moses could not comprehend. And we who live this side of Calvary know things that were not revealed to those who lived before or under the Old Covenant. In the final words from Job's friends turned foes, the most important void in that knowledge is revealed—a void that the gospel has filled. In the midst of a long journey through Job, it is good for these words to launch us into the gospel, the good news these men did not know.

The words of Bildad represent the last whimper of a wilting argument. The constant assertion of the reward-retribution paradigm has finally been silenced by Job. But Bildad is baffled. Job's repeated repine is that injustice has been inflicted on an innocent man. Yet Bildad does not see any way Job's claim can be true—for how can a man be right in the sight of God? While Bildad cannot answer that question, his final poem pleads for the good news of Jesus that we know. He first turns his thoughts to the omnipotent power of God.

Dominion and fear are with God;
he makes peace in his high heaven.
Is there any number to his armies?
Upon whom does his light not arise?

God is transcendent, he is above all things. He rules everywhere. None could amass a force to successfully oppose him. But he is not just all powerful; he is also the essence of purity. No spot nor stain can be found in him—which brings Bildad to ask,

How then can man be in the right before God?
How can he who is born of woman be pure?

How can Job's claim of innocence be true? Compared to God, none are innocent. In his presence, surely our sin-stained hearts would be found out. How could a man born of woman be pure? This cannot be. For even the most radiant of things are nothing compared to God.

Behold, even the moon is not bright,
and the stars are not pure in his eyes

To us, the moon and the stars appear as undefiled light. But compared to God, they are less than pure. Their "brightness" is dull aside his light. As man has advanced in his exploration of space, he has shown this to be true. The moon is not pure light, it is a huge dirt ball. And the stars? We know they are of lesser stuff than God. These lofty celestial bodies that send their radiant light to our planet are far less than the radiant purity of God. What then of man?

[H]ow much less man, who is a maggot,

and the son of man, who is a worm!

The echo of these words can be heard in a later time, through a Psalm of David:

> *When I look at your heavens, the work of your fingers,*
> *the moon and the stars, which you have set in place,*
> *what is man that you are mindful of him,*
> *and the son of man that you care for him?*
>
> *Psalm 8:3-4*

The grandeur of the lights that fill our night sky have captured the awe of men from time immemorial. But these heavenly bodies are merely the work of the *fingers* of our heavenly Father, who is greater than them all. How then does this great God give man a second thought? Bildad, like David after him, stands in wonder as to how this can be.

I believe Bildad has moved from his role of protagonist in the assault against Job's character to a baffled man who simply finds that Job's claim does not compute. It makes no sense to him. He does not see a path by which any man, who is but a worm, could be pure before God. In this, Bildad asks the question that every person should pursue.

To understand that there is a God who made all things forces a person to face the ultimate question—how can I be right before this God? Anyone who honestly seeks the answer to this question is confronted with the state of their own heart. I know my heart condition, and you know yours. And what I know about myself leaves me with a verdict that *purity* is not a word that should ever be used to describe me. I am sure the verdict is the same for you. Not because I know your heart, but because the One who knows all hearts perfectly has given us that verdict: "all have sinned and fall short of the glory of God" (Romans 3:23). Herein is the ultimate expression of inclusiveness. We are in this together, my friends. We all have the same desperate need. Left to ourselves, there would be no hope. Because "the wages of sin is death" (Romans 6:23).

Bildad could see this. For all his shortcomings, he knows a man born of woman cannot be pure—and would, therefore, have no hope of standing before God. For this dilemma, he had no answer. His theology could not clear up this conundrum. So, he closes his mouth and speaks no more. And his friends are reduced to silence with him.

But here is where we can be grateful to live this side of Calvary. For, in fact, there was one born of woman who was pure. What to Bildad was unthinkable has happened.

> *But when the fullness of time had come, God sent forth his Son, born of woman, born under the law, to redeem those who were under the law, so that we might receive adoption as sons.*
>
> *Galatians 4:4-5*

Don't let the familiarity of these two verses cause you to miss their profundity. These words should make us gasp at the awesomeness of what the Father has done. This beloved Son, through whom all things were created, entered our world through a woman. But most importantly, she was a virgin. The defiling seed of Adam had no role in his birth. Unlike all who have occupied a womb before and after him, Jesus was not an offspring of a man. The stain of sin did not contaminate his being. He was pure. But that, in itself, would do nothing for our perilous state before God. No, there is more. This one born pure became God's offering for us. John the Baptist saw it coming and declared, "Behold, the Lamb of God" (John 1:29). And what he did in serving as God's pure offering for us paved the path by which men can be right before God.

> *For our sake he made him to be sin who knew no sin, so that in him we might become the righteousness of God.*
>
> *2 Corinthians 5:21*

There is the solution to Bildad's dilemma. The great exchange. We receive the righteousness of God as a gift through faith, faith in the finished work of Jesus on the cross—because he bore the wrath of God for us. In so doing, this one born pure purifies those he calls to himself.

You see, even the book of Job ultimately leads us to Jesus—as does the entire Old Testament. Not only through its prophetic whispers, but also through the questions it *cannot* answer, like Bildad's. This is just one way the story of Job's suffering should drive us to the finished work of Christ. Any personal affliction that we bear should do likewise. It should all drive us to our Redeemer at the cross, whose trail of blood leads to the tomb, which now is empty. It is because our Savior walked out of that tomb alive that we have hope in the midst of whatever suffering we may bear. Let your pain and perplexity draw you to the Savior who died on Calvary for you, thereby conquering death. For

In His arms He'll take and shield thee,
Thou wilt find a solace there.[18]

---

18   Words from "What a Friend We Have in Jesus" by Joseph M. Scriven, 1855.

44

THE MAJESTY OF GOD

Read Job 26:1-14

Like a roaring fire that consumes its own fuel, the heated arguments of Job's friends have been spent. Job has resigned himself to the disappointment that these companions will bring no comfort in his affliction. His sarcastic words make it clear that they have fallen short:

How you have helped him who has no power!
How you have saved the arm that has no strength!
How you have counseled him who has no wisdom,
and plentifully declared sound knowledge!
With whose help have you uttered words,
and whose breath has come out from you?

Job sounds exhausted by the encounter. Yet he summons the strength to reply. With a long sigh, he reveals his thoughts—where all this back and forth with his friends has left him. Sadly, they have given no strength for his weakness and no wisdom for his perplexity. In short, they have been of no help. So, in a series of final speeches, he puts it all in perspective.

In one sense, what follows in the next few chapters reads like the rambling of a man who can't get his thoughts together. It is easy to be confused by the discontinuity of chapters 26 to 31. But this is not one long speech. The separate introductions in chapter 26, 27, and 29 indicate time had passed between each introduction Job spoke. Yet none of these gaps is filled by words from Job's friends—which is why I asserted their fuel has been spent. Job speaks, then pauses, ponders, and speaks again. He provides his silent audience with his closing thoughts as his mind surveys where all that has happened has left him. We will not hear from these friends again, as Job will spar with them no more. They are done with empty words, but Job has not ended his enlightened musings. Their silence gives him more room to think and speak.

Perhaps there is a lesson for us even in this. Most of us are uncomfortable with silence in the presence of others. But when we are sitting with another who is in distress, silence can be good for us both. It prevents us from saying what should be kept to ourselves, and it also gives those in distress space to think and freedom to share their thoughts. The latter are hindered if we speak too quickly or too much. As James exhort us, we should "be quick to hear, slow to speak" (1:19).

As we arrive at this point in our journey of these protracted speeches, we might find ourselves feeling a bit like Job—exhausted by the length of his trial through affliction and the conflict with his friends. But the drama has more to teach us, and the most important scene is yet to come. Before we get there, though, Job has much to say. His words in these speeches touch on truths helpful to ponder. We will miss food for our souls if we hastily pass over them. To get the most out of his words, we need to pause and chew on each speech for a while.

In his first oration, this man in a lowly and miserable state points us to the majesty of God. Bildad has, in his final words, spoken of the greatness of God. So, Job picks up this theme himself to remind his friend that the ways of this great God are past finding out.

The dead tremble
> *under the waters and their inhabitants.*
Sheol is naked before God,
> *and Abaddon has no covering.*

The rule of God extends even to the realm of the dead. Viewed by the ancients as a place below the oceans and its myriad creatures, it does not lie out of God's sight. No, no matter how deep its location, it "is naked before God." Even the works of Abaddon, another term for the realm of the dead, is not hidden from God. But this God of whom Job speaks does not merely see all; he also upholds the created order.

He stretches out the north over the void
　and hangs the earth on nothing.
He binds up the waters in his thick clouds,
　and the cloud is not split open under them.
He covers the face of the full moon
　and spreads over it his cloud.
He has inscribed a circle on the face of the waters
　at the boundary between light and darkness.

Job moves his sight from below the sea to the realm above ground. And what he sees is amazing. Astrophysicists tell us the earth's position is determined by gravitational forces—but what are those forces that hold planets in their orbits? Job reminds us that they are but the hangers of God. And what about those cloud puffs just above the land? Isn't it amazing that such massive amounts of water are held high in the sky? The average cloud contains enough water to give it a total weight of over one million pounds. Yet who fears walking under those wisps of cotton in the sky?

If you go outside on a moonlit night and place your thumb just the right distance from your face, you can blot out the moon. Of course, the moon is still there. You've actually done nothing to the moon but merely blocked your line of sight. What God can do is infinitely greater. Whether Job's reference is to an eclipse of the moon or true cloud cover is uncertain. Nonetheless, God casts a massive covering hiding the face of this huge satellite orbiting our earth.

From looking up at the sky, Job moves to survey this terrestrial ball. He sees that God set the boundaries of the sea. He even demarcates night and day, darkness and light—probably a reference to the horizon. But God not only sets the foundation and boundaries of the earth; he also shakes them by his command.

> *The pillars of heaven tremble*
> *and are astounded at his rebuke.*

The ancients saw the distant mountains, with their cloud cover, as the foundations (pillars) holding up the sky above. Yet with just God's word, they tremble. The One who holds all things in place can unsettle it all with his rebuke.

Amazing as his creation may be, God's authority is not limited to the natural—he also subdues the supernatural forces of evil. They are no match for his power.

> *By his power he stilled the sea;*
> *by his understanding he shattered Rahab.*
> *By his wind the heavens were made fair;*
> *his hand pierced the fleeing serpent.*

Job here seems to draw from the mythological tales of his day to speak of God's power over evil (Rahab). If you are troubled with references to mythological tales in Job, remember he is poetically painting a picture—using as his palette objects and ideas familiar to his listeners to point them to greater things. In the mind of the ancients, the chaos of the sea represented forces of evil. Their ways were a cauldron of destruction. Indeed, Job might well be demythologizing the ancient ideas of evil, correcting errant notions. The ancients may have seen them as untamable forces, but God silences them all—he shatters all those (like Rahab) that oppose his rule.

> *Behold, these are but the outskirts of his ways,*
> *and how small a whisper do we hear of him!*
> *But the thunder of his power who can understand?*

Job's poetic portrait is just "the outskirts of his ways"— they represent a glimpse of the edge of his robe. "Oh, Bildad, this God is so beyond our understanding!"

The words of Job remind us that glimpses of God's majesty are all around us—if we will just open both our eyes and our minds. Still, how often do we walk under the night sky and fail to see the evidence of the glory of God in the stars? Do we hear their song of his majesty? How rarely do we think of his divine order when the darkness is ended by light and day overtaken by darkness? When we hear reports of earthquakes and hurricanes, are we reminded that all of creation shudders at his rebuke?

Foolish are those who pay tribute to people who build great bridges and towers, but fail to acknowledge the great Builder and Sustainer of creation. In contrast, the wise praise our Creator for his glorious works. The outskirts of his majesty are close enough to see, to smell, to hear, and to feel. Let us not miss it! May he empower us to see his majesty that is displayed before our eyes every day.

45

UNCOMPROMISING INTEGRITY

Read Job 27:1-6

Compromise is at the heart of successful negotiations. Democratic governance freezes when political parties refuse to compromise and find common ground. Contract negotiations between labor and management stall when neither side will give an inch. And compromise is the glue that holds successful treaties between nations together.

But not all things are negotiable—or at least they should not be. Compromise is sometimes ugly. For all of us, there are places we must draw a line in the sand to mark where we will not go. Among the most important area where compromise is wrong is on the matter of truth. Speaking or embracing a lie because of outward pressure should be anathema to those who follow Jesus. Those who hold fast to the truth, even in the face of external pressure, possess the admirable virtue we call *integrity*. It is a virtue that seems uncommon in our day. But it is one that has been demonstrated by Job throughout his long journey with affliction—and it is explicitly on display in the opening verses of chapter 27. Job's integrity is so unshakable that he makes an oath in the hearing of witnesses—his three friends ...and the God he serves.

As God lives...
> *as long as my breath is in me...*
> *the spirit of God is in my nostrils...*
> *till I die*
> *I will not put my integrity away from me.*

For the ancients to make such an oath was to invite God to slay them if they were not speaking truth or would not keep the words of the oath. Job is dead serious about this. His commitment to integrity, to speaking truth and only truth, will not be set aside no matter what comes. Indeed, he holds this commitment despite feeling that God has turned on him:

...who has taken away my right,

...who has made my soul bitter

As he declared previously, Job confesses his sense that his trial left him abandoned by God. Regardless of the state of things, Job will not pack it in and go the way of the wicked. He will not allow circumstance to cause him to compromise. Nor will the pressure from his friends cause him to cave in:

Far be it from me to say that you are right

The goading from his friends to admit hidden sin as the cause of his calamity was incessant. In speech after speech they chided him for his false piety, each taking turns whipping him with their words. How easy it would have been to relieve the pressure by declaring he was wrong and they were right. But he did not and he will not. Because he is not wrong and they are not right. Job knows this and vows,

I hold fast my righteousness and will not let it go;

my heart does not reproach me for any of my days.

It is not that Job is unwilling to examine his heart and admit what is there. After all, this is a man who offered sacrifices *in case* his children sinned against God in their hearts. But he has looked carefully and found nothing to reproach himself. He does not see what his friends declare must be there. It would be a falsehood to admit to being wrong when he is not. His steadfastness is amazing.

It is harder to do *everything* when you live in constant pain. The blaring siren of unrelenting pain wears on you. It is easy to surrender when living with constant physical distress. Job was a man worn down by his physical affliction. We must not forget the depth of unrelieved physical suffering that journeyed with him through this dialogue. For some time now, he has also faced the dogged assault of his would-be comforters. Despite all this pressure, he holds fast to his integrity. He is a man of remarkable fortitude. No wonder God pronounced him blameless.

Integrity is a virtue commended throughout Scripture. The call to walk with integrity echoes across the pages of the Bible and is illustrated in men like Joseph and Daniel.

> *Whoever walks in integrity walks securely,*
> *but he who makes his ways crooked will be found out.*
>
> Proverbs 10:9

> *The integrity of the upright guides them,*
> *but the crookedness of the treacherous destroys them.*
>
> Proverbs 11:3

A life of integrity yields the fruit of security. There is no fear of being found out, no dread of hidden things becoming visible—which is why such people confidently appear before God.

> *Who shall ascend the hill of the Lord?*
> *And who shall stand in his holy place?*
> *He who has clean hands and a pure heart,*
> *who does not lift up his soul to what is false*
> *and does not swear deceitfully.*
>
> Psalm 24:3-4

The integrity of our souls is paramount to our ability to stand before the Lord. For among the abominations that the Lord detests is lying lips.

> *There are six things that the Lord hates,*
> *seven that are an abomination to him:*
> *haughty eyes, a lying tongue,*
> *and hands that shed innocent blood,*
> *a heart that devises wicked plans,*
> *feet that make haste to run to evil,*
> *a false witness who breathes out lies,*

and one who sows discord among brothers.
Proverbs 6:16-19

Perhaps nothing shows our integrity more clearly than our words. Sometimes we are tempted to lie to gain pleasurable things. At other times, we are tempted to lie to avoid painful consequences. The pressure to do so can be massive.

Though the nature of that pressure and the truth to be compromised has varied, Christians have always faced pressure to compromise their integrity. Early Christians were asked to do something very simple—declare Caesar as Lord. They didn't even have to deny that Jesus was Lord, for the Romans were quite comfortable with a pantheon of deities. But to refuse to say the simple words "Caesar is Lord" would cost them their lives. Uncounted numbers were, like Job, unwilling to let go of their integrity. They would not speak a lie, even to save their very lives. Following in their footsteps, Martin Luther was told to recant his beliefs. But he held fast and would not deny what he knew to be true. His conscience was clear, so he stood fast.

Christians in the West are facing a different kind of pressure to their integrity than Job and early Christians. We are under pressure to deny biblical truth that has become culturally unpopular. And the call to compromise truth and affirm lies often comes from "friends." It is a call to denounce the Bible's teaching on marriage and sexuality. The pressure to do so escalates with each passing year. For those who stand fast, jobs may be lost and platforms may be pulled out from under them. Livelihoods are at risk. As a consequence, we have seen numerous Christians jettison biblical truth to avoid the world's reproach. They have bought the lie of the spirit of the age. Integrity has dissolved in the face of incessant pressure to abandon the teachings of Scripture.

The simple truth is that there are many in our day who would like Christians to become silent and invisible, absent from the public square. We are facing a test of our integrity—

whether we will compromise what we know to be true. To stand fast will mean a loss of educational options and career opportunities. It will mean living with public shunning and an effort to cancel our voice and lives from respectable society. We will become, in a very real sense, outcasts in our own land. Will we hold fast to the truth? Will we refuse to cave in and speak lies?

After her husband's loss of children and possessions, compounded by severe physical affliction, Job's wife asked, "Do you still hold fast your integrity?" Job's answer remained uncompromising: "I will not put my integrity away from me." May God empower us to do likewise—no matter the cost.

46

CURSING YOUR ENEMIES

Read Job 27:7-23

Contradictions are hard to live with. People who say one thing yet practice the opposite perplex, frustrate, and anger us—especially when the one living the contradiction is ourselves. But few things trouble the Christian more than what appear to be contradictions in the Bible. Things are said in one part of Scripture that seem to go against what is said elsewhere. The latter part of Job 27 presents us with one of those contradictions. It appears to fly in the face of our Savior's call to love and pray for our enemies. But if we will see it in the entirety of the story of Job, we will see that it actually foreshadows gospel truth. It ends up as one of the clearest displays of grace in the book of Job.

Job has declared his commitment to hold fast his integrity. So deep is this commitment, that he makes an oath in verses 2-6. In doing so, he calls down the judgment of God upon himself if he is not truly innocent of the charges his friends have laid against him. But the ancients had an added way of strengthening one's claim to innocence. An oath was paired with a curse—a curse against those who brought the false accusation. It is this curse to which Job now turns.

Let my enemy be as the wicked,
  and let him who rises up against me be as the unrighteous.

Job here shifts from his innocence to the guilt of his false accusers. Akin to the imprecatory Psalms of David, he pronounces a curse on his enemies. In particular, he relegates them to be numbered "as the wicked" and "as the unrighteous."

This is not simply an exercise of labeling—declaring their true character. No, he is assigning them to the fate of the wicked and the unrighteous. "Let my enemy be as ...let him who rises up against me be as..." He is calling a curse upon their head, a curse that will lead to the fate that he goes on to describe. Most disturbingly, it is a fate without hope.

For what is the hope of the godless when God cuts him off,
when God takes away his life?
Will God hear his cry
when distress comes upon him?
Will he take delight in the Almighty?
Will he call upon God at all times?

The writer of Hebrews reminds us that "It is a fearful thing to fall into the hands of the living God" (10:31). For when God's judgment comes upon a man, there is no means to avoid one's fate. There is no path to escape. Such is the fate of the wicked, the unrighteous who persist in their evil. And it is the destiny Job calls down upon his opponents. These would-be counselors of Job think they know the ways of God, but they do not—so, Job now instructs them.

I will teach you concerning the hand of God;
what is with the Almighty I will not conceal.
Behold, all of you have seen it yourselves;
why then have you become altogether vain?

It is plain that he is addressing his friends for their puffery. In their vanity, they have convinced themselves that they are seeing things with wisdom. They think they have insight into God, his ways, and what is going on in Job's life. Eliphaz, Bildad, and Zophar have cast Job as a guilty man deserving of his afflictions. In their minds, it is all the sure hand of God's judgment upon Job. But Job turns the tables on them. He warns them that their prior descriptions of the fate of the godless will come upon them for their evil toward him.

This is the portion of a wicked man with God,
and the heritage that oppressors receive from the Almighty

Job then goes on to describe the earthly consequences of God's judgment upon the life of the wicked, those who oppress the weak. It all sounds familiar, with echoes of the prior words of these friends' descriptions of the wicked's fate. Job is, in a very real sense, throwing their own words back at them. Because it is they who are guilty of offense, not him. Thus, it is they who will experience this fate.

Sounds awful, doesn't it? Is Job justified in turning on his friends in this way? It seems so unlike our Savior. Actually, it is not. What did Jesus say about the disciple who turned on him?

> The Son of Man goes as it is written of him, but woe to that man by whom the Son of Man is betrayed! It would have been better for that man if he had not been born.
>
> *Matthew 26:24*

Jesus declared a woe, a coming judgment, upon his betrayer. Did he not treat the scribes and Pharisees similarly (Matthew 23)? In fact, he cast woes upon entire towns:

> Then he began to denounce the cities where most of his mighty works had been done, because they did not repent. "Woe to you, Chorazin! Woe to you, Bethsaida! For if the mighty works done in you had been done in Tyre and Sidon, they would have repented long ago in sackcloth and ashes. But I tell you, it will be more bearable on the day of judgment for Tyre and Sidon than for you. And you, Capernaum, will you be exalted to heaven? You will be brought down to Hades. For if the mighty works done in you had been done in Sodom, it would have remained until this day. But I tell you that it will be more tolerable on the day of judgment for the land of Sodom than for you."
>
> *Matthew 11:20-24*

The Apostle Paul also denounced those who mistreated him: "Alexander the coppersmith did me great harm; the Lord will repay him according to his deeds" (2 Timothy 4:14). Obviously, declaring judgment upon opponents is not isolated to the Old Testament.

So, what about Jesus' words to love our enemies and pray for those who abuse us? We must realize this is the other side of the same coin. Scripture is clear that judgment will fall upon the wicked. None are more wicked than people who abuse God's children—those who are as the apple of his eye. And it is good and right that such oppressors, and those who observe their evil, be told of the judgment that will come upon such men. Yet the same heart desires to see repentance and the offender experience the grace that results. The Apostle Paul is a monument to the momentous change that occurs when repentance and faith arrive. And he went on to warn his kinsmen of the judgment that would befall them for their unbelief, while at the same time yearning to see them repent.

A foretaste of this marvelous story of grace is seen through Job himself. This one who in chapter 27 declares the fate of his opponents ends up interceding on their behalf. To see that, we must jump ahead to the drama's closing chapter. It's well worth our time to do so. God has appeared in the whirlwind, displaying his majesty for Job to see as never before. Then, the Lord turns to rebuke Eliphaz, Bildad, and Zophar. Read the words carefully.

> *After the Lord had spoken these words to Job, the Lord said to Eliphaz the Temanite: "My anger burns against you and against your two friends, for you have not spoken of me what is right, as my servant Job has. Now therefore take seven bulls and seven rams and go to my servant Job and offer up a burnt offering for yourselves. And my servant Job shall pray for you, for I will accept his prayer not to deal*

with you according to your folly. For you have not
spoken of me what is right, as my servant Job has."
So Eliphaz the Temanite and Bildad the Shuhite and
Zophar the Naamathite went and did what the Lord
had told them, and the Lord accepted Job's prayer.

Job 42:7-9

Do you see the gospel in this accounting of Job's friends? To whom did they bring their seven bulls and seven rams to make the offering for them? Who interceded with God on their behalf? Here's the other side of the coin. The friend who warned of judgment to come upon them served as their intercessor. The innocent one interceded for the guilty. God, in turn, heard and granted his intercession on their behalf.

Is this not what Jesus has done for us all? But the innocent one did not just make an offering on our behalf—he was the offering. The prophet Isaiah put it this way:

But he was pierced for our transgressions;
he was crushed for our iniquities;
upon him was the chastisement that brought us peace,
and with his wounds we are healed.

Isaiah 53:5

When Jesus took the disciples on the road to Emmaus through an Old Testament journey, we don't know if he opened their eyes to the book of Job. He could have, though. For the gospel is here—as it is everywhere in Scripture. Simply a foretaste, but a wondrous glimpse. The innocent interceding for the guilty. It's what Job did. It's what Jesus did. And to Jesus, we owe eternal thanks!

47

WHERE IS WISDOM FOUND?

Read Job 28:1-28

My best insights into a topic often come to me when the debate is over. When the vigor of the discussion has dissipated, I think more clearly and can better see the heart of the issue. Chapter 28 suggests Job had a similar experience. The debate with his friends has been spent. As he collects his thoughts, his mind's eye is drawn to the true nature of the problem at hand—that which has caused such friction with his friends.

Job is both pained and confused by his persisting affliction. He doesn't understand what God is doing in his life, though he is like cured concrete in his confidence that God is in control of all that has happened. In their arrogance, his friends became unflinching in their unjust accusations. Now that the heat of the debate has subsided, Job sees that they all require wisdom that is beyond their reach. The cessation of their discourse has allowed Job to discern the true need, though he had glimpses of it earlier. So, he now turns his attention to the great void in their debate, the need for wisdom and its source. But the route he takes to get there is fascinating. He takes his hearers on a journey, one that begins by extolling the ingenuity of man—ingenuity illustrated by man's ability to plumb the depths of the earth for precious things.

Surely there is a mine for silver,
and a place for gold that they refine.
Iron is taken out of the earth,
and copper is smelted from the ore.

Man puts an end to darkness
  and searches out to the farthest limit
  the ore in gloom and deep darkness.
He opens shafts in a valley away from where anyone lives;
  they are forgotten by travelers;
  they hang in the air, far away from mankind; they swing
  to and fro.

It is common knowledge today that there are precious metals and minerals in the belly of the earth. But how did the ancients discover this? How did they know where to dig to find veins of iron ore? Even creatures whose sight is much greater than humans' sight are ignorant of these things deep in the earth.

That path no bird of prey knows,
  and the falcon's eye has not seen it.
The proud beasts have not trodden it;
  the lion has not passed over it.

None of the great hunters on earth have done what man has done—probed into the depth of the dirt to find precious things. How did men first devise the means to make shafts to enter and mine these valuable elements far below the surface? Where did they learn to refine metal from the minerals they were embedded in? We take such knowledge for granted, but it is remarkable that man discovered all of this. He has applied his ingenuity to dig out precious things from deep within the earth's crust—even to the point of reshaping the earth itself.

Man puts his hand to the flinty rock
  and overturns mountains by the roots.
He cuts out channels in the rocks,
  and his eye sees every precious thing.
He dams up the streams so that they do not trickle,
  and the thing that is hidden he brings out to light.

Man goes to great lengths to mine hidden treasure, even in our day. He goes to such extremes that he "overturns mountains" and "dams up streams" to extract "the thing that is hidden." The effort and ingenuity that man applies to this goal is profound. Yet what about true treasure?

But where shall wisdom be found?
And where is the place of understanding?

Minerals and metals are not Job's literal concern, just an analogy to point to something greater. Man has discovered how to extract precious things from the earth, but has he devised a way to find wisdom? Does he know where to dig for this treasure of inestimable value?

Man does not know its worth,
and it is not found in the land of the living.
The deep says, "It is not in me,"
and the sea says, "It is not with me."
It cannot be bought for gold,
and silver cannot be weighed as its price.

Man cannot even put a proper price on wisdom. It is not something he will find by digging. Nor can all his wealth purchase it. It seems beyond the grasp of men.

From where, then, does wisdom come?
And where is the place of understanding?
It is hidden from the eyes of all living
and concealed from the birds of the air.
Abaddon and Death say,
"We have heard a rumor of it with our ears."

How can we acquire what cannot be purchased with silver and gold? How does one extract what "is hidden from the eyes of all living"? Clearly, we must learn its source. It is there that we must go to find it. But where is there?

God understands the way to it,
and he knows its place.
For he looks to the ends of the earth
and sees everything under the heavens.
When he gave to the wind its weight
and apportioned the waters by measure,

when he made a decree for the rain
and a way for the lightning of the thunder,
then he saw it and declared it;
he established it, and searched it out.
And he said to man,
"Behold, the fear of the Lord, that is wisdom,
and to turn away from evil is understanding."

If God is the source of wisdom, then it is to God that we must turn. Only he "understands the way to it." Job realized his friends' words were mere distractions on the path toward wisdom. They could not give him wisdom. The best they could do, but failed to do, was to point him to God.

Do we believe this? Do we believe that God is the source of wisdom, that only he can meet our true need in our times of affliction? It is easy to vocally assent to this as an abstract truth. When things are going well, we quickly affirm that God is the true source of wisdom. But what happens when our life becomes a boiling cauldron of calamity? What do we do then? Where do we turn?

Have you ever been lost while driving to a new destination? Were you better served in your confusion to drive around in circles or consult a map? Foolish is the person who relies on his own senses when disoriented in a new landscape. Likewise, when disoriented by the battering of a trial—physical, spiritual, or emotional—it is foolish to try to make sense of it in our own wisdom. Yet how easy it is to allow our own mind to be the guide in such moments. We forget one of the clearest warnings in Scripture about the danger of self-deception:

There is a way that seems right to a man,
but its end is the way to death.

Proverbs 14:12

Job's friends were led to foolishness because they spent too much time in their own heads. Job himself was plagued by excessive time ruminating on his troubles. But now he sees clearly what is needed. Wisdom for times of trouble is not to be found in our own minds, it is found in God. Thankfully, God has not been silent on this matter of suffering and what he can accomplish through it. Scripture has many exhortations to people who are suffering, as well as stories of lessons learned from those who have walked the path of affliction.

Are you, my friend, tested by trouble today? You need to be in the Word of God more than ever. You should *increase* your time in the Bible and prayer when suffering strikes. If reading is hard, then listen to the recorded word. Look for times in your schedule to capture time for reading the Scriptures. You dare not trust your own understanding—you must gain the wisdom of God.

Behold, the fear of the Lord, that is wisdom,
and to turn away from evil is understanding.

48

PINING FOR THE PAST

Read Job 29:1-25

The wealthiest among men often become so by a relentless pursuit of money and a ruthless passion for power. They have risen to the top by stepping on and crushing others. Not so with Job. This greatest man of the east was admired not for his wealth but for his wisdom, compassion, and commitment to eliminating injustice. Sadly, that is all in the past. He no longer holds the prestige of the townsfolk nor the capacity to help others. Ruminating on the loss is painful.

Chapter 29 gives us important insight into Job's life before successive calamities ruined him. It portrays the life of a remarkable man who was held in the highest esteem. Despite his position, he fought for the little guy—using his position as an elder among elders to bring justice for the oppressed and help for the needy. It is a marvelous example of how the godly who rise to positions of power should conduct themselves. Important as those points may be, it is not the theme of this chapter. Rather, the tenor of the text is one of pining for the past. Job longs for the days that have been lost. Listening to his lament should cause us to think about the right way to view what has been lost through affliction—because affliction always brings loss.

Oh, that I were as in the months of old,
*   as in the days when God watched over me,*
when his lamp shone upon my head,
*   and by his light I walked through darkness*

Can you sense Job's longing in these words? His wistful review of the past pains him. He is not just remembering the past—he deeply desires to go back to the way things were. And who can blame him? For that was a day when "God watched over me" and "his lamp shone upon my head." The sure hand of God's blessing on his life was obvious. He sensed God's presence in a very real way.

as I was in my prime,
> *when the friendship of God was upon my tent*
when the Almighty was yet with me

But Job feels that time is no more. Comparing the present with the past represents a stark contrast.

when my steps were washed with butter,
> *and the rock poured out for me streams of oil!*

Perhaps Job has a distorted view of the past—exaggerating the good and ignoring the bad. More likely, he uses these words to speak of a life abundantly blessed by God. For that was a time "when the Almighty was yet with me." As he reminisces, we see how this blessing was manifested.

When I went out to the gate of the city,
> *when I prepared my seat in the square,*
the young men saw me and withdrew,
> *and the aged rose and stood;*
the princes refrained from talking
> *and laid their hand on their mouth;*
the voice of the nobles was hushed,
> *and their tongue stuck to the roof of their mouth.*

In ancient days, the city gate is where the elders would gather for people to bring their charges against offenders. Cares and concerns would be laid at the elders' feet for judgment. Here is where disputes would be resolved. Job's esteem among them was so great that his arrival provoked a hush—for Job's voice was better to be heard than any other who had gathered with them. Importantly, he did not abuse this position of power. Instead, he used his influence to ensure justice to the oppressed, care for the needy, and rescue for people in the clutches of unrighteous men.

because I delivered the poor who cried for help,
and the fatherless who had none to help him.
The blessing of him who was about to perish came upon me,
and I caused the widow's heart to sing for joy.
I put on righteousness, and it clothed me;
my justice was like a robe and a turban.
I was eyes to the blind
and feet to the lame.
I was a father to the needy,
and I searched out the cause of him whom I did not know.
I broke the fangs of the unrighteous
and made him drop his prey from his teeth.

This man, whom the Lord has repeatedly labeled blameless, was the righteous judge every complainant before a court would hope for and every oppressor feared. And in this lofty and blessed position, Job found peace and comfort.

Then I thought, "I shall die in my nest,
and I shall multiply my days as the sand,
my roots spread out to the waters,
with the dew all night on my branches,
my glory fresh with me,
and my bow ever new in my hand."

Job was confident his comfort would continue. He felt secure and assured of many days. But it was not to be. Calamity crushed his plans. His world collapsed around him, leaving ruin in its wake. "Oh, to return to the former days!" is Job's plaintive plea. And when loss strikes us, it easily becomes our plea as well.

There is a warning here for all who have experienced loss—whether the loss be a loved one, a physical ability, an important relationship, a job, or a dream. We can, in a very real way, become captive to the past. In fact, an unwillingness to move on from the loss can give rise to bitterness. Naomi, mother-in-law to Ruth, allowed this to happen in her life. When she returned to her people,

> She said to them, "Do not call me Naomi; call me Mara, for the Almighty has dealt very bitterly with me. I went away full, and the Lord has brought me back empty. Why call me Naomi, when the Lord has testified against me and the Almighty has brought calamity upon me?"
>
> Ruth 1:20-21

Perhaps you have seen those so gripped by a loss that they cannot let go of the past, or maybe you're one of those people. The past holds your attention and affection. The time for a consuming grief has passed, but you cannot let go of what has been lost. It is also true that calamity is not the only cause of loss. If the Lord tarries and we are given length of days, we will all be forced to face loss. Our bodies will not be able to do what was once accomplished without a second thought. The Preacher of Ecclesiastes poignantly describes the increasing limitations that come with aging:

> in the day when the keepers of the house tremble, and the strong men are bent, and the grinders cease because they are few, and those who look through the windows are dimmed, and the doors on the street are shut—when the sound of the grinding is low, and one rises up at the sound of a bird, and all the daughters of song are brought low—they are afraid also of what is high, and terrors are in the way; the almond tree blossoms, the grasshopper drags itself along and desire fails, because man is going to his eternal home
>
> Ecclesiastes 12:3-5

Our legs (keepers of the house) will become unstable. We lose teeth (grinders), forcing a change in diet. Vision fails (the windows are dimmed), making it harder to do things. Sleep becomes elusive (causing us to rise at the sound of a bird). Reaching for things up high and the simple act of walking become dangers. Our hair turns white (the almond tree blossoms). Mobility becomes an act of sheer determination. Not a pretty picture, is it? Nonetheless, it is realistic. Declining physical ability is a common companion to aging. Those who age well can handle this loss and their growing limitations with grace. Those who do not easily become grumpy and bitter, consumed by self-pity.

How do we avoid falling into the cesspool of self-pity over our losses—or get out if we have already landed there? The key is to look forward rather than backward. Instead of pining for the past, we should long for our promised future. The Apostle Paul points the way:

> For I consider that the sufferings of this present time are not worth comparing with the glory that is to be revealed to us.
>
> Romans 8:18

Paul was no plastic saint. He understood the very real pain of present afflictions. But he knew this was nothing compared to the glory promised to all who are in Christ Jesus. That is what we must set our eyes upon, not the past. Look to what is to be gained, not at what has been lost. The hope of glory far exceeds anything lost on this earth.

49

BEARING INDIGNITY

Read Job 30:1-32

Having reflected on the lofty position he has fallen from, Job now turns a spotlight on his lowly present state. But it is not the loss of health, wealth, or children that is his focus. No, it is the loss of dignity that consumes him in this chapter. To suffer indignity is to experience shame and humiliation through mistreatment—an act that offends one's sense of self-worth. While it is true that men often suffer from an inflated view of self, it is equally true that we possess an innate sense that our lives have value, because they do. We should not be treated like feral dogs, outcasts from society. As image-bearers of our Creator, each of us represents a life of immeasurable value.

Moreover, the Bible points to the reality that there is a divine order to things. While this may challenge the egalitarian sensibilities of some, there is a place for giving certain people their due. We are to give "respect to whom respect is owed, honor to whom honor is owed" (Romans 13:7). We are repeatedly called to honor our parents. They should hold a special place in our affections and attitudes. We are called to honor kings and rulers by virtue of the position they hold. Such a posture promotes the well-being of a people collected as a society. In addition, the aged who display godly wisdom are to be held in high esteem by all. They are of great value to a society, and in the church. So, we should honor the elders among us who display the wisdom of godly maturity. Job once knew such esteem. As he rehearsed in the preceding chapter, he held a place of prestige among men. Alas, however, that is no longer the case.

But now they laugh at me,
*   men who are younger than I,*
whose fathers I would have disdained
*   to set with the dogs of my flock.*

Job has become the object of scorn. But it is not just *how* he is being treated that pains him; it is also *who* is behind this ill treatment. They are the dregs of society—young men whose fathers were not fit to work with the dogs who guarded Job's flocks.

What could I gain from the strength of their hands,
*   men whose vigor is gone?*
Through want and hard hunger
*   they gnaw the dry ground by night in waste and desolation;*
they pick saltwort and the leaves of bushes,
*   and the roots of the broom tree for their food.*
They are driven out from human company;
*   they shout after them as after a thief.*
In the gullies of the torrents they must dwell,
*   in holes of the earth and of the rocks.*
Among the bushes they bray;
*   under the nettles they huddle together.*
A senseless, a nameless brood,
*   they have been whipped out of the land.*

It is sons of fools that mock him. They are worthless fellows who have been "driven out of human company," chased out like thieves. They dwell in the barren places and are "senseless, a nameless brood." Yet they have the audacity to laugh at Job, tormenting him in his trial.

And now I have become their song;
*   I am a byword to them.*
They abhor me; they keep aloof from me;
*   they do not hesitate to spit at the sight of me.*

Even the outcasts from among men want nothing to do with Job. They despise him, taunting him with their derogatory ditties. Oh, what indignity this greatest man of the east now bears! The rubble of human society thinks he is beneath them. And why this turn of events?

Because God has loosed my cord and humbled me,
they have cast off restraint in my presence.

What is done to him has been done by God. It is God who has humbled him. But like enemies outside a city wall that has collapsed, the unrighteous seize the opportunity and come upon Job in waves.

As through a wide breach they come;
amid the crash they roll on.
Terrors are turned upon me;
my honor is pursued as by the wind,
and my prosperity has passed away like a cloud.

Can you sense Job's feeling that he is being attacked on all sides? His extended family has forsaken him. Fellow elders he once sat among have abandoned him. His three friends from afar have turned on him. And the most worthless of fellows seize the opportunity to add to his affliction. Though he cries for help, none will come to aid him.

Yet does not one in a heap of ruins stretch out his hand,
and in his disaster cry for help?
Did not I weep for him whose day was hard?
Was not my soul grieved for the needy?
But when I hoped for good, evil came,
and when I waited for light, darkness came.

Dwell on that last line for a moment. Have you ever been there—longing for light but finding nothing but darkness? Can you feel Job's despair? No wonder he closes with these words:

My lyre is turned to mourning,
and my pipe to the voice of those who weep.

Joy is gone. There is no place for glad music ...just the voice of weeping. Heavy words from a man who has incurred indescribable indignity. But Job is not alone in having suffered indignity heaped upon him by lesser men, opposition traced back to the schemes of Satan. There is one who bore even greater indignities—and did so willingly.

When we think of the suffering of our Savior, we understandably tend to focus on the physical suffering of the beating, the nails, and his suffocating while hanging on the cross. Then there is the weight of sin, as God bundled his wrath toward sin and sent it hurling through the eons of space and time onto his own Son as he hung on the cross. All of these were terrible sources of suffering our Savior bore. But there is more. We should not overlook the utter indignities he bore.

The King of kings experienced his first night of earthly sleep in a feeding trough. Would you put *your* newborn son there? He was chased out of his infant home by Herod's deadly tirade—the true king of Israel forced to flee to a foreign land by a wicked usurper. What nation treats their royalty like that? When he returned, his family settled in the backwater town of Nazareth, so they could go unnoticed by those who might wish him harm. Shouldn't a royal son reside in the nation's royal city—the place where kings dwell? In his human youth, the One who created all things subjected himself to the authority of a man and woman of humble means. A precious couple for sure, but one that needed the redemption *he* came to bring. And when he began his public ministry at the age of thirty, the people of Nazareth, where he had first labored, rejected him.

But such were just the beginning of the indignities he bore. Later, he was hunted down by men bearing torches, clubs, and swords—who witnessed his indignity as he was betrayed by a kiss. Later, they spit in his face. Then, they blindfolded him and bid him to play their mocking game, guessing who slapped him in the face. They held a mock royal ceremony, crowning him with a crown of thorns and kneeling before him with the jeering taunt, "Hail, King of the

Jews!" The crowds who witnessed his miracles and listened to his wisdom turned on him, crying out for a ghastly death sentence. Is this how a people treat their king? Like a common criminal, he was hung naked on a cross before a watching crowd—who mocked his claims and challenged him to come down from the cross.

No greater indignity has ever been experienced than what Jesus bore. It shocks our sensibilities to think of the Son of God being treated this way. Yet he did it all willingly—for us. Such was the depth of his love. He gladly paid this price as the cost of our salvation. When indignities come our way, let us remember what the Savior has borne for us. Let the small taste of his sufferings create in us a greater measure of understanding of the depth of his love for us.

The only one who was truly worthy of a place of honor on earth suffered great indignities for us. He did it for us. What a small thing it is when we suffer for him.

50

LIVING IN THE FEAR OF SIN'S CONSEQUENCES

Read Job 31:1-40

It is beyond dispute that Job was a man of unequaled character in his day. The Lord repeatedly pronounced Job as "blameless." The pious nature of his personhood would be remarkable regardless of his state in life. But for the wealthiest and most prominent man in his society, such impeccable integrity is unheard of. Reading through the drama of Job may bring us to ask what produced such piety. The answer is given by Job himself in chapter 31. He lived in fear of sin's consequences—including calamity from the hand of God.

We who live in the age of grace are disinclined to see fear as a right motivation for godly behavior. Nonetheless, the Bible provides this motivation, and not just through the example of Job. The New Testament contains many warnings—to believer and unbeliever alike—of the consequences of sin. These warnings are given to motivate us to steer clear of sin. If our theology defangs these warnings, we not only have a bad theology, we also remove one of the most powerful means to spur us on to godly living. And Job's life shows us the power of such motivation.

This chapter contains Job's final appeal. It is his last assertion of innocence. The way he does this may be unfamiliar to modern readers, but he follows a well-trodden path among the ancients. We are familiar with defendants giving an oath before court testimony, swearing to "tell the truth and nothing but the truth, so help me God." Among the ancients, no stronger declaration of innocence could be made than by pairing your claim with a curse upon yourself if the claim were proven false. Thus, using the pattern of speech, "If I have ...then let ...," Job directly refutes not only several charges made by his friends but also other sins common to man.

From the outset of his final appeal, Job shows that he is motivated by the fear of sin's consequences, calamity that may come as the fruit of iniquity.

> *I have made a covenant with my eyes;*
> *how then could I gaze at a virgin?*
> *What would be my portion from God above*
> *and my heritage from the Almighty on high?*
> *Is not calamity for the unrighteous,*
> *and disaster for the workers of iniquity?*
> *Does not he see my ways*
> *and number all my steps?*

The first sin Job claims innocence from is the sin of lust. To "gaze at a virgin" is something deeper than simply noticing a young woman's beauty. It is to look upon her with illicit intent. But Job has committed to avoiding this sin. Why? Because he knows the consequences that will come upon him from the hand of God. Calamity would rightly fall upon those whose eyes draw them into lust. And while his fellow citizens on this earth may remain ignorant of his lust, God would see it.

> *If my heart has been enticed toward a woman,*
> *and I have lain in wait at my neighbor's door,*
> *then let my wife grind for another,*
> *and let others bow down on her.*
> *For that would be a heinous crime;*
> *that would be an iniquity to be punished by the judges;*
> *for that would be a fire that consumes as far as Abaddon,*
> *and it would burn to the root all my increase.*

If lust would bring consequences, how much more so adultery? Truly, such "would be an iniquity to be punished by the judges." The depth and breadth of the calamity for such sin would be immeasurable. It would consume all that is of worth in his life.

If I have rejected the cause of my manservant or my maidservant,
when they brought a complaint against me,
what then shall I do when God rises up?
When he makes inquiry, what shall I answer him?
Did not he who made me in the womb make him?
And did not one fashion us in the womb?

Similarly, Job is committed to avoiding injustice—for he knows that God rises up to avenge the oppressed. Though he stands in a position of prestige, he knows all people have been created by God, giving them inestimable value that should be reflected in how we treat one another.

if I have raised my hand against the fatherless,
because I saw my help in the gate,
then let my shoulder blade fall from my shoulder,
and let my arm be broken from its socket.
For I was in terror of calamity from God,
and I could not have faced his majesty.

It could not be more plainly stated. Job was motivated in his compassion toward the needy by his fear of calamity from God if he ignored the cries of those he could help. How could he face God, who had blessed him with wealth, if he did not use that very same wealth to help those created in the image of God?

If I have made gold my trust
or called fine gold my confidence,
if I have rejoiced because my wealth was abundant
or because my hand had found much,
if I have looked at the sun when it shone,
or the moon moving in splendor,
and my heart has been secretly enticed,

> *and my mouth has kissed my hand,*
> *this also would be an iniquity to be punished by the judges,*
> *for I would have been false to God above.*

Idolatry, the greatest sin of all, would also bring punishment. To be "false to God above" would bring ruin. This is the pattern that runs throughout this chapter. Job declares his understanding that the sins he lists would bring punishment, including calamity that would upset his blessed life on earth. He wants none of that, so he has committed himself to the piety that God acknowledged. In doing so, Job displays wisdom in its truest sense. Does not the book of Proverbs spur us to godly choices because of the adverse consequences of choosing the alternative?

But, many will ask, shouldn't we be motivated to walk with piety out of our love for God, rather than the fear of consequences? This question actually creates a false dichotomy. *Both* should motivate us in our choices in life, for both are presented in the Bible.

> *"You have heard that it was said, 'You shall not commit adultery.' But I say to you that everyone who looks at a woman with lustful intent has already committed adultery with her in his heart. If your right eye causes you to sin, tear it out and throw it away. For it is better that you lose one of your members than that your whole body be thrown into hell. And if your right hand causes you to sin, cut it off and throw it away. For it is better that you lose one of your members than that your whole body go into hell."*
>
> *Matthew 5:27-30*

These words of Jesus plainly provide motivation to avoid lust and other sins because of their consequences. The potential for dire consequences calls for decisive action. Sometimes warning is given by observing sin's consequences in the lives of others. Acts 5:1-11 records the sudden death of Ananias and Sapphira for lying to the Holy Spirit. As a consequence of this summary act of divine execution, "great fear came upon the whole church and upon all who heard of these things."

Many of our churches remind the gathered congregation of an important warning from the Apostle Paul before each celebration of the Lord's Supper:

> *Whoever, therefore, eats the bread or drinks the cup of the Lord in an unworthy manner will be guilty concerning the body and blood of the Lord. Let a person examine himself, then, and so eat of the bread and drink of the cup. For anyone who eats and drinks without discerning the body eats and drinks judgment on himself. That is why many of you are weak and ill, and some have died. But if we judged ourselves truly, we would not be judged. But when we are judged by the Lord, we are disciplined so that we may not be condemned along with the world.*
>
> *1 Corinthians 11:27-32*

Those whose sins are forgiven are not immune to the temporal consequences of sin. This, like all such warnings, needs to be taken with the utmost seriousness.

Sin is horrible in the sight of God. It is also horrendous in the consequences it brings into our lives and the lives of those we love. Perhaps we would display greater piety in our lives if we, like Job, lived in fear of the calamity sin brings.

51

PATIENCE AND HUMILITY

Read Job 32:1-22

For many chapters we have sat as an audience observing the drama of Job's dark trial and listening to the discourse with his detractors. Unlike Job and his protagonists, we have been privy to events unfolding on the other side of the curtain—events that explain the why behind Job's trial and the truth behind his unswerving claim to blamelessness. We have shaken our heads while listening to the ill-founded accusations of Job's friends. We've also longed to give Job inside information, an understanding that it is not God who has turned on him, but a great adversary he seems ignorant of. Suddenly, another character jumps from the shadows and joins the drama. His name is Elihu. How did he get here? Does he know what we know? Or is his knowledge limited to what is known by the four characters already on stage? And ...how long has he been there, listening to what has transpired? Why didn't we notice him before now?

Like Melchizedek in the story of Abraham, Elihu's appearance is sudden and mysterious—as is his disappearance. He is just one of many characters whose minor role in the grand narrative of the Bible leaves us wanting to know more. Apparently, however, we are given all we need to know for the Lord's purposes in his revelation to us. With this, we can and should be satisfied. Chasing rabbit trails to satiate our curiosity about this man will only distract us from the central purpose of the drama.

So these three men ceased to answer Job, because he was righteous in his own eyes. Then Elihu the son of Barachel the Buzite, of the family of Ram, burned with anger. He burned with anger at Job because he justified himself rather than God. He burned with anger also at Job's three friends because they had found no answer, although they had declared Job to be in the wrong. Now Elihu had waited to speak to Job because they were older than he. And when Elihu saw that there was no answer in the mouth of these three men, he burned with anger.

This narrative, breaking the lengthy and seemingly endless lines of Hebrew poetry, points to a pivot in the story. Job is exhausted in waxing eloquent, as are his friends. Neither has convinced the other and they have thrown in the towel, leaving the opening Elihu has been waiting for. The specificity of Elihu's personhood—naming his father, his greater heritage, and his hometown—argues against the notion of Job as a mythical story. But the most important thing to note about Elihu is his anger, a fact repeated four times in these five verses. He is not just angry, he "burned with anger." The intensity of his anger was so great that he declares it demanded a release valve be opened.

Can we learn from the words of an angry man? Some commentators have apparently concluded not, as they dismiss Elihu as a bombastic intrusive youth who adds nothing valuable to the account. *Au contraire*, I would declare. The inclusion of his lengthy speech in Scripture suggests there is something edifying for us to learn, as is true of all things in the Word of God. And the first thing of importance that we learn is his posture. By this I do not meaning standing, sitting, or supine. Rather, I mean his patience and humility—virtues too rare in our modern day, virtues too often absent in my life. Listen to the perspective from his own words:

And Elihu the son of Barachel the Buzite answered and said:
I am young in years,
  and you are aged;
therefore I was timid and afraid
  to declare my opinion to you.
I said, "Let days speak,
  and many years teach wisdom."

Elihu's patience was rooted in his humility. How long he listened to the discourse we are not told. But his words suggest he wasn't just there at the tail end. He restrained himself through the dialogue, for he knew his place. Apparently considerably younger than Job and his friends, he knew that, in general, their wisdom would exceed his. There is a proper respect to be given to one's elders. So, he refrained from speaking and just listened. And he kept this posture despite the rising rage within him. He didn't just wait because it was polite; he *expected* to be enlightened by the words of his elders. He was looking for their wisdom.

Behold, I waited for your words,
  I listened for your wise sayings,
  while you searched out what to say.
I gave you my attention,
  and, behold, there was none among you who refuted Job
  or who answered his words.

Elihu was humble enough to *want* to learn from others. He knew he possessed no monopoly on wisdom, so he sought it where it may be found. This is not to suggest we should listen to just anyone or without discernment. But Elihu gave his attentive ear to these four leading men of their day. By their position and experience they had earned a hearing. Elihu gave them that hearing and, in doing so, found "there was none among [them] who refuted Job or who answered his words."

The truth is that being among the elders does not guarantee wisdom, nor does youthfulness mean it is absent.

What is thought and said must stand or fall on its own merit— not the merit of the one speaking. Elihu understood this.

> *But it is the spirit in man,*
> *the breath of the Almighty, that makes him understand.*
> *It is not the old who are wise,*
> *nor the aged who understand what is right.*
> *Therefore I say, "Listen to me;*
> *let me also declare my opinion."*

Ultimately, Elihu knew that true wisdom came from on high. It may be absent with the aged or abundant within youth. Words, from wherever they arise, must be heard and measured to determine if they represent wisdom. Be that as it may, there was still a rightful place for patience and humility. Knowing that years of experience and thinking about things can give wisdom beyond what youth may grasp, Elihu patiently listened to Job and his friends. It was not until he heard them out and found their words wanting that he interjected his own thoughts on the matter. This in itself is wise and virtuous. It is an example that merits our consideration.

Hearing others out is hard. With frustrating frequency, I find myself formulating replies before others have even finished making their case. Perhaps you have been there as well. James has a good word for us: "[L]et every person be quick to hear, slow to speak, slow to anger" (James 1:19). If I were ever to get a tattoo, emblazing those words on the back of my hands might prove helpful. It takes commitment to listen thoroughly, especially if we object to early elements of an argument. Elihu surely did. But he patiently waited until Job and his friends were done presenting their case. His actions were not only wise; they also displayed humility.

Elihu greatly respected his elders. He did not have the attitude of an upstart. He knew his place in the grand scheme of things, acknowledging his own limitations by carefully

267

listening to those with more years behind them. Still, he did not cross the line between respect and flattery.

I will not show partiality to any man
or use flattery toward any person.
For I do not know how to flatter,
else my Maker would soon take me away.

Giving deference to elders and those with expertise is proper; ingratiating oneself to others through flattery is sinful. Elihu understood the difference. We must as well.

But what about his "burning with anger"? Frankly, it makes his patience and humility all the more admirable. It took tremendous self-control not to speak before Job and his friends were done. Have you ever constrained words while angry, especially while others are speaking nonsense? Not many of us are successful in that task. And his anger was generated by a righteous cause. While Job's friends saw his suffering as retribution for sin, Elihu saw Job's response as sinful. "He burned with anger at Job because he justified himself rather than God." Yet he held his tongue and waited his turn. Patience and humility were on display. In this, we would do well to follow his example.

52

GOD'S PURSUIT OF SINNERS

Read Job 33:1-33

On the last day of my freshman year of high school, a group of friends decided to visit a popular swimming hole. Shortly after arriving, a friend everyone knew could not swim shocked those gathered when he jumped in to join those already in the water. Shock turned to horror when he did not surface. In the frantic effort to rescue him, another swimmer climbed out on a tree branch overhanging the water—enabling him to dive to the depth where our friend was thrashing about deep in the murky water. Sadly, my drowning friend did not understand that the hand that was grabbing and pulling him upward was there to help. In the agony of drowning, he misunderstood his rescuer's intent. As a consequence, he fought off his rescuer and perished.

Elihu sees Job in the same spot as my drowning friend. Job believes God has visited him to bring harm. He believes that his crushing calamities show that God has turned against him. Elihu seeks to help Job understand that God's hand on his life is intended to rescue him. In doing so, Elihu reminds us of what is at the heart of God's dealing with people in our world. He is pursuing them to save them from the pit. Often, however, people misread his intent.

Since Adam and Eve tasted the forbidden fruit, the grand story of the Bible is God's pursuit of his children to save them from the penalty of their sin. It is true that Elihu knows little about the details of the Lord's marvelous plan of salvation. The nature of grace and faith, the efficacy of the atonement, and so much more are absent from his understanding. But this he knows with certainty—God, through various means, pursues men to rescue them from perishing. Compassionately, he invites Job to see his suffering through this lens. "God is not against you, Job—he is pursuing you for your good." And through this invitation, he reminds us of the precious truth that our gracious God pursues sinners to rescue them. It is a reality we should savor.

> *But now, hear my speech, O Job,*
> *   and listen to all my words.*
> *Behold, I open my mouth;*
> *   the tongue in my mouth speaks.*
> *My words declare the uprightness of my heart,*
> *   and what my lips know they speak sincerely.*

With laser focus, Elihu turns to Job. Having listened to the ping-pong-like discourse with Eliphaz, Bildad, and Zophar, he assures Job that he speaks with righteous intent.

> *The Spirit of God has made me,*
> *   and the breath of the Almighty gives me life.*
> *Answer me, if you can;*
> *   set your words in order before me; take your stand.*
> *Behold, I am toward God as you are;*
> *   I too was pinched off from a piece of clay.*
> *Behold, no fear of me need terrify you;*
> *   my pressure will not be heavy upon you.*

He reminds Job that they are kindred souls. Like him, Elihu is just a man, "pinched off from a piece of clay." He does not come to add to his burden; he will not assault him with words. Yet, after briefly summarizing Job's claims, he confronts what he sees to be Job's error.

> *Behold, in this you are not right. I will answer you,*
> *   for God is greater than man.*
> *Why do you contend against him,*
> *   saying, "He will answer none of man's words"?*

Job's error is that he has contended with God. Job has challenged what God is doing in his life and believes he deserves an account from God for those actions. So, Elihu reminds Job of the ways and the reason God visits men on this earth.

For God speaks in one way,
  and in two, though man does not perceive it.
In a dream, in a vision of the night,
  when deep sleep falls on men,
  while they slumber on their beds,
then he opens the ears of men
  and terrifies them with warnings,
that he may turn man aside from his deed
  and conceal pride from a man;
he keeps back his soul from the pit,
  his life from perishing by the sword.

Sometimes, Elihu tells us, God speaks to men through terrible dreams—visions that provoke dread. He did so to Nebuchadnezzar, king of Babylon. He did so not to destroy but to bring about repentance. The vision, followed by its fulfillment, seems to have done just that (see Daniel 4:34-37). God, at times, uses visions to "turn man aside from his deed" to keep "back his soul from the pit." It is his grace that brings these terrors in the night.

Man is also rebuked with pain on his bed
  and with continual strife in his bones,
so that his life loathes bread,
  and his appetite the choicest food.
His flesh is so wasted away that it cannot be seen,
  and his bones that were not seen stick out.
His soul draws near the pit,
  and his life to those who bring death.

At other times, God uses physical suffering to awaken men to their need. Pain can be, as C. S. Lewis said, a megaphone by which God gains our attention. Sometimes, physical ailments are a needed pause button in our lives— forcing us to desist from normal activity and giving time for introspection. Sadly, too many sufferers fail to seize this opportunity when God provides it. But physical limitations can truly be a gift from God. A dear friend of mine who was on a sure path to the pit suffered a stroke after yet another injection of an illicit drug. As he lay in his hospital bed, he was awakened to where his destructive path would lead and surrendered his life to Christ. He will always bear the limitations from that physical affliction. But through it, he now also bears the name of Christ wherever he goes.

> If there be for him an angel,
>> a mediator, one of the thousand,
>> to declare to man what is right for him,
> and he is merciful to him, and says,
>> "Deliver him from going down into the pit;
>> I have found a ransom."

And then there are those marvelous moments when God sends an angel, a messenger from heaven, to speak to men. Cornelius, as recoded in Acts 10, was visited by God in this way. It was the first step in him finding "a ransom." I have written previously about whether God stills speaks to us in these ways today. The key to understand here, though, is the reason he does so.

> Behold, God does all these things,
>> twice, three times, with a man,
> to bring back his soul from the pit,
>> that he may be lighted with the light of life.

Could it be said more plainly? Whether it be through terrors of the night, agonies of the flesh, or angelic messengers, God's hand comes upon men to "bring back his soul from the pit." And don't miss the persistence of his pursuit. "God does all these things, twice, three times, with a man." He is a patient pursuer of men for their good. Aren't you thankful that he is? Where would you and I be if he had not pursued us?

But the lengths to which the Father goes to pursue men is seen most clearly in the incarnation of his Eternal Son—of which Elihu knew nothing. The purpose for this mysterious union of God and human flesh was given by our Lord himself: "For the Son of Man came to seek and to save the lost" (Luke 19:10). The gospel, the good news, is that the God of heaven pursues sinners. In that pursuit he has paved the way for sinners to be rescued—through the shed blood of his son.

Here is a way we can be like Elihu: help people to see what God is doing in this world. Through his Son, he is pursuing them—rescuing them from perishing. Like Elihu, we can tell them that our God rescues sinners. This is the message the world needs to hear. This is the message that is our privilege to give. Are you looking to tell someone today?

53

IS GOD UNFAIR?

Read Job 34:1-37

We all hate unfairness—especially when it happens to us. From the youngest of age, our voices rise with bitter complaint when we feel we have not been treated fairly. We are inclined to label any loss or failure to gain what we desire as unfair, even more so when someone else gets a better deal. But one area where the issue of fairness is sure to arise throughout life is the matter of persistent suffering. If we believe in the providence of God—that he not only controls all that happens but also uses all events to accomplish his purposes—we may find persistent suffering leading us to think that God is unfair. This was the central conclusion within Job's complaint. Elihu understood this, so he turns now to refute this accusation, which he sees as an act of rebellion by Job.

Hear my words, you wise men,
and give ear to me, you who know;
for the ear tests words
as the palate tastes food.
Let us choose what is right;
let us know among ourselves what is good.

Whether Elihu is addressing Job's friends or a wider audience that has gathered to listen in is unclear. What is clear is his call for them to judge the opinion he is about to give, and to discern what is good—specifically whether Job's words are sound.

For Job has said, "I am in the right,

and God has taken away my right;
in spite of my right I am counted a liar;
  my wound is incurable, though I am without transgression."

Elihu sums up Job's basic complaint: he is blameless of any transgression that would merit his suffering and is therefore being treated unfairly. In particular, he is being treated unfairly by God, and what is happening to him is not right. But Elihu sees things differently. He disagrees with Job's conclusions and invites those listening to see this as well.

What man is like Job,
 who drinks up scoffing like water,
who travels in company with evildoers
 and walks with wicked men?
For he has said, "It profits a man nothing
 that he should take delight in God."

Elihu seems to have fallen into an error similar to Eliphaz, Bildad, and Zophar's. He has latched onto words spoken by Job in lament, taking umbrage with his tone and content. He accuses Job of overflowing with scoffing and walking "with wicked men." His claim that Job believes there is no profit in a man's "delight in God" is somewhat dubious. Though his words about Job seem to lack charity, he addresses the question of God's fairness with clarity.

Therefore, hear me, you men of understanding:
 far be it from God that he should do wickedness,
 and from the Almighty that he should do wrong.
For according to the work of a man he will repay him,
 and according to his ways he will make it befall him.
Of a truth, God will not do wickedly,
 and the Almighty will not pervert justice.

His message is pointed—God does "not pervert justice." God is never unfair ...*never*. The reasons this is so should be obvious to all. First, because God is sovereign over everything.

Who gave him charge over the earth,
 and who laid on him the whole world?

If he should set his heart to it
and gather to himself his spirit and his breath,
all flesh would perish together,
and man would return to dust.

No one handed the world to God and asked him to oversee it. No, he made it all and upholds it all by the power of his word—without which "all flesh would perish together and man would return to dust." Does Job understand *who* he has accused of being unfair? God, by his very nature and sovereign power, cannot be unjust in any way, shape, or form. No, it is impossible for the One who is God over all to be unjust in his actions.

Shall one who hates justice govern?
Will you condemn him who is righteous and mighty,
who says to a king, "Worthless one,"
and to nobles, "Wicked man,"
who shows no partiality to princes,
nor regards the rich more than the poor,
for they are all the work of his hands?

Elihu asserts that in addition to being sovereign over all, God also shows no partiality. He is a righteous governor who curries favor with no one. He has made them all. And in his transcendent being, he is far above all. It is, therefore, impossible that he should be unfair to anyone.

For his eyes are on the ways of a man,
and he sees all his steps.
There is no gloom or deep darkness
where evildoers may hide themselves.
For God has no need to consider a man further,
that he should go before God in judgment.

His third point is that God could not even be unfair inadvertently because he sees all. No doing of men is hidden from his sight. He does not need anyone's testimony to render a right judgment. And since these things are true, how does a mere man dare to question God?

When he is quiet, who can condemn?
When he hides his face, who can behold him,
whether it be a nation or a man?

Elihu believes it is audacious for a man to argue with God, as Job had done. Hence, he pulls no punches in characterizing what he believes is Job's error.

"Job speaks without knowledge;
his words are without insight."
Would that Job were tried to the end,
because he answers like wicked men.
For he adds rebellion to his sin;
he claps his hands among us
and multiplies his words against God.

Elihu minces no words. Job is "without knowledge" and has gone the way of wicked men. He is a rebel who needs to repent. Has Elihu fallen into the trap of the trio before him, declaring a blameless man guilty because of affliction? Not really, for they saw Job's suffering as evidence of prior sin—which they believed provoked retribution in the form of suffering. Elihu argues that Job's *response* to suffering is sin. His *reaction* to the suffering is where Job's rebellion lies. Job's questioning of the justice of God, because he does not understand the actions of God, is irreverent.

The Apostle Paul also addressed this issue of the fairness of God in his sovereign choices. In recounting the Lord's choice of Jacob over Esau—before they were even born—Paul asks:

What shall we say then? Is there injustice on God's part? By no means! For he says to Moses, "I will have mercy on whom I have mercy, and I will have compassion on whom I have compassion." So then it depends not on human will or exertion, but on God, who has mercy. For the Scripture says to Pharaoh, "For this very purpose I have raised you up, that I might show my power in you, and that my name

277

might be proclaimed in all the earth." So then he has mercy on whomever he wills, and he hardens whomever he wills.

Romans 9:14-18

The sovereign choices of God are inscrutable—impossible for us to fathom in our finite understanding. More importantly, as the One who is sovereign over all, he answers to no one.

But who are you, O man, to answer back to God? Will what is molded say to its molder, "Why have you made me like this?" Has the potter no right over the clay, to make out of the same lump one vessel for honorable use and another for dishonorable use?

Romans 9:20-21

Paul's words may be uncomfortable, but they are not unclear. God does not answer to us. His actions are not subject to our scrutiny. He owes us no explanations. Does that seem harsh? If so, why? Is it because we are thinking more highly of ourselves than we ought—and less of God than we should?

The sovereign God of the universe works out all things according to his purposes. In doing so, he is accountable to no one. After all, that is part of what it means to be God.

54

SEEK GOD, NOT RELIEF

Read Job 35:1-16

How should people living with persistent suffering pray? The answer to this question is immensely important. For how you pray when in the crucible affliction will largely determine whether your trial crushes you or refines you. It will determine whether your suffering makes you bitter or better. What you ask for in the midst of affliction both reveals *and* molds your heart. This is especially true for an enduring trial—one in which the pain won't stop. Whether its source is physical, spiritual, emotional, or relational matters little. What matters greatly is how you approach God as a result of that suffering. It is this truth to which Elihu now turns, and the direction he guides Job toward in the concluding chapters of his speech.

And Elihu answered and said:
"Do you think this to be just?
Do you say, 'It is my right before God,'
that you ask, 'What advantage have I?
How am I better off than if I had sinned?'
I will answer you
and your friends with you."

Having just argued that God is never unfair in his treatment of men, Elihu now confronts Job about his unjust manner of speaking to God. Job is demanding his right to receive an answer from God about the why behind his calamities. He believes God is treating him as a sinner who has turned his back on God, rather than the blameless man he claims to be. Job's friends provided no convincing answer to this charge, so Elihu steps in to fill the gap.

> Look at the heavens, and see;
>> and behold the clouds, which are higher than you.
> If you have sinned, what do you accomplish against him?
>> And if your transgressions are multiplied, what do you do to him?
> If you are righteous, what do you give to him?
>> Or what does he receive from your hand?
> Your wickedness concerns a man like yourself,
>> and your righteousness a son of man.

Elihu begins by reminding Job of God's transcendent nature. "Look above you, Job. There is an immeasurable expanse above you—yet God is farther still." He tells Job that nothing he does or says adds to or subtracts from God. God neither gains nor loses from the hand of men. Men's deeds, whether good or bad, impact their fellow men, but not God. Arguably, Elihu's view of God is too small—at least his sole focus on God's grandeur. For God is touched by our infirmities and saddened by our rebellion. His hand moves in both compassion and anger toward humans. The Bible teaches us that God is *both* transcendent and near. But Elihu is seeking to point Job to the majesty of God, his divine otherness. This is something men often forget when they pray in the midst of suffering.

> Because of the multitude of oppressions people cry out;
>> they call for help because of the arm of the mighty.
> But none says, "Where is God my Maker,
>> who gives songs in the night,
> who teaches us more than the beasts of the earth
>> and makes us wiser than the birds of the heavens?"

Did you catch his point? When the oppressed cry out they seek relief, "help because of the arm of the mighty." They appeal to one stronger than their oppressors to bring relief. In other words, they want God's help. But—and here is his key point—they fail to seek God himself. They look not for their Maker, only for a deliverer. As a result, they do not gain what they seek.

> *There they cry out, but he does not answer,*
> *because of the pride of evil men.*
> *Surely God does not hear an empty cry,*
> *nor does the Almighty regard it.*

Your heart may be inclined to revolt at these words, but if our prayer is limited to requesting relief from our personal pain, we should not expect an answer from God. Prayers that are self-focused do not move the hand of God. James put it this way: "You ask and do not receive, because you ask wrongly, to spend it on your passions" (James 4:3). The word *passions* means desires or pleasures. James is referring to requests made to God based on what would be pleasing to us. In our self-centeredness, we seek to avoid pain or hardship. Thus, when affliction strikes, our hearts are inclined to desire relief above all else—even more than God himself. We tend to think only of our comfort.

Yet the grand story of the Bible makes it very clear that relieving personal suffering would have, at times, prevented a greater good for others or even for the one suffering. Joseph's slavery and imprisonment was the route by which he was ultimately able to preserve the house of Jacob— and thereby preserve the Messianic line. What he endured for years led to a greater good. The blind man we are told about in John 9 endured decades of hardship because of his blindness. Jesus gave the reason why: "that the works of God might be displayed in him." Sooner relief would have been to his personal advantage. Yet it would have thwarted the plan of God to magnify himself through his Son by granting this man sight in his adulthood. We could add to these Paul's thorn in the flesh—the persistence of which was designed for his own good, to keep him from boasting. Relief from this affliction would not have been in his best interest. And there is no clearer example of God's greater purposes through enduring affliction than the indescribable suffering of Jesus on the cross, whereby he served as the propitiation for our sins and relieved us of an unpayable debt that would have otherwise led to our damnation. But it required suffering instead of relief.

Like Job, we are unlikely to know the why behind our sufferings on this earth. Their purposes in the providence of God are probably impenetrable. To respond with pure self-interest may put us in the position of praying counter to God's purposes. Relief may not be what is best—for us or others. But what is always right to seek in times of affliction is "God my Maker." For he is the One "who gives songs in the night."

We who live in the age of electricity and smartphones that light up the night are far from the experience of the ancients. They did not hide behind dead-bolted steel doors and alarm systems. For them, nighttime was scary. The veil of darkness hid dangerous things, which could draw near unnoticed. The sounds of the night went unidentified and often struck terror in the hearts of those who heard them. Peace in the night was a precious experience. Elihu reminds Job that the God of heaven "gives songs in the night." Whether the darkness is real or metaphorical, his presence brings peace when darkness falls—including the darkness that comes from affliction.

What does all this mean as to how we should pray when pressed in the crucible of affliction? It means we must first seek God. We must pray that he would open our eyes to see him—even in the darkness that comes through suffering. For we may be sure that he is at work in our affliction. In his providence, he has a purpose. We need not know that purpose to ask him to use it for his glory and our good. After all, isn't that the truth Romans 8:28 points to?

And we know that for those who love God all things work together for good, for those who are called according to his purpose.

Yes, the providential purposes of God can be hard to bear. They were for Joseph, the blind man of John 9, the Apostle Paul, and Jesus. And they were very hard for Job to bear. Nonetheless, there was a purpose behind his suffering. And there is a purpose behind every affliction we experience as well. Of that fact the Bible is perfectly clear. So, if in the providence of God we experience sore affliction, we must seek him above all else. For it is he who will give us the strength to endure until his purpose is accomplished. And as we endure, we hold on to this precious promise:

And after you have suffered a little while, the God of all grace, who has called you to his eternal glory in Christ, will himself restore, confirm, strengthen, and establish you.

1 Peter 5:10

Am I suggesting that requesting relief as a part of our prayer is wrong? No, I am not. But when we do ask for relief, we should qualify it in the same manner as Jesus: "Nevertheless, not my will, but yours, be done." His will above our comfort. Are we willing to follow the example of Jesus and pray that way?

55

LEARNING THROUGH AFFLICTION

Read Job 36:1-21

Have you ever read a book that was mostly empty prose or mindless dialogue—yet tucked in the midst was a nugget of invaluable truth? Though nearly overlooked in the mass of forgettable text, the snippet was worth considering. Indeed, it made ploughing through the volume worthwhile. It may be best to see Job 36 in this manner. While Elihu has an inauspicious beginning in this chapter, he slips in a challenge that's helpful for any who bear an enduring affliction. In fact, it foreshadows a fascinating and instructive element of the earthly experience of the Lord Jesus. You don't want to miss it, because it is sure to help you in your journey as a pilgrim on this earth.

Elihu begins like a baseball pitcher who is determined to deliver a pitch that sends the batter back to the dugout. He opens with a dramatic windup, one that displays his confidence in what he is about to throw toward his opponent. And like an overconfident pitcher, his arrogance is on full display.

Bear with me a little, and I will show you,
for I have yet something to say on God's behalf.
I will get my knowledge from afar
and ascribe righteousness to my Maker.
For truly my words are not false;
one who is perfect in knowledge is with you.

Sensing a growing impatience in Job, Elihu pleads for more time—time to deliver his best stuff. *Bombastic* would be a valid term to describe his assertion here. He claims to speak "on God's behalf." He will not draw on the "wisdom" of the gathered crowd. No, he seems assured that he has wisdom from God. In fact, he tells Job that "one who is perfect in knowledge is with you." That is quite the claim, but one easily refuted.

If Elihu had "perfect knowledge," he would know that the cause of Job's calamity is Satan. He would also know that Job's affliction has not arisen because of sin, but rather to show that Satan's claims about the character of Job are false. But Elihu does not seem to know any of these realities. Thus, his claim of "perfect knowledge" and to speak for God are exaggerated, at best. Indeed, he now moves on to repeat the error of Eliphaz, Bildad, and Zophar.

> Behold, God is mighty, and does not despise any;
>> he is mighty in strength of understanding.
> He does not keep the wicked alive,
>> but gives the afflicted their right.

Elihu rightly asserts the strength of God, including his "strength of understanding." No injustice escapes his notice because he knows all. But then comes the curve in Elihu's pitch—he asserts the same reward-retribution paradigm as his predecessors in this drama.

> He does not withdraw his eyes from the righteous,
>> but with kings on the throne
>> he sets them forever, and they are exalted....
> He opens their ears to instruction
>> and commands that they return from iniquity.
> If they listen and serve him,
>> they complete their days in prosperity,
>> and their years in pleasantness.
> But if they do not listen, they perish by the sword
>> and die without knowledge.

God, Elihu argues, may bring affliction upon even kings if they behave arrogantly. But if "they return from iniquity,"

God will be gracious and allow them to "complete their days in prosperity." Like Job's three friends, he equates prosperity as a sign of blessing from God and affliction as evidence of guilt. Thus, affliction is ended by repentance. But if there is no repentance, there is only death and disaster.

The godless in heart cherish anger;
they do not cry for help when he binds them.

The implication is that there is only one path for Job to find relief. It is not an explanation from God that he needs, but rather repentance toward God. The Lord is not unjust in his dealings with Job, Elihu asserts. Thus, Job must be guilty and needs to acknowledge this—so that he might avoid the fate of those who "do not cry for help when he binds them." He goes on to tell Job:

But you are full of the judgment on the wicked;
judgment and justice seize you.

Elihu believes the source of Job's trouble should be obvious. It is judgment for his wickedness. What else could it be? The depth of his suffering could have no other cause. With this, Elihu slips down the same slope as Eliphaz, Bildad, and Zophar. And yet in the midst of this misjudgment, he makes an observation and delivers a warning that cracks open a door to important truths.

He delivers the afflicted by their affliction
and opens their ear by adversity.

Truth misapplied is still truth. When the high priest Caiaphas declared that it was expedient that one man die for the sake of the nation, he did not realize he spoke a greater truth—a prophecy actually (John 11:49-52). He meant it was better that Jesus die than for Israel to lose its freedoms within the yoke of Rome, as well as the Sanhedrin to lose its power. But his words actually spoke of the substitutionary death of Jesus (though Caiaphas did not realize this), the one man who died for all. Similarly, though Elihu spoke these words to point Job to his guilt, they actually point to a greater truth worth contemplating. For whenever we experience affliction, God can use it for blessing, for our benefit. He is doing something for us, not to us.

Note that Elihu declares that "he delivers the afflicted *by* their affliction." In other words, the affliction itself is a form of deliverance. How can that be? Affliction is an attention-grabbing experience. It halts us in our tracks like a giant stop sign. In bringing affliction, God "opens their ear by adversity." In affliction, we can hear things we might otherwise miss—things from God.

Every sufferer is also a sinner. That does not mean the suffering is caused by specific sin, but the affliction can reveal the sin remaining in us. A time of affliction can force us to pause, take stock of our lives, and address habits of the heart that need to change. Our initial response to suffering may unveil sin we've been blind to. Apart from the need to kill residual sin, we all also need to grow. Importantly, a time of affliction teaches us obedience—placing us on a more holy path in our earthly pilgrimage. Indeed, suffering was a means by which even Jesus learned obedience.

> *In the days of his flesh, Jesus offered up prayers and supplications, with loud cries and tears, to him who was able to save him from death, and he was heard because of his reverence. Although he was a son, he learned obedience through what he suffered.*
>
> Hebrews 5:7-8

The Father did not spare his Son the experience of suffering. We are inclined to think only of what his suffering did for us. But his suffering also did something for Jesus. Through his suffering, "he learned obedience." I do not pretend to understand the mystery of that—the Eternal Son learning during his incarnation. Yet in his humanity, suffering was used as a learning tool in Jesus' life. And it can do the same for you and me.

At the same time, there is also a warning from Elihu that we need to heed, a warning regarding how we respond to affliction.

Take care; do not turn to iniquity,
  for this you have chosen rather than affliction.

The intended lessons from affliction that enters our lives can be lost by our responses. If we respond sinfully, we will not learn obedience. If escaping the pain becomes our priority, we may "turn to iniquity." Alcohol, divorce, tax evasion, and embezzlement are common paths people choose to avoid the pain of trials. Others release their agony in anger toward and abuse of others. These are the paths our adversary would like us to take.

How are we responding to the affliction that enters our lives? Are we, like Jesus, learning obedience? Or are we going down the path to iniquity?

56

THE GOD BEHIND THE CHAOS

Read Job 36:22–37:24

Chaos theory is a fascinating scientific concept that enables scientists to predict seemingly random or chaotic events. This theory is grounded in the notion that order on a small scale produces chaos on a large scale. In other words, behind what seems to be chaotic behavior are causes that can be discovered. It is the framework by which meteorologists predict the weather. The flashes of lightning, the nerve-racking cracks of thunder, and the swirl of rain and clouds all appear to be evidence of an atmosphere out of control. But if you understand the small events producing this pandemonium, it is quite predictable. The world was introduced to this concept by MIT mathematician and meteorologist Edward Lorenz in 1961. But many millenia before Lorenz, Elihu extolled the existence of order behind the chaos of storms—not just order, but also purpose.

Job is a man living in the rubbles of a storm that has decimated his life. Sabean marauders, fire from heaven, raiders from Chaldea, and a wind from the wilderness shattered his well-ordered life. Then, out of nowhere, disease descended that left him in utter misery. In the midst of the ruins, he sees no purpose. After three friends failed to be of much help, Elihu appears on the scene convinced he sees what is behind the chaos. In his fourth and final speech, he takes an interesting turn to help Job see what is behind the mayhem in his life. That order arises from the One who is behind the chaos—God himself.

Behold, God is exalted in his power;
   who is a teacher like him?
Who has prescribed for him his way,
   or who can say, "You have done wrong"?

Having warned Job not to respond to his affliction by turning to iniquity, he now seeks to turn Job to a vision of the majesty of God—the One who "is exalted in his power." Neither Job nor others should tell God what he ought to do nor question what he has done. No, when our thoughts turn to God, it should be to magnify his name.

Remember to extol his work,
   of which men have sung.
All mankind has looked on it;
   man beholds it from afar.
Behold, God is great, and we know him not;
   the number of his years is unsearchable.

Men should never forget that God is inscrutable, that his ways are beyond finding out. As those who behold his works "from afar," we must acknowledge that his will and ways cannot be fully grasped by humble humans. That he is in control and has a purpose in all that he does should be beyond question. When we look the farthest our eyes can take us, to the atmosphere above, we see and hear events ordered by the God of heaven. It is he who paints turmoil on this tapestry above.

For he draws up the drops of water;
   they distill his mist in rain,
which the skies pour down
   and drop on mankind abundantly.
Can anyone understand the spreading of the clouds,
   the thunderings of his pavilion?
Behold, he scatters his lightning about him
   and covers the roots of the sea.

Elihu draws Job's eyes to the pavilion above him, where remarkable drama unfolds. Many an artist has sought to reproduce on manmade tapestry the wonder of the clouds—whose formation, shapes, and movement have fascinated us from the youngest of age. Yet from those docile puffs of cotton come immense stores of water, powerful thundering, and lightning that streaks across the sky. But this swirling chaos has a purpose.

For by these he judges peoples;
he gives food in abundance.

Storms can be ruinous or refreshing. They can destroy or give life. Through them, God can punish or bless. And in the thundering and pelting of rain, he has a purpose. If nothing else, such profound action in the sky reminds men that God is there.

Its crashing declares his presence;
the cattle also declare that he rises.

The attention-grabbing sights and sounds of a storm should remind us that there is a God in heaven—the Maker who controls it all. The busyness of our lives is disrupted and our attention is drawn upward when the sights and sounds of a storm reverberate across the sky—announcing his presence.

At this also my heart trembles
and leaps out of its place.
Keep listening to the thunder of his voice
and the rumbling that comes from his mouth.
Under the whole heaven he lets it go,
and his lightning to the corners of the earth.
After it his voice roars;
he thunders with his majestic voice,
and he does not restrain the lightnings when his voice is heard.
God thunders wondrously with his voice;
he does great things that we cannot comprehend.

It was with good reason that Martin Luther surrendered his life to God in the midst of terror brought by cracks of lightning, roaring thunder, and pelting rain. He knew that only the God of heaven could rescue him in the midst of this meteorological mayhem. In truth, the Reformation began with the storm God brought on a desolate road in Germany that day. For it was the means he used to change the course Luther had charted for his life. Yet who in that day knew this greater purpose behind that particular storm? To them, it was just a random event. But it was not.

> Hear this, O Job;
>> stop and consider the wondrous works of God.
> Do you know how God lays his command upon them
>> and causes the lightning of his cloud to shine?

As Luther would do thousands of years into the future, Elihu invites Job to turn his eyes to the God who is behind the storm. "Stop, Job, and consider him carefully." And we would do well to do the same. The majesty of God is there, if we would simply stop and see. Yet do our thoughts turn to God when a storm arrives? Are our thoughts drawn to the One who is behind it all? Or do we, like most of the world, see meteorological storms as random events with no cause or purpose?

What about the storms of life? When our lives are turned upside down through affliction, do we see God there? If God is behind myriad small events that produce chaos in the atmosphere, is he also pulling all the levers that have led to the chaos in our lives? Yes, he is. And when he pulls those levers, what he does is always right—always. But ...it does not always look that way to us, does it? How do we live with the disquiet in our souls when it seems that what he is doing is not fair, when we cannot see how goodness could come out of the chaos? We remember this:

> The Almighty—we cannot find him;
>> he is great in power;
>> justice and abundant righteousness he will not violate.
> Therefore men fear him;
>> he does not regard any who are wise in their own conceit.

We remember the majesty of God, that he will never violate justice and righteousness. So, we stand in awe of who he is and what he does—unless, of course, we are foolish enough to think ourselves wiser than he.

Elihu points us to the question that every meteorologist should ask before they begin their workday: What is God going to do in our atmosphere today? In doing so, Elihu also helps us see how we should respond to the chaos that sometimes enters our lives. Instead of being tossed by the turmoil, we should seek the purpose of the God who is behind the commotion that vexes our soul. For even when it is indiscernible to our eyes, he always has a purpose. That knowledge itself should be a source of peace whenever storms blow our way. May God empower us to see that he is always in the eye of the storm. Always. It is his doing, and we can trust him there.

57

WHEN GOD APPEARS

Read Job 38:1

The drama of theophanies—appearances of God on earth—grab our attention. They remind us that God is always watching and listening to what is happening on this earth. These infrequent accounts recorded in Scripture tell us that sometimes he responds to what he sees or hears by making an appearance. The rarity of such appearances makes them even more profound. But perhaps none is as pregnant with power as his appearance in the whirlwind to Job.

Elihu has set the stage for this exhilarating entrance. He turned Job's eyes to the atmosphere above him, focusing his mind on the meteorological events controlled by God. He speaks of wind, thunder, lightning, rain, snow, and ice. Elihu paints a verbal picture of the chaos of storms that display powerful forces—all of which are controlled by God. He winds down his description by pointing to the calm after the storm has passed.

> *And now no one looks on the light*
> *when it is bright in the skies,*
> *when the wind has passed and cleared them.*
> *Out of the north comes golden splendor;*
> *God is clothed with awesome majesty.*
>
> *37:21-22*

The darkness of the storm clouds, blown away by the wind, gives way to the brightness of the sun in the sky. And now, men must shield their faces from this blazing glory emanating from the sun. The storm displayed the power of God, but the solar brightness displays his majesty. It is too brilliant to behold. Then, when the discourse has gone silent, a whirlwind appears. Not a picture painted with words, but an actual whirlwind.

Then the Lord answered Job out of the whirlwind and said

The stunning nature of the Lord's arrival is impossible to reproduce on paper. Job has been pleading for an audience with God. For days on end, he has cried out with all earnestness for God's presence. He has, in fact, challenged God to make an appearance and explain the why behind Job's undeserved suffering. Elihu has argued that Job does not know what he is asking and is impertinent for doing so. He then draws Job and the greater audience to the God behind the chaos of storms as he paints a picture of God's power through atmospheric events. When he is done with his speech, a genuine change occurs in the atmosphere—a whirlwind. The direction from which it came we are not told. How long they observed its advance is not recorded. But then, the voice of God sounds forth from this tempest, indicating God is in the whirlwind. He has arrived on the scene. What Job pled for is happening. It must have been awesome beyond measure!

This is not the only time God appeared in a storm. His appearance to Moses on Mount Sinai was accompanied by frightening atmospheric chaos.

> *On the morning of the third day there were thunders and lightnings and a thick cloud on the mountain and a very loud trumpet blast, so that all the people in the camp trembled. Then Moses brought the people out of the camp to meet God, and they took their stand at the foot of the mountain. Now Mount Sinai was wrapped in smoke because the Lord had descended on it in fire. The smoke of it went up like the smoke of a kiln, and the whole mountain trembled greatly. And as the sound of the trumpet grew louder and louder, Moses spoke, and God*

answered him in thunder. The Lord came down on Mount Sinai, to the top of the mountain. And the Lord called Moses to the top of the mountain, and Moses went up.

Exodus 19:16-20

Though some have tried, no cinematographer could ever capture the full power of the Lord's appearance on this occasion. The breathtaking nature of his arrival struck fear in the people—and rightly so, for the Holy God had come upon them. Men meeting with God in such a real way was unheard of. Wasn't God way, way up there somewhere? But he had come down to speak to his people, the people he had just delivered from bondage and would enter into a covenant relationship with. Surely, this was a moment none of them ever forgot. Nor would Job, Elihu, Eliphaz, Bildad, and Zophar forget their dramatic encounter.

Other appearances of God have also been marked by profound visible evidence of his arrival. He appeared to Moses in the burning bush (Exodus 3). He guided Israel through the wilderness in a pillar of cloud and fire (Exodus 13:21). When the tabernacle was completed, a cloud descended as the glory of the Lord filled the tabernacle—making it impossible for Moses to enter (Exodus 40:34-35). The Lord appeared to Ezekiel in a similarly dramatic fashion: "a stormy wind came out of the north, and a great cloud, with brightness around it, and fire flashing forth continually" (Ezekiel 1:4).

Each of these earthly encounters with the living God left the people with no doubt that the Lord had arrived on the scene. Yet there were also subtler theophanies, appearances that made it clear the Lord was there, but in human form. The Lord's appearance to Abraham before the destruction of Sodom and Gomorrah (Genesis 18), Jacob's nocturnal wrestling experience (Genesis 32), and the fourth man in the fire with Daniel's friends (Daniel 3) all foreshadow the humble arrival of the second person of the Trinity as a babe in Bethlehem. On each of these occasions, not all eyes would realize who was there.

Reading such accounts may create in us a desire for a special appearance from God, or at least an uncontestable sign that he is among us. When such thoughts arise, we do well to remember that his most prolonged presence on this earth was missed by most who experienced it. Throughout his incarnation, most did not perceive that the presence of Jesus meant God was in their midst. The scribes and Pharisees kept demanding a special sign to signify his personhood, all while missing the irrefutable evidence before their eyes. The crowds only saw one who was doing amazing things—healing their diseases and filling their bellies—rather than who these acts revealed him to be. Even his closest followers, the Apostles, did not see clearly who stood before them. They missed what was in plain sight. Recall his exchange with Philip:

> *Philip said to him, "Lord, show us the Father, and it is enough for us." Jesus said to him, "Have I been with you so long, and you still do not know me, Philip? Whoever has seen me has seen the Father. How can you say, 'Show us the Father'? Do you not believe that I am in the Father and the Father is in me? The words that I say to you I do not speak on my own authority, but the Father who dwells in me does his works. Believe me that I am in the Father and the Father is in me, or else believe on account of the works themselves.*
>
> John 14:8-11

Like Philip, we can fail to see his ever-present person abiding in us. Yet his promise to do so, in the person of the Spirit, was made on the heels of his challenge to Philip.

> *And I will ask the Father, and he will give you another Helper, to be with you forever, even the Spirit of truth, whom the world cannot receive, because*

*it neither sees him nor knows him. You know him,
for he dwells with you and will be in you. I will not
leave you as orphans; I will come to you. Yet a little
while and the world will see me no more, but you
will see me. Because I live, you also will live. In that
day you will know that I am in my Father, and you
in me, and I in you.*

John 14:16-20

This truth should take our breath away every bit as much
as God appearing in a whirlwind did for Job. Christ in us?
How amazing is that? Yet it is true for everyone who has
been born again. The Spirit of God has taken up residence in
his people. Not simply *with* us, but *in* us!

When affliction strikes, we may find ourselves wondering
where God is. Like Job, we may call out for God to make an
appearance. In doing so, we are being as foolish as Philip—
for he is there dwelling within. I do not pretend to fully
understand the mystery of the Spirit's constant presence,
special movements of the Spirit within the people of God,
and God's special visitations (such as Peter and Paul both
experienced). But I find myself asking whether we should
less often ask for a visitation from God and more often ask
him to open our eyes to see his already-there presence. I
believe I most often need my eyes of faith to be opened than
to receive added evidence of his presence and care. Like
Philip, I need to see that he is already there.

It is unlikely that God will visit any of us in a whirlwind.
He doesn't need to, for he has already come in the person of
his Spirit. Seeing and savoring that presence is all we really
need. Is it enough for you?

58

WHEN THE TABLES TURN

Read Job 38:2-38

How do you best answer the hard questions people ask about suffering, injustice, and the seemingly random nature of disasters that strike the lives of the innocent? How do you help people in the midst of their affliction understand that suffering is not without purpose? Some have devoted their lives to creating and sharing apologetic answers—giving reasons for the why behind God's inexplicable doings on this earth. Interestingly, God himself appears to see no reason to give direct answers to such questions. Instead, he points to the route for finding trust during life's storms.

Job has peppered his poems of lament with questions for God. He wanted answers to the why behind his suffering and a reason for the apparent injustice of it all. He felt he was owed an audience with God, that his charges might be answered. But when God appears, he turns the tables and interrogates Job. He does so not to gain information, but rather to give illumination. The rhetorical questions he poses are intended to force Job to see beyond what he can comprehend. They are structured to bring Job to a fuller knowledge of the grandeur of the One behind all that happens in this world—the One whose will is decisive in all things. For if Job can see that, his turmoil will turn to trust. And we can be similarly enlightened if we see what Job saw.

Who is this that darkens counsel by words without knowledge?
Dress for action like a man;
I will question you, and you make it known to me.

299

Like a bolt of lightning, God's words must have quickened Job's heart and mind. He had no idea who was in the whirlwind until God spoke. Rather than answer his questions, the thunderclap-like voice challenges Job. Who does he think he is? Through his ignorance, Job has darkened the counsel of God—the divine order of things. He has questioned whether things are working as they should, whether his circumstances are just. "Let's see if you're really up to this, Job. Prepare yourself, for I have some questions for you," says the Lord. This was not a turn Job expected, but the One in charge has decided the course for this encounter. It is about to get very intense.

Where were you when I laid the foundation of the earth?
Tell me, if you have understanding.
Who determined its measurements—surely you know!
Or who stretched the line upon it?
On what were its bases sunk,
or who laid its cornerstone,
when the morning stars sang together
and all the sons of God shouted for joy?

The contrast here is between Job ("you") and God ("I"). And the contrast could not be starker. The Lord takes Job back to the beginning of the physical universe and asks if he was there when it all unfolded in its splendor. Of course Job was not there. The only audience was the "sons of God," the heavenly hosts referred to throughout the book of Job. Not being there, Job has no idea what holds the universe in place. He knows not its height, depth, nor breadth. In truth, Job knows nothing of the beginning of the universe—which shows how little he really knows.

Or who shut in the sea with doors
when it burst out from the womb,
when I made clouds its garment
and thick darkness its swaddling band,
and prescribed limits for it

and set bars and doors,
and said, "Thus far shall you come, and no farther,
and here shall your proud waves be stayed"?

Nothing appears more untamed than the tempest of the sea, which is why it often serves as a metaphor for evil. Yet the most turbulent of forces—physical and spiritual—are hemmed in by God. He prescribes their limits, "set[s] bars and doors" to determine the boundary of their movements. Did Job watch as these boundaries were put in place? Of course he did not.

Have you commanded the morning since your days began,
and caused the dawn to know its place,
that it might take hold of the skirts of the earth,
and the wicked be shaken out of it?

People's lives revolve around the rhythmic rising and setting of the sun. Yet who created this cycle our lives are so deeply embedded in? Indeed, it is this very light that sneaks up on men and reveals the deeds of the wicked that are undertaken under the cover of darkness.

Have you entered into the springs of the sea,
or walked in the recesses of the deep?
Have the gates of death been revealed to you,
or have you seen the gates of deep darkness?
Have you comprehended the expanse of the earth?
Declare, if you know all this.

Job's knowledge of the physical universe is very small. There are vast corners of it that he has never probed. He would not even know how to get to them if he wanted to. Even today, we make a big deal of the fact that we have sent probes to the edge of our solar system. Nonetheless, that distance is miniscule compared to the full expanse of the universe. And when you look up into that vast space, the sights are amazing.

Can you bind the chains of the Pleiades
or loose the cords of Orion?
Can you lead forth the Mazzaroth in their season,

301

or can you guide the Bear with its children?
Do you know the ordinances of the heavens?
  Can you establish their rule on the earth?

There is even order in the massive array of stars in the heavens—so much so that we can name and characterize star clusters such as Pleiades and constellations like Orion. But who creates this order? Who turns their gaze upon the earth? It was not Job, that's for sure.

Can you lift up your voice to the clouds,
  that a flood of waters may cover you?
Can you send forth lightnings, that they may go
  and say to you, "Here we are"?
Who has put wisdom in the inward parts
  or given understanding to the mind?
Who can number the clouds by wisdom?

The Lord now brings Job back closer to the land on which he stands, to the atmospheric storehouse of water just above his head. But Job exerts no more control over these than he does over the star clusters and constellations that are so far away. Through this physical sweep of the universe, God confronts Job with the reality of both his ignorance and impotence. Compared to the grandeur of God, Job is nothing. And neither are we. I presume we will all agree with that, but exactly how is this comforting?

We sometimes wrestle with the same problem that challenged Job. What we experience does not seem right in our eyes. Call it unjust, unfair, or undeserved—we feel like we've gotten a raw deal. It simply doesn't measure up to our standard of what should be for the children of God. And therein lies the problem. We think we are the standard bearers, that we can determine whether the experiences of life measure up. But of course, we are fooling ourselves. And to question God, as in accusing him of being unfair, is to darken his counsel—his decisive choice for our life. It is to repeat the folly of Job. Through his verbal tour of the physical universe, the Lord points Job to a truth expressed so plainly to the prophet Isaiah (55:8-9):

For my thoughts are not your thoughts,
*   neither are your ways my ways, declares the Lord.*
For as the heavens are higher than the earth,
*   so are my ways higher than your ways*
*   and my thoughts than your thoughts.*

I don't understand how a giant silver tube launches thirty-five thousand feet into the air and transports me from one city to another. But I trust the pilot knows what he is doing and will get me there safely. Nor do I understand how all that has entered my life will work together for my good and the Lord's purposes. But I do know the pilot of my life—and he knows things I know nothing about. I can trust that he knows where we are going and how best to get there. And you can trust him too.

59

THE ONE WHO ORDERS THE WILD KINGDOM

Read Job 38:39–39:30

At a young age, I informed my parents that I wanted to become a zoologist. My father—an engineer who spent much of his career involved in our nation's lunar launches—was not impressed. "Unless you want to spend your life shoveling elephant dung in a zoo," he said, "you might want to pick another career." His warning dissuaded me from majoring in zoology, but it did not dull my desire to learn about the animal kingdom. When I later became a Christian and began studying the Bible, I was delighted to see how often the Lord points to the animal kingdom to teach us important spiritual truths. In this section of Job, we have a profound example of this use.

In his encounter with Job, the Lord begins by confronting this troubled soul with the creation of the universe. The grandeur of the physical universe shows Job how little he understands about the wonders of the world and its workings. It is all so great, and in comparison, Job is so small. Then, God moves from cosmology to zoology, the world of wild animals. He begins and closes this section with predators and prey—a tension-filled dynamic that shows provision through violence. It exemplifies the truth that even hard things have purpose.

Can you hunt the prey for the lion,
*   or satisfy the appetite of the young lions,*
when they crouch in their dens
*   or lie in wait in their thicket?*
Who provides for the raven its prey,

when its young ones cry to God for help,
and wander about for lack of food?

Weeks before writing these words, I watched a documentary on lions. The scenes were both amazing and appalling. The stealth, speed, and strength displayed by these animals is astounding. But the tearing of flesh and splashing of blood shocks the sensibilities of those not used to hunting or butchering their dinner. The juxtaposition of beauty and blood creates a tension. Does the violence of this interaction between predator and prey have a purpose? Zoologists tell us it does. Predators cull the herd by preying on the weak among them—preserving food supplies and speed of movement for the rest of the herd. And the weak provide nourishment for the hunters. When they are all done, the scavengers of the bird and mammalian kingdoms do a gross but needed task of ridding the land of the carrion. This too is a provision of the Lord, when the "young ones cry to God for help."

If the blood and gore between predator and prey is a provision from God, is there also purpose behind the conflict and calamities that enter our lives? Can the tension-filled dynamic among members of the animal kingdom help us deal with the tension created by affliction from the hand of a good God? Can't this dynamic teach us important truth about God and his workings in this world?

Do you know when the mountain goats give birth?
Do you observe the calving of the does?
Can you number the months that they fulfill,
and do you know the time when they give birth,
when they crouch, bring forth their offspring,
and are delivered of their young?
Their young ones become strong; they grow up in the open;
they go out and do not return to them.

The Lord moves his narrative from the tension of life and death to the rhythm of pregnancy, birth, and youth. Who tells the mountain goat when gestation is complete and it is time for the young to enter the world? The wild goats know what to do. They need no herdsman from Job's employ to guide them. And their young? Well, they grow without the help of men and know when they are ready to strike out on their own. This all happens by the grand design of God—no steadying hand of men is needed. These are all things Job does not understand.

Next, after pointing Job to the untamable wild donkey and ox, he speaks of an aberration in the wild world of animals—the ostrich neglecting her young.

The wings of the ostrich wave proudly,
  but are they the pinions and plumage of love?
For she leaves her eggs to the earth
  and lets them be warmed on the ground,
forgetting that a foot may crush them
  and that the wild beast may trample them.
She deals cruelly with her young, as if they were not hers;
  though her labor be in vain, yet she has no fear,
because God has made her forget wisdom
  and given her no share in understanding.
When she rouses herself to flee,
  she laughs at the horse and his rider.

As birds go, the ostrich is bizarre. A flightless bird that can run over 40 mph, it lays eggs as long as a dollar bill. The behavior of the female can seem both callous and careless. Unusual among birds by using a group nest, the dominant female will push the eggs of other females out of the nest—leaving them exposed to being trampled on or consumed by predators. When her young hatch, she abandons their care to the male. Her behavior seems so ...unmotherly. Yet it is God who has made her this way. He is the one who "made her forget wisdom."

Then, without hesitation, the Lord moves Job from folly to fright.

Do you give the horse his might?
  Do you clothe his neck with a mane?
Do you make him leap like the locust?
  His majestic snorting is terrifying.
He paws in the valley and exults in his strength;
  he goes out to meet the weapons.
He laughs at fear and is not dismayed;
  he does not turn back from the sword....
With fierceness and rage he swallows the ground;
  he cannot stand still at the sound of the trumpet.
When the trumpet sounds, he says "Aha!"
  He smells the battle from afar,
  the thunder of the captains, and the shouting.

What is more terrifying than a warhorse? Its taut muscles release like a slingshot at the sound of battle. This animal that knows no terror produces it in those he races toward. Yet the One who made the ostrich careless also made the warhorse terrifying. Each fulfills its purpose in the grand scheme of things.

Finally, Job's eye is drawn to the sky again.

Is it by your understanding that the hawk soars
  and spreads his wings toward the south?
Is it at your command that the eagle mounts up
  and makes his nest on high?...
From there he spies out the prey;
  his eyes behold it from far away.
His young ones suck up blood,
  and where the slain are, there is he.

The beauty of the hawk and eagle soaring in the sky is a prelude to a lethal descent. These birds are prowling for prey below. They look for and create death. And when they are done, there will be blood and gore on which their young will feast. Others must suffer for their young to survive.

This is the world that the Lord has made. There is death and terror all around. This is not the stuff of children's fables.

The real world of animals is not some happy kingdom of diverse species joyfully interacting in daylong picnics. No, it is a world of conflict and suffering. Claws, fangs, and talons threaten. Run fast and hide quickly, or you will become prey for the predator.

Why did the Lord paint this portrait for Job? What does the tension portrayed teach us? Perhaps it is this: the world God has made defies simple explanations. While there is much wonder, there is also much suffering. The moral calculus behind this complexity is beyond our ability to compute. We are fooling ourselves if we think we can grasp it all. Real life is harder than the most complex jigsaw puzzle. It is not possible for us to fully see how joy and suffering fit into the mosaic that is our lives, for their purpose is often elusive. The contrast of pleasure and pain make it seem that something must be amiss. But it is not. The One who made it all did so with purpose. None of this occurs by accident— not in the natural world and not in our lives. It is all by his design. So, we can trust the Designer, even when it is hard. This is what Job comes to see. Will we do likewise?

60

HUMBLED BEFORE GOD

Read Job 40:1-5

I often talk too much. It is, I suppose, something of an occupational hazard for all professors. My calling, and that of my compatriots in the academy, is to explain difficult things to audiences large and small. But the practice of doing this for decades can lead to an arrogance about one's understanding of how the world works. Out of the habit of unraveling complex concepts, one can emerge with an unhealthy confidence in his or her ability to understand hard things. Sometimes it takes a painful experience to knock you down from the lofty heights you have elevated yourself to.

If I understand Job correctly, he suffered from this ailment himself. In fact, I believe it is the cause of his struggles. Not the cause of his calamities, but the source of his struggle to live with his afflictions. Specifically, to be at peace with his lot in life. He was, after all, "the greatest of all the people of the east" (1:3). When he went to the gate of the city—the meeting place of the elders—"the princes refrained from talking and laid their hand on their mouth ...men listened to me and waited and kept silence for my counsel" (29:9, 21). So esteemed was his wisdom that all in the land of Uz deferred to his judgment. He understood things others did not.

Accustomed to explaining things to others, Job was certain he had deciphered the cause of his own suffering. Unshaken in his confidence that God's hand was decisive in all things, he knew his suffering was from the Lord. He also knew he was innocent of transgression that would merit his afflictions. Thus, he concluded, God had turned against him and was treating him as an enemy. So, he demanded an audience with God so that he might be given a reason for this turn in their relationship.

As the audience, we know Job is missing key information about the cause of the various tragedies he experienced. There are cosmic doings he knows nothing about. Unlike us, he does not know what has been going on behind the curtain. His confidence in his ability to understand his experience is sorely misplaced. Indeed, this is what God shows him through his visit in the whirlwind. But God does not intend to directly answer Job's question. Rather, he brings Job to recognize that he does not and cannot understand the complexities behind the myriad of things that the Lord is doing in the world. It is a lesson we would do well to learn along with Job.

Having taken Job on a verbal tour of cosmology and zoology, the Lord pauses to see if the message is sinking in.

And the Lord said to Job:

"Shall a faultfinder contend with the Almighty?

He who argues with God, let him answer it."

Abruptly, the Lord shifts attention from creation to the "faultfinder" who has been foolish enough to "contend with the Almighty." It appears Job did not fully comprehend whom he has been questioning. Yet he is beginning to come to grips with this salient truth. Now, God is the one demanding an answer. And Job is overwhelmed.

Then Job answered the Lord and said:

"Behold, I am of small account; what shall I answer you?

I lay my hand on my mouth.

I have spoken once, and I will not answer;

twice, but I will proceed no further."

Do not miss what these words tell us transpired within Job thus far in the encounter. Job has moved from a demanding petitioner to a dumbfounded person. He might have held a lofty position among the people of Uz, but before God he is "of small account." The verbal tour of God's doings in the world has brought him down quite a few notches. What he has seen thus far has been sobering. At this moment, he realizes that he did not know what he was getting into when he asked for an audience with God. He understands that he has played the fool. So, he pledges to shut his mouth. He dares not even answer, for fear more foolishness will flow.

God is not done with Job, but it is worth pausing at this point—as God himself has done in his speech to Job. We should make sure we do not pass too quickly over the illumination the Lord has given Job thus far. Like God's inquiry of Job, it is good to ask if the truth is sinking in for us. For the theophany Job has experienced shows that though he thought highly of God, he did not think highly enough. Though his belief in the sovereignty of God was unshakable, even in the face of deep affliction, he still did not see all of God that he needed to see or could see. His vision of God was too small ...far too small.

Could the same be true of us? Is our vision of God too small? I am certain that it is, for none of us can fully comprehend God. Throughout our pilgrimage on this earth, shouldn't we be seeking and yearning for a greater comprehension of the person of God? If Job missed truths about God in the cosmos he could readily see, may it be that we are missing what can be seen as well? Could we be missing the depth of what the heavens declare? Do we forget to regularly look upward?

The heavens declare the glory of God,
and the sky above proclaims his handiwork.
Psalm 19:1

Every Christian should be a star gazer. For the sky above is a visible manifestation of the glory of God. Astronomers tell us there are 100 thousand million stars. What power does it take to hang and hold such a quantity of massive luminous spheres in their place? And between all those stars is an incalculable amount of space. The average distance between stars in our galaxy is 5 light-years, or over 270,000 times the distance between the earth and our sun. But all these stars are not hung at random. The universe is so finely tuned that if any number of factors were altered by a miniscule amount, life would not be possible on this earth. One small change, and we are gone.

How powerful is God if he set all that in place and controls it all? What depth of mind can design the intricacies of such infinite space? No wonder David said,

> When I look at your heavens, the work of your fingers,
>   the moon and the stars, which you have set in place,
> what is man that you are mindful of him,
>   and the son of man that you care for him?
>
> Psalm 8:3-4

Is that what you see and think when you behold the moon and stars? Are your thoughts drawn to God? Or do you, like me, often walk underneath this vast array without seeing and hearing what the heavens declare? And what about the rest of the created world? How often do we pass by and fail to hear their song of the Creator?

Maltbie Babcock, a Presbyterian minister and hymn writer, was one who walked in conscious awareness of the Creator behind the world in which he lived. It is said that before his morning walks near the shores of Lake Ontario, he would declare, "I'm going out to see my Father's world." He captured this mindset and its impact through his hymn of that name.

> This is my Father's world,
> And to my listening ears
> All nature sings, and round me rings
> The music of the spheres.
> This is my Father's world:

I rest me in the thought
Of rocks and trees, of skies and seas—
His hand the wonders wrought.

This is my Father's world,
The birds their carols raise
The morning light, the lily white,
Declare their Maker's praise.
This is my Father's world:
He shines in all that's fair;
In the rustling grass I hear Him pass,
He speaks to me everywhere.

This is my Father's world.
O let me ne'er forget
That though the wrong seems oft so strong,
God is the ruler yet.
This is my Father's world:
Why should my heart be sad?
The Lord is King; let the heavens ring!
God reigns; let the earth be glad!

May God open our eyes to see him in his world. And as a result, may we rest in the confidence of his control. For we know our God reigns. Now and forever more.

61

WOULD YOU ASSUME THE ROLE OF GOD?

Read Job 40:6–41:34

While I was working as an intern in a community pharmacy over four decades ago, a patient strode up to the prescription counter with the bluster of an important man in a hurry. When told it would take fifteen to twenty minutes to fill his prescription, he gave a disgusted retort: "All you've got to do is put some pills in a vial and put a label on it! Why should it take that long?" Weary of dealing with impatient patients on a busy day, the pharmacist-in-charge invited the man to come behind the counter and fill his own prescription. After he hemmed and hawed a bit, the patient incredulously asked, "How would I know if the dose is right or if it will interact with my other medications?" The man realized he was not prepared to assume the job of the pharmacist and had spoken rashly.

Likewise, though with far greater profundity, when God next speaks to Job from the whirlwind, he asks if Job is ready to assume the role of judge of the universe. Confronted with the power needed for the task, Job will respond in humble admission of his foolish presumption. He had set himself as judge—judge of the doings of God no less—but this was pure folly.

Then the Lord answered Job out of the whirlwind and said:
"Dress for action like a man;
*   I will question you, and you make it known to me.*
Will you even put me in the wrong?
*   Will you condemn me that you may be in the right?*

Have you an arm like God,
and can you thunder with a voice like his?"

After repeating his challenge from the first of his two speeches, the Lord zeroes in on the core problem with Job's line of thinking. In questioning the justice of his circumstances, Job had accused God of treating him unjustly. He has, in effect, assumed for himself the role of judge of the universe. "Are you really ready to do that, Job?" God effectively asks. "Can you truly assume that role?" To be judge over the universe requires the power to subdue its unruly members. This is power Job does not possess. To demonstrate this, the Lord goes on to ask Job if he can subdue three great forces in the world: the prideful, the powerful, and that which petrifies men—the forces of evil.

Adorn yourself with majesty and dignity;
clothe yourself with glory and splendor.
Pour out the overflowings of your anger,
and look on everyone who is proud and abase him.
Look on everyone who is proud and bring him low
and tread down the wicked where they stand.
Hide them all in the dust together;
bind their faces in the world below.
Then will I also acknowledge to you
that your own right hand can save you.

Lacking "an arm like God" and not possessing "thunder with a voice like his," exactly how does Job think he would subdue the proud? Does he think he can "abase" the proud, "bring him low," and "tread down the wicked"? With great irony, the Lord then declares to Job, "When you accomplish that, I'll acknowledge that you have the power to save yourself." But, of course, this is something Job will never accomplish. He does not possess the power to subdue the prideful.

Behold, Behemoth,
which I made as I made you;

315

he eats grass like an ox.
Behold, his strength in his loins,
 and his power in the muscles of his belly.
He makes his tail stiff like a cedar;
 the sinews of his thighs are knit together.
His bones are tubes of bronze,
 his limbs like bars of iron.

Whether Behemoth is real or symbolic, the reference is to a creature of immense power. Alluding to this creature's virility, the Lord portrays him as a beast among beasts— manly above all others, if you will. Docile on the surface (he eats grass, not other creatures), he poses no obvious threat to others ...unless one is foolish enough to try to rein him in.

Can one take him by his eyes,
 or pierce his nose with a snare?

This speaks of the untamable nature of this powerful creature. He cannot be subdued by men. Yet God made him just as he made Job. Once again, Job is confronted with his inability to fulfill the task and assume the role of judge for the universe. But there is yet greater power needed for the role.

Can you draw out Leviathan with a fishhook
 or press down his tongue with a cord?
Can you put a rope in his nose
 or pierce his jaw with a hook?

Job is here confronted with another untamable creature. This one is not just powerful, he is terrifying. At the very sight of him, men are petrified.

Behold, the hope of a man is false;
 he is laid low even at the sight of him.
No one is so fierce that he dares to stir him up.

So fierce is this creature that no one "dares to stir him up." Why? Because once he is aroused, none can subdue him. The best weapons of men are worthless against this foe.

The arrow cannot make him flee;
 for him, sling stones are turned to stubble.

Clubs are counted as stubble;
he laughs at the rattle of javelins.
His underparts are like sharp potsherds

Though many have sought to identify him, there is no creature in God's wild kingdom that matches this description. While a crocodile's skin may be tough, it is not impenetrable. But other elements of the description exclude any known species.

His sneezings flash forth light,
and his eyes are like the eyelids of the dawn.
Out of his mouth go flaming torches;
sparks of fire leap forth.
Out of his nostrils comes forth smoke,
as from a boiling pot and burning rushes.
His breath kindles coals,
and a flame comes forth from his mouth.

A smoke-exhaling, fire-breathing, armor-platted creature of the deep that men fear to awaken? This description makes the creature sound mythological. Clearly, Job understood the reference—why else would God have used it? But this is not the only reference in the Bible to this terrifying creature. In speaking of Israel's redemption, the prophet Isaiah declares,

> *In that day the LORD with his hard and great and strong sword will punish Leviathan the fleeing serpent, Leviathan the twisting serpent, and he will slay the dragon that is in the sea.*
>
> *Isaiah 27:1*

The book of Psalms also makes several references to Leviathan, portraying him as a multi-headed sea creature (Psalm 74:12-14; 104:25-26). In many ancient mythologies, evil was personified as a fierce, untamable dragon that visited men out of the tempests of the sea. That is most likely the symbol of Leviathan in Scripture as well. It portrays what no man can subdue—the terrifying forces of evil.

317

The tenor of the text of the Lord's second speech is telling: just as it takes great power to create the universe, it takes unimaginable power to subdue its indomitable members. Undoing the wrongs and making them right is no task for mere men, even a blameless man like Job. Job, this dear man whom God loves, needs to settle his heart and leave to God what only God can do. Trying to figure it all out will only frustrate him, while trusting will bring peace.

There are times that I, like Job, play the fool by trying to play God. I want to control what is beyond my ability to control—the hearts of others, the diseases that plague me, the circumstances of my life, and many other things. Perhaps you are the same? God has never visited me in such moments in a whirlwind, but he has in his word. One sure word from Jesus has always brought me peace when things seem out of control. You may find this truth to bring you peace as well:

> *With man this is impossible, but with God all things are possible.*
>
> *Matthew 19:26*

62

COMFORTED IN THE AFFLICTION

Read Job 42:1-6

In the drama that was Job's trial, we have watched the turmoil build within him. His calmness and steadfast faith astounded us when calamity first struck. But as his physical suffering continued unabated, his emotions began to frazzle. The slow grind of unending physical pain took its toll. It often does in people. What vents from his mouth as he weakens would have been unthinkable when tragedy initially arrived. In chapter 3, he declared that he wished he had never been born, or at least that he had been stillborn. He goes on to wonder why God didn't just snuff him out now. In fact, he hoped God would. He did not become suicidal, but he welcomed the idea of the Lord ending his days.

The more he dwelt on his plight, the worst things got. Then came the unhelpful "wisdom" from his three friends. They too were confounded by the suffering of this man known by all to be upright. Having spent too much time in their own heads, they concluded Job must be hiding sin that brought retribution from God. Their false accusations and unsound theology added to his pain—and the confusion of the situation. They wore him down even further. Knowing he did nothing to merit retribution from God, Job concluded the hand of the Almighty had turned against him. Aggrieved over the injustice of his circumstances, he lost control of his thoughts and words. His mind went places it should not have. In his pain and confusion, he felt undone by a God who refused to explain himself.

If I read the heart of Job correctly, there is no grain of doubt about the sovereignty of God in his circumstances. He knew God's hand was decisive in every detail of his experience. On that truth he remained steadfast. But he struggled mightily with a sense of injustice—for he could see no other explanation for his experience. He doubted that God was doing good when things looked bad. He was convinced that God had become his enemy. How else could his suffering be explained?

The fundamental struggle for Job was to find peace in the midst of his affliction, rather than through relief from the affliction. Job is like most of us. Escape from affliction seems to be the only reasonable response for a loving God who is for us. When he doesn't bring the relief we ask for, what does that mean? Is he against us? Has he forsaken us? Have you ever wondered that? Have your circumstances left you feeling abandoned by God? If so, you are not alone. Consider the words of David, later repeated by our Savior:

> *My God, my God, why have you forsaken me?*
> *Why are you so far from saving me, from the*
> *words of my groaning?*
> *O my God, I cry by day, but you do not answer,*
> *and by night, but I find no rest.*
>
> *Psalm 22:1-2*

Many a saint has struggled with the silence of God—a silence they believe is shown by no change in their circumstances. Yet ...what if the needed change is not in our circumstances? What if the necessary change is not external, but internal? What if the circumstances causing our pain are the means by which God will change our hearts? Then, relief is not what we need. Rather, it is to find comfort through trusting God's providence in the midst of our circumstances. This is exactly what Job experiences through his encounter with God in the whirlwind. And if we will listen carefully, we can find the same comfort in our circumstances—however painful they may be.

Then Job answered the Lord and said:
"I know that you can do all things,
and that no purpose of yours can be thwarted."

The Lord's jet-tour through creation has solidified for Job an important truth. God is in control, and nothing will stand in the way of him accomplishing his purposes. Nothing. Not prideful men, powerful beasts, nor even the terrifying forces of evil. Nothing can withstand him. Coming to this point, Job musters the courage to repeat and then answer the Lord's opening question.

"Who is this that hides counsel without knowledge?"
Therefore I have uttered what I did not understand,
things too wonderful for me, which I did not know.

Job now understands that he spoke of things he did not comprehend. The workings of the world and what God is accomplishing is all beyond his grasp. God has a purpose in all he does, though we may not understand it. Job realizes his deductive reasoning—which led him to conclude that God had turned against him—was faulty to the core. As a result, what flowed from his lips was foolish beyond belief. Having come to his senses, he also comes to grip with the Lord's second challenge.

"Hear, and I will speak;
I will question you, and you make it known to me."
I had heard of you by the hearing of the ear,
but now my eye sees you

Job has been put in his place. His visit with God has opened his eyes. Oh, he knew God before this. He had heard of this God who rules over all things. He had made many sacrifices to him over the years. Yet now, his vision of God has been exponentially expanded. Interestingly, through this encounter with the Creator and Ruler over all, he has not received a reason for his sore affliction. But that no longer matters. He no longer needs an explanation. Nor does he seek relief from his suffering. For through this visit from God, he has received something better.

Therefore I despise myself,
*   and am comforted in dust and ashes.*

The entire drama of Job has been moving to this verse. Misunderstand this and you will miss the purpose of the book. You will fail to grasp the most important lesson Job teaches us, and you will not gain the greatest help it provides. This will seem audacious to write, but I believe many translations mislead us on this very point. As a result, we easily misconstrue what has happened.

You may note that I have quoted the variant reading from the ESV in verse 6. The traditional reading ("repent in dust and ashes") can mislead us about what Job is expressing. When we read the word *repent*, we think of a turning from sin. But the word *repent* in this verse is the same Hebrew root for the word translated *comfort* in 2:11—describing the purpose behind his three friends' arrival. Everywhere else this root word is used in Job, it is translated to denote comfort. The word speaks of changing your mind or perspective of your experience.

When Job declares "I despise myself," he is acknowledging "a fault deserving correction, but not a wickedness deserving punishment."[19] He spoke hastily and in the turmoil of his pain, but it was not sin needing repentance. As made plain in the verses that follow, the Lord does not convict Job of sin nor demand sacrifice for atonement—as he does from Job's friends. Distraught in his circumstances, Job has spoken out of his agony. This was folly, not sin. What changes for Job in these verses is not his circumstances but his heart in the midst of his unchanged circumstances.

Job, you will recall, has been sitting in ashes—perhaps to bring some comfort to his sore-covered body. When

---

19   Quote from Andersen, Francis I. *Job.* Tyndale Old Testament Commentaries, Donald J. Wiseman (ed), IVP Academic, 1976, pp. 314-315.

his friends arrived, they flung dust in the air to visibly demonstrate their sense of the grievous nature of Job's lot. So, there they all sat, covered in dust and ashes. After God's visit in the whirlwind, Job's circumstances remain unchanged. The sores are still there, and his children are still not. He is still sitting in dust and ashes. But what has changed is his heart. Because now, he has been comforted in knowing that God always acts with purpose. With this, he is now at peace.

In this, the drama of Job shows the greatest need for those who suffer enduring affliction. It is to stop waging war against your circumstances. Stop cursing the day that calamity arrived and your life became a train wreck. Stop trying to make sense of it all. Stop the endless pursuit to find an escape hatch. Instead, plead with God to use the painful circumstances to change your heart. Ask the Lord to give you a greater vision of himself from within the valley of the shadow of death. For you see, when saints suffer, God can do a great work within them. He did so in Job, and he will in you.

63

VINDICATION AND RESTORATION

Read Job 42:6-17

In my many readings of the book of Job through the years, I have often found myself wishing it ended with verse 6. The restoration of Job's health and prosperity seemed to undo all that has been gained through his lengthy experience leading to contentment despite his terrible circumstances. But I have changed my view on what is seen by some as the epilogue to the drama. Because what happens to Job after his encounter with God in the whirlwind actually points us to a comforting reality—a reality that can help us in the midst of affliction. The truth is, for every saint of God, there is the promise of future vindication and immeasurable blessing. For most of us, that will not happen on this side of eternity. But happen it will, and in greater measure than was recorded for Job. This is truth worth dwelling on. First, though, we must see how God deals with Job's misguided friends.

> *After the Lord had spoken these words to Job, the Lord said to Eliphaz the Temanite: "My anger burns against you and against your two friends, for you have not spoken of me what is right, as my servant Job has. Now therefore take seven bulls and seven rams and go to my servant Job and offer up a burnt offering for yourselves. And my servant Job shall pray for you, for I will accept his prayer not to deal with you according to your folly. For you have not spoken of me what is right, as my servant Job has." So Eliphaz the Temanite and Bildad the Shuhite and*

*Zophar the Naamathite went and did what the Lord
had told them, and the Lord accepted Job's prayer.*

Up to this point, Job's friends had been observers in the
drama with God in the whirlwind. This changes as the Lord
turns and speaks to the ringleader, Eliphaz. He tells him that
their words have not been right. In particular, their words
about God were wrong. Not just erroneous, but sinful. So, he
demands a sacrifice. The reason for seven each of bulls and
rams is not explained. Regardless, the sacrifice itself was
clearly insufficient. They also needed someone to intercede
for them—the one they erroneously thought was hiding sin.
Job was to be their intercessor.

Surely this was a jaw-dropping moment for Eliphaz,
Bildad, and Zophar. Deeply convinced in their reward-
retribution way of judging life, they saw Job as the one who
had offended God. Now, the tables are turned, and they are
the ones who need repentance. Indeed, the Lord makes it
clear that in the agony of his laments, Job had not sinned.
They "have not spoken of me what is right, as my servant
Job has." One may interpret Job's words through his laments
in various ways, but sinful does not fit with the Lord's
assessment. Job's friends must make sacrifice for their
words, but Job does not for his. This is why verse 6 is best
read as speaking of comfort and not repenting. Job turned
from his turmoil and rested in *trust*—trust in the God of
the whirlwind. What is recorded for us in verses 7-9 is the
vindication of Job. He was, true to his claim, blameless after
all. God's demand to Eliphaz makes that clear.

Yet there is a greater vindication than what happened
on earth. Recall that this whole affair started when Satan
accused Job before the Divine Council of serving God under
false pretense. The crushing calamities that he brought
upon Job were designed to provoke him to curse God to his
face. But Job did not do this. In the end, Satan's accusations
were proven false. Job was vindicated before men on earth

and the host in heaven.

Nonetheless, Satan's defeat on this conflict did not end his inclination to attack the children of God. The Apostle John identifies him as "the accuser of our brothers ...who accuses them day and night before our God" (Revelation 12:10). Perhaps hard to comprehend, but there is a malicious presence before the throne of God who means us harm. As he did with Job, he slanders us. And he will bring events into our lives to prove his accusations. We should remember this when calamity strikes. We must know our foe. The devil sees trials as an opportunity for his vindication. His intent is to cause us to turn from God. When pain, loss, and tribulation come into our lives, it is above all else a *spiritual* battle. We cannot allow the obvious physical or emotional elements to cause us to overlook this. Satan wishes to see us undone.

But do not be troubled by this knowledge. For there is coming a day when that too will end. The archangel Michael will lead an army of angels and forever toss this diabolical traitor out of heaven (Revelation 12:7-9). The slanderer will be silenced. In the meantime, the battle continues. The accusations fly. And we are tested. As the testing batters us, we should not lose heart. Rather, we can confidently declare the words of the Apostle Paul: "I know whom I have believed, and I am convinced that he is able to guard until that day what has been entrusted to me" (2 Timothy 1:12). Ours is a defeated foe. His lies will not hold. Vindication is assured. But there's more.

> *And the Lord restored the fortunes of Job, when he had prayed for his friends. And the Lord gave Job twice as much as he had before. Then came to him all his brothers and sisters and all who had known him before, and ate bread with him in his house. And they showed him sympathy and comforted him for all the evil that the Lord had brought upon him.*

And each of them gave him a piece of money and a ring of gold.

Job's testing was costly. He lost his health and wealth, all to prove the slanderer wrong. But when the testing was done, the Lord "restored the fortunes of Job." Actually, Job received double. Those who had abandoned him in his plight returned. They came with sympathy and their presence brought comfort. They provided tangible help in the form of money and gold. In short order, all Job had lost was restored.

And the Lord blessed the latter days of Job more than his beginning. And he had 14,000 sheep, 6,000 camels, 1,000 yoke of oxen, and 1,000 female donkeys. He had also seven sons and three daughters. And he called the name of the first daughter Jemimah, and the name of the second Keziah, and the name of the third Keren-happuch. And in all the land there were no women so beautiful as Job's daughters. And their father gave them an inheritance among their brothers. And after this Job lived 140 years, and saw his sons, and his sons' sons, four generations. And Job died, an old man, and full of days.

This is not a fairy-tale ending. It is a true accounting of the Lord's blessing upon this man who has been at the center of the drama. His status as the greatest man of the east was surely regained. He even had another ten children, as well as uncounted grandchildren. These must have brought him great comfort. He lived to a ripe old age and died "full of days."

Despite the restoration of health, wealth, and progeny, his testing most certainly left scars. Deep trials usually do. Above all was the loss of his ten beloved children. Their voices fell silent, their faces disappeared from view, and the warmth of their touch was never felt again. I know the hole left in the soul from the loss of one child. I cannot fathom the gaping hole left by the loss of ten. No amount of wealth or added children could fully heal that wound. It was a burden he bore until the end of his days.

Testing may have left you in the same position. Even if the battle has ended, the battle scars endure. The measure of restoration you have experienced is wonderful, but all is not wonderful. There are residual effects that continue—memories, unhealed relationships, the wisps of rumors. Whether it is the trial itself or its aftereffects that endure, some trials bring changes that are unrecoverable this side of heaven. But therein lies our hope. For life this side of heaven will not endure. And for followers of Jesus, what follows is immeasurably better than anything this side of heaven. There, our losses will become gain. That should color how we view our suffering in this life. Like Job, suffering should ultimately humble us before God.

> *Humble yourselves, therefore, under the mighty hand of God so that at the proper time he may exalt you, casting all your anxieties on him, because he cares for you. Be sober-minded; be watchful. Your adversary the devil prowls around like a roaring lion, seeking someone to devour. Resist him, firm in your faith, knowing that the same kinds of suffering are being experienced by your brotherhood throughout the world. And after you have suffered a little while, the God of all grace, who has called you to his eternal glory in Christ, will himself restore, confirm, strengthen, and establish you.*
>
> *1 Peter 5:6-10*

In the depth of pain and sorrow that endures, never forget that "he cares for you." Knowing this, we can resist Satan and remain firm in our faith. After all, in the light of eternity, our suffering is just "a little while." And then comes restoration rooted in "his eternal glory in Christ." This is a restoration that will undo all that has been lost since the Fall in the

Garden of Eden. It will far surpass the earthly restoration of Job. This is our hope and comfort. Let us rejoice in it!

64

IN THE AFTERGLOW OF THE DRAMA

James 5:7-11

What is your next step when you come to the end of a good story? Do you close the back cover and savor the journey? Does your mind wander back through the experiences the author has shared? Do you ask how you might see the world differently now that you have looked at it through the lens of the story you just read? The book of Job invites us to do all these things and more.

James, the brother of Jesus, invites us to see the story of Job as a great source of practical help for living life. Job's is a story not to be forgotten. It imprints on our hearts and minds things that will aid us on our earthly pilgrimage. So, let us see what these things are while the afterglow of the story still burns within us.

> *Be patient, therefore, brothers, until the coming of the Lord. See how the farmer waits for the precious fruit of the earth, being patient about it, until it receives the early and the late rains. You also, be patient. Establish your hearts, for the coming of the Lord is at hand. Do not grumble against one another, brothers, so that you may not be judged; behold, the Judge is standing at the door. As an example of suffering and patience, brothers, take the prophets who spoke in the name of the Lord. Behold, we consider those blessed who remained steadfast. You have heard of the steadfastness of Job, and you*

have seen the purpose of the Lord, how the Lord is
compassionate and merciful.

Patience is a virtue we must cultivate. This need is rooted in the reality that the journey of life is often difficult. As songwriter Andrew Peterson puts it, "This life is not long, but it's hard."[20] Jesus told us that "in the world you will have tribulation" (John 16:33). And to face the hardness of life, we need patience to endure. Because the test of our endurance will continue "until the coming of the Lord." We are in this time of trouble for the long haul.

This is truth we must face head-on. Pain, grief, and sorrow will periodically punctuate our lives until Jesus returns. These experiences are to be expected. They should neither surprise nor unsettle us when they arrive. Denying yourself, taking up your cross, and following Jesus does not set you on a path of ease. It never has and it never will. The record of the history of the church abounds with suffering saints, many of whom suffered in unimaginable ways. Sometimes those hardships came at the hand of opponents of the gospel. Other times they came at the hand of our great adversary. At all times they have been the consequence of living in a sin-cursed world. Mutating genes cause cancer and birth defects, wandering microbes bring pandemics, the earth convulses, cars collide, and evil people do wicked things to other people—all because we live in a broken world. And true healing of this broken world will only come when Jesus makes it new. Until then, we suffer. So, we need patience.

But this patience is rooted in deeper soil than simply in the inevitability of suffering. For saints who suffer are also sinners. Even when our affliction is not *because of* specific sin, suffering can *expose* sin in our hearts. Most commonly, this occurs through our response to affliction. Suffering

---

20   Quoted from "Faith to Be Strong" by Andrew Peterson, *After All These Years – A Collection,* ©
      Centricity Music, 2014.

often uncovers hidden idols of the heart. And once exposed, we are given the opportunity to smash those idols. Therein lies a blessing through suffering. Tribulations, whatever their proximate cause, can be sanctifying. They loosen our grip on the things of this world. And that is a good thing.

Calamity can also be illuminating. In particular, it often enables us to see God in ways that a carefree life never would. It certainly served this purpose in Job's life, and it can do so in ours. Through the slow grind of pain or the agony of grief, we can see God with a clarity previously unknown.

But none of these benefits of suffering will accrue to us if we are not patient in the midst of affliction. If we rail against the pain, against God, or against others, we will miss the refining potential. The trial will make us bitter rather than better. James knows this, which is why he points us to our need for patience.

This is a lesson we cannot afford to miss. In the turmoil of testing, confusion often descends upon us. Affliction disorients us, and we lose our way. As the pain endures, our view of God may become clouded. Like Job, we may think he is trying to ruin us. But he is not. No, he is seeking to refine us. And we must learn to be patient as he chips away the rough spots on our heart. James likens the kind of patience needed to that of a farmer waiting for the rain to water the crops.

I am blessed to have several friends who are farmers. One characteristic common in each of them is that they never appear to be in a hurry. They don't rush through things. The perpetual cycle of waiting for rain to water their crops, knowing they cannot control when it will come, has molded them. They have learned the virtue of patience. James encourages all of us to be like that.

"Establish your hearts," James tells us. Batten down the hatches, secure the sails, and prepare ourselves to ride through the storms of life. Don't try to fight it; ride it out. Bear with the tempest and trust the Lord—who is coming soon—to do his work in us through the storm. And realize that in the tempest of trials, we will be tempted to grumble. Like the children of Israel wandering through the wilderness, our hardship may cause our hearts to take a hard turn. Recognize this weakness and look to those who can encourage you in your journey.

The prophets of old should be one group we find courage through. Jeremiah certainly comes to mind. What this man endured is hard to fathom. But like us, he was made of frail flesh. In the face of constant opposition, he remained steadfast as a mouthpiece for the Lord. Can't you and I do the same in our trials? Was he really made of tougher stuff than us?

And then there is Job. "You have heard of the steadfastness of Job, and you have seen the purpose of the Lord, how the Lord is compassionate and merciful." The story of Job should help establish our hearts, prepare us for times of trouble. Job's account is in the Bible to enlighten us. James specifically reminds us that in the drama of Job we "have seen the purpose of the Lord." Think on that for a moment. We did see it, did we not?

As an audience, we were privy to events Job was ignorant to—the reason for the fateful turn in his life. We were let in on the cosmic conflict going on behind the curtain. But Job never knew. No explanation was given for his many afflictions. Yet through it all, he was steadfast in his confidence that God's hand was decisive in all things. And what he learned in the end was that he didn't need to know the why for his afflictions. He only needed to know the God whose hand controlled it all. That was sufficient. Confronted with incomparable portraits of God's majesty, Job stopped fighting against his trial. He found comfort in knowing God was in control, even though the affliction remained—as he sat in dust and ashes. But that is not the end. Job gained invaluable insight about the Lord who had brought his woes.

The end of Job reveals something about God that Job did not see before, an element of his character that he never expressed in his passionate poems. And James tells us it is a key message for us: "how the Lord is compassionate and merciful." The drama of Job does not simply reveal that God is sovereign. It also reveals other elements of God's character that we need to hold on to in times of testing. He is compassionate and merciful.

I would not want to be at the mercy of a sadistic surgeon. But a compassionate surgeon who seeks to do me good even when the path to that end is through pain? That's a surgeon I will trust my well-being to. A God who is control of all things would be frightening if he did not care about me. But the God who *is* in control of all things is *both* compassionate and merciful. This is the God in whom I place my trust.

We must keep our eyes on the truth that the God who is in control of our circumstances is compassionate and merciful. We can, therefore, trust our very being into his hands. However hard enduring the trial may be, we can be confident that he is not doing something to us—he is doing something for us and through us.

Thank you, our glorious Father, for your sustaining comfort when we are suffering in dust and ashes.

ACKNOWLEDGMENTS

Many thanks are owed to uncountable authors and preachers the Spirit has used to open my eyes to the Scriptural truths reflected in this book. Their insights and phrases have surely found their way into my thinking and words. Any failure to acknowledge specific uses is unintentional. As they have helped me in my earthly pilgrimage, my hope is that these meditations will be used in some small way to help others. I owe a deep debt of gratitude to Dr. Brent Aucoin for his line-by-line reading of the entire manuscript, providing constructive help to improve the text. I have again been blessed by the remarkable skill and attention to detail of Christina Roth. Her work as an editor is second to none. My beloved wife (to whom this work is dedicated) has, as always, been my first and most helpful editor. More importantly, she has proved that "two are better than one" when on a journey through this trying experience we call life.

BIBLIOGRAPHY

Alter, Robert. *The Hebrew Bible: A Translation with Commentary. Volume 3: The Writings.* W. W. Norton & Company, 2019.

Andersen, Francis I. *Job.* Tyndale Old Testament Commentaries, Volume 14, Donald J. Wiseman (ed), IVP Academic, 1976.

Ash, Christopher. *Job: The Wisdom of the Cross.* Preaching the Word, R. Kent Hughes (ed), Crossway, 2014.

Brown, Colin (ed). *The New International Dictionary of New Testament Theology,* Volume 1. Zondervan, 1986.

Fyall, Robert S. *Now My Eyes Have Seen You: Images of Creation and Evil in the Book of Job.* New Studies in Biblical Theology, Volume 12, D. A. Carson (ed), IVP, 2002.

Gibson, John C. L. "The Book of Job and the Cure of Souls." *Scottish Journal of Theology* 42:303-317, 1989.

MacArthur, John. *2 Corinthians.* The MacArthur New Testament Commentary, Volume 18. Moody Publishers, 2003.

Parsons, Greg W. "Guidelines for Understanding and Proclaiming the Book of Job." *Bibliotheca Sacra* 151:393-413, 1994.

Rienecker, Fritz and Rogers, Cleon. *Linguistic Key to the Greek New Testament.* Zondervan, 1982.

Robertson, Archibald T. *Word Pictures in the New Testament.*

Volume IV: The Epistles of Paul. Broadman Press, 1931.

Spurgeon, Charles H. *The Suffering of Man and the Sovereignty of God: Twenty-Five Selected Sermons on the Book of Job.* Fox River Press, 2001.

Wiersbe, Warren W. *Be Patient: Waiting on God in Difficult Times.* David C. Cook, 1991.

Zuck, Roy B. (ed). *Sitting with Job: Selected Studies on the Book of Job.* Wipf and Stock Publishers, 1992.

ABOUT THE AUTHOR

Craig K. Svensson, PharmD, PhD, is Dean Emeritus of Pharmacy and Professor of Medicinal Chemistry & Molecular Pharmacology at Purdue University, as well as Adjunct Professor of Pharmacology & Toxicology at the Indiana University School of Medicine. He has served as a Bible teacher, an interim preacher, a seminary board chair, a mission agency board chair, a small group leader, and a visiting seminary lecturer. He and his wife live in West Lafayette, Indiana, where they serve with Faith Church. He is the author of *When There Is No Cure: How to Thrive While Living with the Pain and Suffering of Chronic Illness*, *The Painful Path of a Prodigal: Biblical Help and Hope for Those Who Love the Wayward and Rebellious*, and *Breaking the Grip of Addiction: How Is Drug Addiction Started, Sustained, and Stopped?*

Visit CraigSvensson.com

Made in the USA
Monee, IL
03 March 2024

54152428R00187